Toward a Global PhD?

FORCES AND FORMS IN DOCTORAL EDUCATION WORLDWIDE

Toward a Global PhD?

FORCES AND FORMS IN DOCTORAL EDUCATION WORLDWIDE

Edited by

MARESI NERAD & MIMI HEGGELUND

CENTER FOR INNOVATION AND RESEARCH
IN GRADUATE EDUCATION • UNIVERSITY OF WASHINGTON

in association with

UNIVERSITY OF WASHINGTON PRESS • SEATTLE AND LONDON

Printed in the United States of America
13 12 11 10 09 08 5 4 3 2 1

University of Washington Press
P.O. Box 50096
Seattle, WA 98145–4056, U.S.A.
www.washington.edu/uwpress

CIRGE
Box 353600, College of Education
University of Washington, Seattle, WA 98195, U.S.A
depts.washington.edu/coe/cirge

Library of Congress Cataloging-in-Publication Data
Toward a global PhD? : forces and forms in doctoral education worldwide/
edited by Maresi Nerad and Mimi Heggelund.
p. cm.
Includes bibliographical references and index.
ISBN: 978-0-295-98802-3 (pbk. : alk. paper)
1. Doctor of philosophy degree. I. Nerad, Maresi. II. Heggelund, Mimi.
LB2386.T69 2008 378.2'4—dc22 2007050520

The paper used in this publication is acid-free and 90 percent recycled from at least 50 percent post-consumer waste. It meets the minimum requirements of American National Standard for Information Sciences—Permanence of Paper for Printed Library Materials, ANSI Z39.48–1984.

CONTENTS

ACKNOWLEDGMENTS

The editors are grateful for the cooperation of all of the contributors, as well as for the very effective collaborative writing accomplished by so many teams who produced papers together while serving in research, administrative, and teaching posts at universities that were in some cases hundreds, if not thousands, of miles apart.

The editors wish to acknowledge the assistance of the large number of individuals who have made the 2005 conference, this book, and the follow-up task forces possible. We are grateful to the Ford Foundation for its general support of the Center for Innovation and Research in Graduate Education (CIRGE), especially Jorge Balan, our program officer. A grant from the National Science Foundation (NSF) provided funding for the meeting in Seattle and in the mountains east of Seattle. We want to thank Bianca Bernstein, then director of graduate education of NSF, and Carol Stoel, our program officer for their support. Many people and units of the University of Washington helped with different aspects of the conference. Johnnella Butler, Elaine Chang, Martha Dietz, Sandra Elman, David Fenner, Lee Huntsman, Christine Ingebritsen, Susan Jeffords, Alvin Kwiram, Mani Some, and Gael Tarleton served on our local UW advisory board. Fellow associate graduate deans Donald Wullf, Elizabeth Feetham, and Tom Gething gave additional advice and support. We want to thank the following for the financial assistance for the events on the Seattle campus: Graduate Dean Suzanne Ortega; Dean of the College of Education Pat Wasley; former dean of the College of Engineering Denice Denton; former dean of Arts and Science, David Hodge; and former provost for research Craig Hogan. The College of Education staff: Scott Macklin helped with design, a web site, and documented the conference on video; Connie Petlitzer provided help with web postings; Roberta Hilton and Aki

Kumashiro sorted through the complicated budgeting of an international conference.

Myan Baker, CIRGE organizational development consultant, developed the conference with us and creatively facilitated the meeting. Her experienced conference planning and guidance during the meeting made it possible that a highly diverse group of participants succeeded during the course of five days, to not only cover recent changes and innovations in doctoral education of fourteen countries, but also to agree on a research agenda and a framework for universities to lead societies in shaping doctoral education. She was instrumental in transforming the participants into the *Forces and Forms Global Network*. Katalin Hausel designed the conference logo and Saana Baker adapted it and designed the graphics for the overall conference materials. Rebecca Aanerud contributed substantially to the grants that made the conference and book available. Laura Zanotti helped finalize loose ends of the conference and provided help welcoming the authors and conference participants at the airport.

Renate Sadrozinski and Elizabeth Rudd of CIRGE were outstanding listeners during the meeting and performed miracles in summarizing the country representations. They both were careful readers of the Introduction and Conclusion. Elizabeth's suggestions for the Conclusion improved the chapter substantially. Thomas Trzyna, PhD, a professor of English and member of the Washington Educational Research Center at Seattle Pacific University, who co-authored the Introduction and Conclusion also provided assistance in pulling this book together. Jerry de Jaager lent his clear mind and pen to sharpen the Conclusion. Without the professional editorial assistance of Karalynn Ott, this book and the conference materials would not have seen the light of day. We want to particularly thank her for her patience and endurance with this book project. Michael Duckworth at the University of Washington Press was invaluable at every step of the publishing process.

While this book aims to be the first of its kind in the way it studies the forces and forms of change in doctoral education with a truly global perspective, our work also builds on earlier attempts to look at doctoral education systems from different nations in a comparative way. These include *Doctoral Studies and Qualifications in Europe and the United States: Status and Prospects*, edited by Jan Sadlak (UNESCO-CEPES 2004), and *Graduate Education Reform in Europe, Asia, and the Americas and International Mobility of Scientists and Engineers: Proceedings of an NSF Workshop* (National Science Foundation 2000).

Toward a Global PhD?

FORCES AND FORMS
IN DOCTORAL EDUCATION WORLDWIDE

INTRODUCTION

MARESI NERAD, THOMAS TRZYNA, AND MIMI HEGGELUND

"The most significant development in higher education," according to the September 8, 2005 issue of *The Economist* "is the emergence of a super-league of global universities." This pronouncement acknowledges what many had already been observing: higher education is indeed globalizing. However, as doctoral educators, we believe that the *forces* and *forms* of this process, important to its understanding, are as yet barely studied. This volume explores the consequences of globalization in higher education for doctoral education. Doctoral education lies at the core of a university's research capacity, and is also seen as the primary source of research productivity and innovation in the global knowledge economy. It is therefore a question of vital importance to universities, nations, and the world, whether and *how* a global system of doctoral education is emerging within the global knowledge economy.

The contributors to this book are doctoral education innovators from around the world. They met in September 2005 at the University of Washington, Seattle, (which ranked twentieth in a worldwide ranking of research universities produced by the Shanghai Jiao Tong University that same month) to consider how well doctoral education is responding to global trends. The conference, held at a retreat center in the nearby Cascade Mountains, was convened by the University of Washington's Center for Innovation and Research in Graduate Education (CIRGE), under the leadership of Professor Maresi Nerad. More than thirty doctoral education innovators, including top university administrators, senior members of national research councils and institutes, and doctoral education researchers came together to explore the globalization issue. The group included disciplinary backgrounds ranging from astronomy to engineering, to economics and zoology, and represented fourteen nations as well as one international institution, the European University Institute. Participants came from Australia, Brazil, Canada, Denmark, Germany, Iceland, Japan, Mexico, the Netherlands, New Zealand, Norway, South Africa, the United Kingdom, and the United States of America. The countries selected were those that experienced innovations and changes in doctoral education during the last couple of decades. Participants from China, France, and the Organization for Economic Co-operation and Development (OECD) were also invited, but were unable to attend.

The conference, titled *Forces and Forms of Change in Doctoral Education Worldwide*, consisted of highly interactive meetings and workshops designed to forge the participants into an effective international network of doctoral education experts, to bring to light global patterns of change in doctoral education, and to outline an ongoing agenda for international research and innovations to improve doctoral education globally. Drawing from the collective expertise of conference participants, and from a later collaborator who represents India, this book offers a survey of forces and forms of change in doctoral education around the world and proposes an ambitious agenda for future research.

BEYOND INTERNATIONALISM: FORCES AND FORMS OF CHANGE IN DOCTORAL EDUCATION

The 2005 Seattle conference focused on the "forces" and "forms" of change in doctoral education. These forces include the globalization of the economy; the shift to a knowledge economy; and efforts of policymakers in nation states, supranational and global organizations, and higher education institutions to respond to these broad transformations. Forms of change in doctoral education refer to globalization in two senses: shifts in graduate programs designed to prepare graduates for work in the global knowledge economy and the emergence of a worldwide hierarchy of institutions, degrees, and doctorate holders.

The globalization of the economy means both intensified interaction across and between nations—a form of interaction that can be labeled "inter-national" (Thompson 1999)—and it also means the emergence of global systems and processes, including global flows of people, practices, and ideas and the emergence of "global actors" (actors who are not primarily anchored in national entities). "Inter-national" aspects of the economy remain anchored in national economies, while *global* aspects exist above and beyond national economies and agents and have an autonomous impact upon national entities (Thompson 1999). In Appadurai's (1999) view, globalization means that today "we stand on the edge of a global order characterized by the emergence of a large number of forces which constrain, erode or otherwise violate the workings of national sovereignty" (230). Globalization in both senses—as the intensification of international interactions and the emergence of global forces—is contributing to expansion and innovation in doctoral education around the world.

The increasingly important role of knowledge production for economic success makes doctoral education vital for nations wishing to remain or to become important players in the global knowledge economy. Doctoral education is seen as playing a crucial role in the production of knowledge, and doctorate holders are viewed as a primary source of innovation, research, and development capacity and as workers able to perform well in complex, knowledge-intensive situations. Consequently, governments around the world have begun to expand doctoral training capacity and critically evaluate existing doctoral education. This is leading to reforms and innovations designed to produce graduates better prepared for work in the emerging global knowledge economy. There is broad agreement that doctoral students are poised to become global leaders—and not just in academia. Governments and supranational organizations such as the European Union hope to reap the benefits of a labor force leavened with a higher proportion of doctorate holders who are prepared to work in transnational contexts, and to recognize and solve problems that are international or global in scope.

The "forms" of change in doctoral education include the innovations and trends apparent in the goals, processes, and products of doctoral programs around the world. Many doctoral programs throughout the world are looking for opportunities to equip their students to work in transnational settings with scientists and researchers located across the globe. From the perspective of universities—charged with educating the next generation of researchers, scholars, and leaders—the desire to educate students to work within a global network speaks not only to the technical abilities of sophisticated and quick communication but also to an awareness of the interconnections of global problems. No nation is an island, nor can any afford to be. Globalization can be an opportunity to bring the best minds together to solve the world's most critical challenges. However, nations themselves, competing within this global economy, often have different and not necessarily compatible motivations for globally educating doctoral students.

These forms of change include indications of the beginnings of a possible future global system of doctoral education in which credits and degrees will be universally transferable around the world, and there may be one global system of rankings and evaluations within which all doctoral programs in the world can be ordered. The meaning of this is illustrated by the recent worldwide rankings of research universities by the Shanghai Jiao Tong University. This ranking placed Harvard University at the very top, University of Cambridge was ranked third, and Tokyo University was fourteenth (*The Economist,* September 8, 2005, p. 2). In an internationalized world of higher education, Tokyo University might be the best university in Japan, Harvard University the best in the United States, and Cambridge University the best in the UK—or maybe not. In an internationalized system, the United States, the UK, and Japan might all have different methods of ranking and ordering their universities, and these methods might not even be applicable to institutions outside national boundaries. One indication of a globalized world of doctoral education is the audacity to compare and contrast all of the universities around the world as part of one system.

Globalization in doctoral education, as in everything else, brings with it the legacies of imperialism, colonialism, and Western domination. According to the method used to create the Jiao Tong University rankings, seventeen of the world's top twenty research universities are in the United States, two in the UK, and one in Japan.

If this is the "super-league," as *The Economist* has suggested, or even if the super-league includes the top fifty or top one hundred universities in the world, entire continents have reason to be concerned about their ability to participate in a knowledge economy dominated by those who teach at, and those who take their degrees from, members of that league. The European Union, for instance, seeks to equal the PhD output of US universities. What about places where natural catastrophes and political upheavals have driven away professors and researchers, or where universities have only recently begun to establish standards that will bring them up to an international level of performance?

All nations share a concern about how best to prepare the next generation of leaders who will be able to confront a complex set of social, political, technical, environmental, and health issues within a global setting. Many leaders throughout the world share the view that the planet is entering a period of development in which access to advances in human knowledge and the technological applications of those advances will be critical if every nation is to keep pace with change and participate in a single, integrated world economy. In this period of rapid growth in knowledge and technological change, it is essential for every nation to have an educational system that readies its citizens to understand, apply, and participate in the basic research that is creating this new economy. Technology also enables new types and levels of international research and policy networks. Moreover, technology facilitates connections in the rapidly evolving labor market for highly educated professionals, and technical advances also assist in the education of new generations of PhDs who will be the leading labor force for knowledge-based economies. Taken together, these realities create a powerful motivation for educational leaders today to share information about the most effective ways to educate leaders for these emerging social roles.

CONTRIBUTIONS OF *CIRGE'S FORCES AND FORMS OF CHANGE IN DOCTORAL EDUCATION WORLDWIDE* SERIES OF CONFERENCES

To facilitate the understanding of the forces and institutional forms that are shaping doctoral education worldwide, and to interpret the emerging trends, CIRGE at its conference in September 2005 brought together a group of key players in the field and commissioned a series of papers on recent developments. A grant from the US National Science Foundation (NSF) and support from the Ford Foundation funded this conference; the first in a series of three conferences on *Forces and Forms of Change in Doctoral Education Worldwide.* (Follow up conferences were planned for 2007 and 2009). The initial conference focused on several key issues, including: defining the labor force needed in the twenty-first century, the characteristics of the new labor force, the impacts of technology on research and education, the content and the pedagogy of doctoral education, the transition from post-doctoral education to regular employment, the changing demographics of the doctoral student body, and the financing of doctoral education. Issues of gender, socioeconomic class, race, ethnicity, and regionalism were also on the agenda, as was the growing trend toward privatization of education in some nations.

Objectives included sharing information on innovations and best practices and developing a common vocabulary and shared understanding of the issues. It was expected that this emerging network of leaders (now called the Forces and Forms Global Network) would work toward establishing greater inclusiveness in the realm of doctoral education so that underrepresented nations and groups would have a place at the table and an opportunity to explore methods for increasing their participation in the knowledge economy. The conference was also designed to produce a research agenda on doctoral education internationally, including issues that related to the management and leadership of doctoral programs and universities.

Several recent developments made this conference particularly timely. The 1999 Bologna Accords of the European Union pushed forward the European agenda for increasing collaboration and enhancing the effectiveness of higher education in Europe, and subsequent meetings have focused on doctoral education in particular. In the United States many leading foundations have focused efforts on studying the successes and shortcomings of American doctoral education, the fit between earned degrees and the nation's needs, and other topics. Foundations active in this field include the NSF with its new doctoral programs, Alfred Sloan Foundation with its support for the interdisciplinary master's degree project by the Council of Graduate Schools, The Carnegie Foundation for the Advancement of Teaching, The Pew Foundation Charitable Trust, The Woodrow Wilson National Fellowship Foundation, and the Ford Foundation, among others in its support to CIRGE. Other foundation projects have preceded these, and as the brief study of the following chapters demonstrates, large and small nations alike have been active in creating new studies, panels, quality control commissions, and other institutions in order to improve doctoral education and to guide national research efforts so their citizens are not left out of the emerging economy.

QUESTIONS RAISED

The September 2005 Seattle conference and its commissioned papers were designed to identify both commonalities and differences among systems of education. Was the Bologna Process in Europe creating a more homogeneous system of education? Were other nations adopting or emulating UK, German, or US models of study? Was there pressure within the world to adopt common standards in such areas as doctoral coursework, generic or professional workplace related skills, examinations, supervision, transcripts, credits, and length of study? Were doctoral students being prepared to participate in a new world system of education and research? Did students have mobility once they had degrees? Would their credentials be recognized and valued elsewhere? Were students encouraged to study abroad as part of their doctoral study?

As planned, the conference convened with a diverse panel of international innovators in doctoral education. Over the course of five days, panelists presented papers and engaged in a series of structured and unstructured meetings to explore various dimensions of the issues faced by doctoral studies. Some events were planned carefully so that visitors from developed nations would hear the perspectives of those from less-developed countries. At the end of the conference, participants gathered into study groups that continued to discuss a number of issues in preparation for a second conference that was convened at the University of Melbourne, Australia, in April 2007.

The 2005 conference concluded with the participants agreeing on six topics critical for understanding the role of doctoral education in the knowledge economy and the world and to which they dedicated time to investigate answers over the following sixteen months:

1. The two-directional influence of doctoral education on the global economy and of globalization on doctoral education, and how to deal with the brain drain of doctoral-level researchers out of developing countries.
2. The tension between nation building and local action for development and the necessity for participation in the international scholarly community.
3. Whether there is an international consensus about what comprises doctoral education and what competencies the degree should confer.
4. The creation of internationally meaningful comparative data on doctoral education.
5. How to evaluate doctoral education across national boundaries.
6. The identification of policies that promote the most efficient and useful types of doctoral education.

DEVELOPMENT OF THIS VOLUME

As background for this first conference, participants were asked to describe their countries' doctoral education systems and any changes underway and to emphasize innovations. A common outline was presented as a guide for each country's analyses. Collectively, the papers reveal significant differences among the approaches to doctoral education and the analyses of the problems faced by each national educational system. While the variety of approaches to doctoral education and the different histories of doctoral study in each nation make it difficult to generalize about the state of doctoral education, the last chapter of this book develops a conceptual framework for understanding what we find in the rest of the chapters of this volume and concludes with the research agenda that emerged from the 2005 conference and was articulated in the "Seattle Declaration" developed there.

OVERVIEW OF THIS VOLUME

The bulk of the chapters in this book are grouped roughly by geographic region. We concentrate first on doctoral education systems in Europe;

followed by those in Africa, South America, and Mexico; Australasia; and finally, North America.

Europe

At the turn of the nineteenth century, the German doctoral education provided the model for a new system of emerging doctoral studies: the master-apprentice model of education, which allows senior professors a great degree of autonomy and power over the process of doctoral education. Today, Germany, like other nations with well-established apprentice systems, is working with new codes to define the supervisory structure of doctoral education. A relatively high age at completion of the doctorate and significant attrition are forcing changes such as the implementation of doctoral programs similar to those in the United States. Faculty members in Germany are also being faced with performance-based contracts. At the national level, new accreditation agencies are reviewing the quality of doctoral programs, and the government is beginning to establish "clusters of excellence," including its own type of graduate schools. Barbara Kehm describes all of these changes and articulately presents a concern that appears in many other papers: Will knowledge and therefore doctoral education become just another commodity that is part of a global agenda for technological progress, or will there still be room for systems of education that cultivate scholars who are driven by deep curiosity about problems that may have no obvious practical application?

Howard Green, in his essay on doctoral education in the UK, presents a comprehensive study of the history and function of British universities. He also points out the shortcomings of the current system and describes some of the strategies that are being considered by doctoral programs at the present time. As recently as 1996, doctoral education in Britain was described by an expert as a "cottage industry," characterized by a high degree of autonomy on the part of institutions and faculty members who supervised doctoral students. Like other nations, the UK was faced with attrition and long degree completion times. British doctorates were also losing standing in the international community as graduates were faulted for failing to have sufficient skills in such areas as communication and teamwork—a theme that appears in many of these papers. As in the case of German educators, British experts are reviewing standards for thesis supervision, codes of conduct, the possibility of some common coursework for all doctoral students, and an increased focus on skills that allow doctorates to work effectively in teams, in industry and in government. Institutional audits have been mandated. Like universities on the Continent, British universities are also exploring ways to provide something equivalent to course transcripts for those who complete doctoral degrees. This chapter, like those from Germany, Canada, and the United States, demonstrates that even those nations that are major destinations for foreign students have identified a need to reexamine major elements of doctoral study in response to calls for global standards, mobility, and equivalency in graduate education.

Hans Kristiján Guðmandsson provides a well-documented narrative of changes in doctoral education in the Nordic nations. Home to many fine research universities, the larger Scandinavian nations have a long tradition of cooperation that may serve as a model for the greater European community. A large increase in participation by women since the early 1990s is one of the salient features of doctoral education in the Nordic nations. So is the extraordinary growth and success of scientific and technological research in Iceland, a nation that graduates only a few doctorates on its own soil, but relies on sending students abroad to obtain the very best international credentials. Gudmandsson also provides a picture of the situation in the newly independent Nordic nations, Latvia, Lithuania, and Estonia. A final issue raised by this paper is the average age of those who complete doctorates, which is high compared to the rest of the world.

Andreas Frijdal describes the role of the unique European graduate university (EUI) in Florence, Italy, which was one of the major institutional outcomes of the first fifty years of work on higher education in the European community. While primarily a single-institution study, we included this chapter because Frijdal's essay comments broadly on the Bologna Process and on the degree to which the recommendations of the Bologna Process are being implemented throughout Europe. The EUI has served as a laboratory for Europe by implementing many recommendations and piloting new programs. Recently the EUI created a large number of post-doctoral positions and is leading the way in the discussion of the future of post-doctoral work as a feature of the mobility and knowledge transfer that are to be integral parts of the European educational model.

In Europe, Jeroen Bartelse and Jeroen Huisman write in their discussion of the Bologna Process, that doctoral education is being subjected to intense scrutiny and strong pressures for innovation because of its location "between two worlds: education and research." Debates about improving doctoral education address shortcomings of current training models, including a lack of transparency in requirements for supervisors and candidates, and complaints by employers that doctorate holders often lack communication skills and are over-specialized. The view that doctoral degree holders are vital in the workforce outside academia exerts pressure to increase the number of doctorates and to shift the functions of doctoral programs to include an increasing emphasis on acquisition of transferable skills.

Africa, South America, and Mexico

Ahmed Bawa's chapter on the current state of doctoral education, and indeed on the current state of research in South Africa, speaks powerfully to the growing educational gap in the world. Bawa articulates the concerns of many in the underdeveloped world who fear that in the realm of education, as in other economic realms, the developed Western nations will lure away what little struggling nations still possess in the way of researchers or people of notable talent. South Africa, as he points out, pioneered heart transplant surgery, but today research productivity is dropping, doctorally trained professionals are leaving the country or approaching retirement, and only 10 percent of those who start doctoral programs finish within five years. Bawa frames the issues in terms of a number of ways in which the educational system is "disarticulated." The issues are expressed in terms of mismatches of black and white populations, black and white professors, traditionally black and white institutions, the needs of the society, and the kinds of PhDs that are being turned out. Several possible solutions to the problems are suggested, and the government's attempts to address this "crisis" are both praised and critiqued.

Renato Janine Ribiero describes the Brazilian government's efforts to create an effective system of quality control and the push to assure that a higher percentage of Brazilian university professors complete the PhD. Brazil also has passed a National Graduate School Plan that aims to increase the number of scientific and technological experts in the nation to assure that Brazil participates fully in global economic growth and the knowledge economy. Like Australia, Brazil wishes to have more universities and more doctorates in the less populated regions of the nation, and Brazilian authorities are particularly sensitive to the effectiveness with which national resources are used. Brazil has taken many other dynamic steps to increase the quality of graduate education, and the nation presents evidence that the new quality control measures have been very effective in producing the desired end. Brazil is also working with a plan to send thousands of graduate students abroad to diversify the training of the next generations of Brazilian scientists and academics.

Doctoral education in Mexico is centered at a handful of universities, most of which are in the capital city. Armando Alcantara, Mauricio Fortes, and Salvador Malo offer a historical and contemporary analysis of the challenges faced by Mexican higher education, which has a strong tradition of producing *licensuras*, individuals licensed to practice in particular professions such as engineering and medicine. Communication between the industrial and academic sectors of the Mexican economy poses many problems. The Mexican government has established plans and agencies to help the development of doctoral education in particular and higher education in general, but changes in the central government have led to changes in these plans as well. At this time, relatively few PhDs are produced annually by Mexican universities and the chapter addresses this important issue.

Australasia

In discussing the development of Australian doctoral education, Terry Evans, Barbara Evans, and Helene Marsh point to an early reliance on British models, as well as to many creative responses to the particular needs of that continent, including building up strong undergraduate universities and serving all the distant regions and distinct ethnic groups of the emerging nation. Australia, like the United Kingdom and Europe, is reconsidering the role of coursework in the doctorate. Australia also has had interesting experiences with the creation of new professional doctoral degrees.

Shinichi Yamamoto describes the state of doctoral education in contemporary Japan, a nation that has increased its doctorate production significantly. Japan introduced Western style doctoral education as part of the reforms introduced by the Meiji Emperor in the late nineteenth century. The Japanese government has done a great deal of work to forecast national need and also to monitor the numbers of doctoral and undergraduate students. Government grants support specific types of research and, as in Germany, specific universities have been identified as centers of excellence and offered additional incentives and support for research and scholarly productivity. Japan, like Australia, New Zealand, and Canada, is a major destination for foreign graduate students; though Japan chiefly serves students from other Asian nations, particularly China, Korea, and Taiwan. Japan also has studied a phenomenon important throughout the world—the extent to which PhDs are welcome or can be productive in industrial rather than academic settings.

In discussing doctoral education in India, Narayana Jayaram details enrollment trends, requirements, and current problems. After Indian independence in 1948, higher education there expanded. The number of doctorates granted also increased rapidly, but this was largely due to instituting the doctorate as a requirement for permanent teaching positions in postsecondary institutions. In Jayaram's view, this led to declining standards. Requirements for being allowed to begin doctoral studies include entrance exams, minimum standards for earlier academic achievement, and scrutiny by a committee. However, Jayaram concludes, "in most universities the process is carried out perfunctorily," so that many students are not prepared for doctoral work. Moreover, traditionally the best students choose professional education and the "left over" ones enter doctoral education. The best students who wish to pursue research careers usually go abroad. A continuing problem is quality control. Plagiarism and use of ghostwriters for theses are recognized problems and the University Grants Commission lacks adequate capacity for regulation of Indian universities.

North America

Canada's higher education system shares with Brazil and Australia the phenomenon that its universities are clustered in a few geographic areas of a very physically large country. Garth Williams, in the chapter on Canada's account of doctoral training, points out that Canada's governments have a history of implementing bold national plans for higher education, including a plan that led to the secularization and merger of many former religious institutions and more recent plans to emphasize doctoral training in science and technology. Like the United States, Canada responded to the baby boom by establishing new universities and expanding existing ones. Canadian universities attract many foreign students, and universities in the Francophone area of Canada maintain creative collaborations with universities in France.

Maresi Nerad reviewed the situation in the United States, which produces about 40,000 new PhDs each year, the largest number of any nation. Unlike most of the nations discussed in this book, the United States has a large number of private research universities as well as publicly funded universities. While other nations are turning to quality control models that are similar to American accreditation, in most cases those new accreditation systems are being implemented by governmental bodies, whereas in the United States assessment of research doctoral education is performed by a nongovernmental agency, the National Research Council, by professional disciplinary associations in the case of professional fields, and by each university itself through a system of peer reviews. In very fundamental ways, American education is less centrally controlled, although the United States, like other major industrial nations, provides a great deal of government funding for research that guides the direction of science and technology. American universities face many of the same problems as universities in the rest of the world: low completion rates, long time-to-degrees, sometimes a poor fit between social needs and the fields of graduates, and many PhDs who cannot find academic employment, but increasingly find satisfactory employment in business, government, or nonprofits. Moreover, in spite of the fact that American universities have traditionally required more coursework than doctoral programs elsewhere, American programs recognize the same needs for change in such areas as a common course on epistemology and the scientific method, more interdisciplinary training, more preparation for teaching, and more attention to teamwork, presentation skills, and collaborative research. American universities often have graduate schools, an institutional structure being explored by many other nations. Altogether, this chapter shows that while American doctoral education may attract the emulation and admiration of much of the world, its problems are in fact similar to those faced by graduate education worldwide. The chapter summarizes the various foundation projects currently examining the state of American doctoral education.

Conclusion and Appendixes

The Conclusion, by Maresi Nerad and Thomas Trzyna, with input by Jerry de Jaager and Elizabeth Rudd, points out a number of topics that appear in several chapters without being explored in detail. These may be areas where additional research would be very helpful.

Included is the development of a conceptual framework for understanding doctoral education within globalization. This provides the context for considering key dimensions of globalization in doctoral education that are illuminated by the work presented in this book: commoditization, the market economy, the Mode 2 educational model, brain drain, the use of English, standardization, quality assurance, and the Bologna Accords. It focuses on national and institutional responses to globalization, and on the ways that these responses are affecting the education of individual doctoral students. It synthesizes the innovations described in this volume into an outline of the likely characteristics of future-oriented doctoral education. It concludes with the research agenda that emerged from the 2005 conference (see the Seattle Declaration) that identifies topics critical to understanding the current dynamics of doctoral education and for shaping the future of doctoral education in a global context that preserves diversity.

The material in Appendix A was developed at the end of the 2005 conference. It offers an overview of the commonalities, differences, and future trends in doctoral education around the world. The Seattle Declaration in the appendixes was also one of the outcomes of the conference. It was created as a guiding document intended to steer and encourage a continuing conversation about where doctoral education is going in the future and about setting a research agenda for the newly created international network of doctoral education experts—another outcome of the conference.

We hope this volume will be a useful and informative reference which will spur innovative thought about the future of doctoral education. If you are interested in keeping up with the latest papers, conferences, and task force findings that have emerged from this work, you are invited to visit the CIRGE web site, www.cirge.washington.edu.

BIBLIOGRAPHY

Appadurai, Arjun. 1999. "Globalization and the Research Imagination." *International Social Science Journal* 160: 229–38.

The Economist. 2005. "The Brains Business." Sept. 8.

Thompson, Grahame. 1999. "Introduction: Situating Globalization." *International Social Science Journal* 160: 139–52.

· I ·

DOCTORAL EDUCATION IN EUROPE

1 • GERMANY

BARBARA M. KEHM

INTRODUCTION

During the last ten to fifteen years doctoral education and training in Germany has moved more and more into the focus of policy debates. Several factors contributed to this development. First, since the 1980s the number of doctoral degrees awarded in Germany has more than doubled, with about 25,000 doctoral degrees awarded annually, Germany belongs to those countries worldwide in which the highest number of doctorates are awarded. To provide a context for this figure: In the UK about 14,000 doctoral degrees are awarded annually and in France about 11,000. In the USA approximately 1.2 percent of all citizens above the age of twenty-five have a PhD degree, while the same figure for Germany is 1.8 percent and the average proportion across all OECD member states is 1.0 percent (OECD 2002).

Second, we can observe that research related professional activities for economic and societal development are increasingly important within the emerging knowledge society. Third, labor markets and career opportunities for doctoral degree holders have changed to a certain extent. PhDs are no longer recruited almost exclusively into teaching and research functions within universities and research institutes but also into professional jobs outside academia. Germany has always been a country in which non-academic labor markets were particularly open for doctoral degree holders. Having such a degree traditionally provided access to high-level professional positions not only in universities and research institutes but also in the professions, in public administration, in politics, and in the private sector. The doctoral degree thus fulfilled and continues to fulfill an important function in the reproduction of societal elites (Enders 2005).

With the growing importance as well as the growing numbers of doctoral degree holders, concern about quality, duration, and completion of doctoral education and training increased as well. In the following I will give an overview first of the traditions of doctoral education in Germany and second of the current forces of change at the national as well as at the European level that have contributed to the fact that doctoral education and training has become a "hot topic" on the agenda for reforms in higher education. I will then go through the main issues of concern and reform currently being undertaken in Germany and also illustrate these with a few examples of good practice. In my conclusions I will identify and summarise the main trends in current reforms of doctoral education and try to provide a look into future developments.

TRADITIONS OF DOCTORAL EDUCATION IN GERMANY

The traditional German model of doctoral education and training has frequently been characterized as the "master-apprentice model." That implied that doctoral education did not take place within programs or schools as it did and does in Anglo-American countries, but that it was a rather personal relationship between a doctoral candidate (i.e., they were not considered students but rather adjuncts or assistants) and his or her supervisor. Apart from colloquiums for doctoral students organised by a chair holder and full-professor, if he or she had several doctoral candidates, getting the degree often just involved doing individual research work and producing a thesis, or having a paid position (part-time and temporary) within the framework of a research project or as an assistant for a professor. Until about the end of the 1970s, it was frequent in the humanities subjects that those students heading for an academic career finished their studies with a doctoral degree without getting any other undergraduate or graduate degree first. After that time, however, it became normal to graduate with a Magister, Diplom, or Staatsexamen (the traditional German degrees after four to six years of studies) and then go on to get a doctoral degree. Doctoral degrees can only be awarded by universities. Graduates from *Fachhochschulen*, now called universities of applied sciences, could not change to a university after graduation and get their doctoral degree there but had to do additional course work for one or two years at a university before being accepted as doctoral candidates.

Doctoral candidates often had a paid junior researcher position, were associated to the professor and chair holder and supported him or her in teaching and research. Positions were part-time (50 percent or less of a full-time position) and temporary, mostly for up to four years. The chair holder typically acted not only as supervisor of the dissertation thesis (which more often than not was in his or her field of specialization) but also as first referee of the thesis and as main examiner in the defence. There always was a second referee but this person could not be chosen without the consent of the first one. This implies that the position of a doctoral candidate was one of high personal dependence.

Other but less frequent forms of getting a doctoral degree were scholarships provided by various foundations, political as well as elite, or jobbing part-time and writing the thesis during the rest of the time. Only a rather small proportion of doctoral candidates did their research in industry or enterprises while the thesis was supervised by a professor. Such university-industry cooperation took place in particular in engineering subjects, chemistry, and pharmacy. Dropout was frequent (though no statistics exist) and time-to-degree was on average (though varying considerably between subjects) between four and six years. Over the years the average age upon completion of the degree slowly but continuously increased across all subjects from thirty-one years to thirty-two years and it was thirty-three years by 2003, again with considerable differences among the disciplines. In 2003, it was lowest in the medical fields (31.6 years in veterinary medicine and 32.1 years in human medicine) and highest in the fine arts (37.0 years). It was 36.7 years in the philologies and cultural sciences as well as in sports and physical education. The average age upon completion of a doctorate in mathematics and the natural sciences, in 2003, was 32.2 years, and in engineering it was 34.1 years (Statistisches Bundesamt 2003).

In the German Democratic Republic a basic system for the promotion of junior academic staff through postgraduate programs had been established by the end of the 1960s. Between 1968 and 1970, the award of doctoral degrees increased by two-thirds, from less than 2,900 to more than 4,700 annually. During the same period, the proportion of women who were awarded a doctoral degree increased from 18.5 percent to 30.3 percent. In the twenty-year period from 1970 to 1989 the number of doctoral degrees awarded in the German Democratic Republic increased steadily to almost 22,000 annually. Owing to the transformation process starting in 1990 and the large-scale redundancies of East German academic staff, the number of doctoral degrees awarded fell by one-third. The number slowly increased again after 1993. In 2003, altogether 23,043 doctoral degrees were awarded in both the old and the new federal states of Germany (for this section Kehm 1999).

TABLE 1.1. Doctoral degrees awarded in Germany 1970–2003 according to subject groups and gender (in percent)

	1970[a]			1980			1990			2003		
Subject Groups	*Total*	*Men*	*Women*	*Total*	*Men*	*Women*	*Total*	*Men*	*Women*	*Total*	*Men*	*Women*
Humanities (incl. Sports)	925	722	203	1,089	800	289	1,726	1,116	610	2,597	1,301	1,296
Law/Economics/ Soc. Sciences	1,233	1,174	59	1,232	1,111	121	1,886	1,571	315	3,342	2,291	1,051
Natural Sciences	2,106	2,004	102	2,739	2,399	340	5,177	4,048	1,129	6,412	4,422	1,990
Medical Fields	4,552	3,294	1,258	4,869	3,534	1,335	6,523	3,997	2,526	7,725	3,928	3,797
Engineering	768	763	5	997	983	14	1,400	1,348	52	2,153	1,928	225
Agric. Fields	144	132	12	331	262	69	549	410	139	501	331	170
Fine Arts	-	-	-	153	93	60	236	119	117	313	118	195
Total	9,728	8,089	1,639	12,221	9,838	2,383	18,494	13,353	5,141	23,043	14,319	8,724

[a] Foreign students are not included.

SOURCES: Statistical Yearbook of the Federal Republic of Germany 1973, p. 96; Science Council: Basic and Structural Data of the Situation of the Universities from 1980 to 2000, p. 39; Federal Statistical Office: Education and Culture, Series 11, volume 4.2: Examinations at Universities 2003. Wiesbaden, 2003.

FORCES OF CHANGE

At the beginning of the 1990s the German Rectors' Conference and the Science Council began to draw attention to severe problems that could be seen in the traditional Humboldtian "master-apprentice model" of doctoral education in Germany. Insufficient structure, unclear status of doctoral students, increasing time to successful completion of the degree, high numbers of drop-outs, high degree of personal dependency on the supervisor, lack of interdisciplinary approaches, and insufficient orientation to labor markets outside academia were just some of the problems which could be observed. The German Rectors' Conference suggested the introduction of graduate programs that would incorporate the model of graduate colleges. With the financial support of the German Research Foundation such graduate colleges (Graduiertenkollegs) had been set up starting in 1990 at a number of universities. These took the form of thematically oriented and often interdisciplinary research groups for which there were special admission procedures but which also gave some structure to the phase of getting a doctoral degree and supported the young researchers with scholarships. By 2001, about 285 graduate colleges had been established. Twenty-seven of these are international graduate colleges, i.e., in association with partner universities from abroad (Hüfner 2003).

However, the model of graduate colleges did not become the rule but remained a more or less privileged exception. In November 2002, the Science Council observed that a need to reform the education and training of doctoral students continued to exist in Germany (Wissenschaftsrat 2002). In February 2003 the German Rectors' Conference followed up by publishing further recommendations concerning the organisation of doctoral studies (Hochschulrektorenkonferenz 2003). The goals included in particular a reduction of the average age upon completion of the thesis and award of the degree, the introduction of taught elements into the phase of research training, and the acquisition of additional competences in preparation for employability in non-academic labour markets.

The German Academic Exchange Service (DAAD 2004) in cooperation with the German Research Foundation, and with additional funding from the Federal Ministry for Education and Research (thirty million Euros for the period from 2001 to 2006), have established fifty international postgraduate programmes (IPPs) in a broad range of subjects to advance implementation of the recommendations to reform doctoral education and training in Germany and to strengthen the appeal and competitiveness of German universities in the field of postgraduate education.

INITIATIVES AT THE EUROPEAN LEVEL

Two political events made doctoral education a hot topic not only in Germany but also in practically all European countries. The first took place in 1998, with the "Joint Declaration on Harmonisation of the Architecture of the European Higher Education System" issued in Paris by the Ministers of Education and Research from Germany, France, Italy, and the UK. The declaration was a first step towards creating a unified structure of studies that would further reduce barriers for mobility and exchange. This declaration was not intended to interfere in the content of studies, learning and teaching styles. One year later the so-called Sorbonne Declaration led to the famous Bologna Declaration, which has now been signed by forty-five European countries. The most important part of this Declaration was the intention to create a "European Higher Education Area" until 2010 and introduce the two-tiered structure of studies consisting of a bachelor's degree of about three years' duration as a first degree providing students with an education that enables transition into the labor market (employability is the key word here) and—for a clearly smaller proportion of students—the offer to continue with a master's degree of approximately another two years' duration (this is called the 3 + 2 model).

The European Commission was totally surprised by this undertaking. This was what the Commission had always wanted but was never allowed to do because education was deemed to be a national responsibility. The European Commission began to support the Bologna Process, which started after 1999, meaning the actual implementation on the national level of what had been decided by the ministers. At the same time the Bologna Process triggered considerable reforms in almost all European higher education systems. The ministers also agreed to meet every two years until 2010 to assess the implementation process. They have met in Prague (Czech Republic) in 2001, in Berlin (Germany) in 2003, and in Bergen (Norway) in 2005. In 2007 they will meet in London (UK). As preparation for each of these high-level meetings, a so-called "Trends Report" is issued analyzing the implementation process in the countries involved in the process. The Bergen meeting was additionally prepared by a small group responsible for stock-taking. In many countries smaller and larger studies were commissioned by the national governments to examine national implementation processes.

For our topic concerning forces and forms of change in doctoral education, the Berlin meeting of ministers in 2003 was the most important of the Bologna follow-up meetings so far. In the final communiqué issued at the end of the meeting, the ministers declared their intention to include doctoral education in the new-tiered structure, i.e., bachelor's degree (3 years), master's degree (2 years), and doctoral degree (another 3 years).

The European Commission reacted to this surprising conclusion not only by actively supporting the Bologna Process but also by coming up with a similar goal in the field of research and technological development. At the Lisbon Summit in 2000, a communication from the European Commission to the Council, the Parliament, and the relevant Committees was issued proposing to create a "European Research Area." In his Lisbon speech, the Commissioner for Research, Philippe Busquin, declared a resolve to make Europe the most dynamic and competitive knowledge-based economy in the world by the year 2010. In order to achieve this, it was decided to raise the proportion of the national GDP spent on research and technological development in all member states to 3 percent, thus increasing the number of qualified researchers in Europe and triggering further innovation.

The two processes have begun to merge. Creating a European area of higher education and a European research area in order to become a dynamic and competitive knowledge society on a global scale has not only created a renewed awareness of the importance of universities in terms of their task of research and research training, it has also led to a closer scrutiny of the ways in which research is currently organised (Kehm 2004, 2005b).

CHANGE AGENTS AND IMPLEMENTATION OF REFORMS IN GERMANY

From what has been said so far, it is easy to identify the main change agents driving reforms of doctoral education and training in Germany. Apart from the European developments, which are included in the policy agenda on a national level, driving forces of change are the German Research Foundation, the Science Council, the German Rectors' Conference, and recently also the German Academic Exchange Service. While the Science Council and the Rectors' Conference are influential bodies for agenda setting and making recommendations, the German Research Foundation and the German Academic Exchange Service have money for funding actual programmes, pilot projects, and graduate schools. Funding is distributed on the basis of competitive bidding and those initiatives that are successful are usually thought of as models of good practice.

However, as doctoral education and training continue to be considered a matter that is part of the academic freedom, each professor can decide individually whom he or she is willing to accept as a doctoral student, what the topic for the thesis might be, how much the doctoral student will be involved in the professor's research and teaching, and how much time he or she is willing to spend on supervision. Therefore, the actual change agents can only be the professors themselves, who must to react to incentives, take on the extra time to conceptualise a program, cooperate with other professors to create a critical mass, design courses for the taught part and possibly write an application for funding, and provide more structure in doctoral education and training. Usually a doctoral program cannot be established and implemented by one person alone, but also needs support from the central level of the university. In addition, such an undertaking needs extra funding.

Currently there is widespread agreement that doctoral education and training should be given more structure to improve quality and reduce the duration until completion of the degree. The trend to establish doctoral programmes also includes some taught elements and clearer regulations of supervision and the amount of work expected from the student. And indeed, doctoral candidates in such programmes are considered more frequently to be students rather than young researchers on a paid contract.

It is possible to name one other source for changes in doctoral education and training. Due to recent and ongoing management reforms in the governance of universities and a higher degree of financial autonomy through lump sum budgets, coupled with new forms of accountability and a decrease in detailed state control, performance based contracts have been introduced as a new instrument of steering. Contracts are negotiated between a university and the responsible state ministry as well as between the central level of an institution and the basic units, and in negotiations with newly appointed professors. In quite a few cases performance indicators are applied that seek to increase the number of students successfully completing a program within a defined framework of time. These contracts also specify the amount of external research funding an individual professor or a department is supposed to attract, and an increase in the number of doctoral degrees awarded in those departments or faculties where the numbers are considered to be too low.

As all these reforms are ongoing, it is not yet possible to present hard data or to evaluate successes and shortcomings in implementation. In a study about models of doctoral education and training in Bavaria (Berning and Falk 2005) the authors found that between 51.3 percent of doctoral work in the natural sciences and 85.5 percent of doctoral work in law continue to be according to the traditional "master-apprentice model" while the balance takes place within the framework of graduate schools or doctoral programs with more structure and taught elements. Nevertheless, this study also observed a decreasing importance of the individual dissertation in favour of integration into larger research projects and an increasing importance of more intensive supervision that is often divided among several persons.

ISSUES IN THE ONGOING REFORMS

"More structure" in doctoral education and training is the current key phrase. It does not imply merely a turning away from the "master-apprentice model" and the individual dissertation; it also implies more formalised procedures of selection, supervision and examination, the establishment of programs or schools, and an increase in the taught elements, i.e., some kind of study program. Summarizing the emerging new structure of doctoral education, Hüttl (2005) emphasized three core elements:

- a competitive and performance oriented selection procedure for doctoral candidates;
- the establishment of clear responsibilities on the side of the doctoral student as well as on the side of the supervisor, including the provision of working conditions that are more closely related to the research and the topic of the thesis; and
- an accompanying study program.

In recent years more and more doctoral programs or "graduate colleges" (Graduiertenkollegs) have been established, many of them of an interdisciplinary nature and often with an international orientation, i.e., accepting doctoral students from other countries and providing courses in English. However, such programs need extra funding, and if Bavaria can be used as an example, there is no subject as yet in which more than 50 percent of all doctorates are produced within a structured framework. However, with the implementation of the Bologna reforms, which include doctoral studies as the third cycle in a tiered structure of studies, it can be expected that by 2010 doctoral programs will be more widespread.

The quality of supervision, and in some cases the lack of adequate supervision, has been identified as one of the main problems of doctoral education and training in Germany. Personal dependence on the supervisor, insufficient contact with the supervisor, or exploitation by the supervisor has been identified as typical problem areas in this respect.

Within the framework of doctoral programs and graduate colleges (Graduiertenkollegs) it is hoped that such problems can be remedied. Written agreements (or contracts) between the doctoral candidates and the person responsible for the program are supposed to regulate the responsibilities on each side and provide opportunities for shared supervision and more contact hours.

The oral defence of a thesis is usually a public event. As a rule there will be three examiners, one of whom can be from another university or even from abroad. After a thirty-minute presentation of the results of the thesis, the examiners will ask questions pertaining to the research work as well as to broader disciplinary matters. The public is not allowed to intervene in the discussion between the examiners and the doctoral candidate. After about sixty to ninety minutes, the examiners withdraw to discuss the defence among themselves and agree on a grade. The doctoral candidate is then informed about the result immediately.

There are currently no discussions as yet in Germany to change this procedure; however, if getting a doctoral degree becomes the third cycle of the new tiered structure of studies, including taught elements as well, the weighting of the research work and the oral defence for the final grade will change to include the results of the course work.

Beginning doctoral researchers either have status as paid employees at a university or as students. Outside of doctoral programs and Graduiertenkollegs, doctoral candidates are not considered to be students. They may be contract researchers in projects funded by third parties, they may be junior researchers on half-time paid positions connected to a chair holder, or they may have a scholarship from one of the various German foundations. In the last case doctoral candidates remain enrolled as students at a university. Some universities have also created a special status for doctoral "students." Current regulations for contract research assistants, i.e., the typical paid position for a junior researcher with the opportunity to get a doctoral degree, provide employment for up to four years on a 50 percent basis. Of this 50 percent, one third of the paid working hours can be used for doing doctoral research and writing the thesis, while the rest of the time is spent on supporting the teaching and research duties of the professor, who is normally also the supervisor of the thesis, the main referee of the thesis, and the main examiner in the oral defence. If a doctoral candidate is funding this phase through a scholarship or paid jobs outside academia, the relationship between the doctoral candidate and the supervisor becomes very informal. The doctoral candidate is more or less left alone to deal with the task ahead and will make appointments with the supervisor to receive feedback and keep up contact after having submitted written parts or chapters of the thesis.

The status of doctoral candidates within the working context of a university or a research institute varies considerably according to subject field. The majority of doctoral candidates in the natural sciences, in engineering, and also in economics carry out their research work within the context of an institution or a research project team. In the social sciences and humanities we find considerably higher proportions of doctoral candidates doing their research work and writing their theses with the support of a scholarship or some type of paid work outside the university (Enders and Bornmann 2001). In these cases, the students are not part of research groups and therefore do most of their work independently.

The German trade union that organizes academic and research staff has for some years been making a case to adopt the Scandinavian model for young researchers as paid employees of the university with full social security and all fringe benefits given to regular academic staff. However, looking at the European developments to establish more internationally attractive doctoral programs with (high) tuition fees and refined marketing, and taking into consideration as well the German decision finally to allow tuition fees, it appears that the trend will go in the opposite direction. Sooner rather than later, doctoral programs in Germany will charge tuition fees and enroll candidates with the status of doctoral students. Currently acceptance into a doctoral program or a graduate college is frequently connected with a scholarship. There are no tuition fees as yet. Another sizeable proportion of young researchers getting a doctoral degree will continue to be part-time assistants and junior contract researchers on paid positions within the university.

In general, quality debates in German higher education are closely connected with the idea of making study in Germany more attractive for students from abroad, as well as with increasing Germany's reputation in the European and international competition for excellence. Teaching quality at most German universities is now evaluated on a more or less regular basis, new study programs are accredited by external accreditation agencies, and standards and assessment criteria are being developed according to European standards. Doctoral programs and graduate colleges are also evaluated periodically because they often receive external funding. Due to the competitive bidding for funding programs, graduate schools are evaluated by peers on behalf of funding organizations. However, the newly established German accreditation agencies are only making their first moves towards establishing their right to accredit doctoral programs. The criteria and standards that have been developed so far for the accreditation of doctoral programs are still in a rather early stage and are frequently judged rather critically by the academic community.

In recent years, the federal government and the German states have been negotiating the funding of an "initiative for excellence." For example, the Federal Ministry for Education and Research proposed providing a large amount of money in order to finance selected universities to develop the potential to become elite universities on an international or even global scale. Until 2011, altogether 1.9 billion euros will be available for the universities, of which funding the federal government will provide 75 percent and the states 25 percent. The money is supposed to promote competition for top universities and clusters of excellence. The German Research Foundation and the Science Council will administer the money, develop criteria for spending it, and establish a selection commission. The program consists of three forms of support: graduate schools, clusters of excellence, and concepts for the future of university research. Funding is provided for these activities on the basis of competitive bidding; however, the individual states have insisted on keeping the right to select those universities that are allowed to submit a proposal. That means that real competition will be prevented once again because in each of the states the state ministries will select those universities they think are top institutions. This will assure that the money will be more or less equally distributed among the sixteen German states regardless of the fact that one state, for example, might have five top level universities and another state might have none.

Relationships between higher education institutions and industry in Germany have always been stronger at universities of applied sciences than at other universities. But even at those other universities, as at the technical universities there are strong relationships to industry in subjects like engineering, some of the more applied natural sciences (for example, a doctoral degree is a must in chemistry in order to get adequate employment inside as well as outside academia) and often in economics as well. Since the expansion of German higher education in the latter half of the 1960s and the early 1970s, it became clear that university students needed to explore potential fields for professional activities after completion of their degrees, and many curricula included phases of practical work placements. In the state regulated professions (e.g., teaching, law, medicine) graduates had to complete another eighteen months of practical professional training, which culminates in another examination before they can practice their professions.

Relationships between university and industry in doctoral training are frequent in certain subjects and almost non-existing in the humanities and social sciences. Still, the German labor market for highly qualified graduates with doctoral degrees has always been relatively open. While in other European countries new doctoral programs for professional doctorates have been developed in recent years (particularly in the Netherlands and in the UK), this has not been considered a serious problem in Germany. However, with the establishment of more doctoral programs that include taught elements, more emphasis has been put on the development of generic skills or key qualifications, such as communication, presentation skills and project management skills. These qualifications are supposed to enhance the employability of those doctoral degree holders who graduate in subjects without a defined professional field and to enhance the professional and leadership skills of those doctoral degree holders who graduate in technical and scientific subjects. With the continuing growth in doctoral degrees awarded it has become evident that the majority will not head for a career in academia but rather seek employment in the private and public sector.

For many years, postdoctoral positions in universities were considered to be either a phase of the second formal qualification required in Germany to be eligible for a professorship (the Habilitation) or some type of waiting or holding position until an adequate employment outside the university or a research institute could be found. The principle of "up or out" continues to characterise employment in academia. All positions below the full professor with tenure are basically temporary. Often the Habilitation took another six to ten years to achieve after one had been awarded a doctoral degree. Upon completion of the Habilitation, candidates are awarded the title of "private docent" making them eligible for a call to a chair but providing no guarantee for success. Due to higher education expansion and demographic factors the turnover of chair holders was very low for almost twenty-five years (from about the mid-1970s until the end of the 1990s). This implied that there were quite a few highly qualified persons often older than forty years of age with no opportunity to remain in academia. These individuals were often regarded as overqualified and over-specialized for non-academic labor markets. Currently a new round of this cycle is taking place. Many professors go into retirement, young persons are called to a chair, and then there might be another phase of rather low turnover.

In order to avoid this, the Federal Ministry for Education and Research created a fast track to a professorship, called "junior professor," which did not require a Habilitation. The junior professorship became part of a change of the framework law for higher education in 2002. Doctoral degree holders with very good grades and not older than in the beginning of their thirties can apply for such positions that enable them to be independent in their teaching and research. They receive a contract for six years, and their work is evaluated after three years. Those universities willing to introduce this type of position into their system were given additional funding that the junior professor could use to establish and build up a research group and the necessary infrastructure. The universities had to provide a fully tenured professorship after successful completion of the six-year phase of junior professorship. Again, three of the German states (Bavaria, Thuringia, and Saxony) went to court to complain about the procedure through which the change of the framework law was undertaken, but the underlying reason for their suit was undue interference of the Federal Government into their responsibilities.

The high court issued a judgement in July 2004 that ruled that the change of the framework law did not follow required procedure and that the intention to make the junior professorship the regular way to become a professor was wrong. All this was accompanied by political debates and discussions in relevant bodies and organisations about whether or not the Habilitation should be abolished. The creation of junior professorships was not altogether forbidden, but the effect of the ruling is that there are two ways to gain a professorship and eventually two classes of professors. However, since the beginning of the 1970s, there has been another class of professors already, i.e., those who were given a chair without a Habilitation on the basis of merit and reputation. While this practice is not common, neither can it be said to be rare.

A survey concerning the careers of doctoral degree holders inside and outside academia, carried out by Enders and Bornmann (2001) in 1999, was able to show that in the emerging knowledge society more and more highly qualified holders of doctoral degrees are required, i.e., that no "overproduction is taking place." However, such highly qualified persons need a number of competences over and beyond their actual subject related qualifications in order to become flexible knowledge workers in the new knowledge economy. This will certainly have implications for this particular phase of qualification as well as for the traditional German pathways of becoming eligible for a professorship.

SUMMARY AND CONCLUSIONS

The traditional German structures for organizing doctoral education are currently in an accelerating process of change. At the national level concerns about the long duration of doctoral education as well as the quality of supervision have been voiced for quite some time. A solution to these problems was seen in the establishment of doctoral programs, to give more structure to the qualification process and to guarantee better supervision and possibly shared supervision. With the inclusion of doctoral studies as the third cycle of study in the framework of the Bologna process, an international and competitive dimension has been added to existing national concerns. It could be said that doctoral education and training is undergoing a paradigmatic change in Germany insofar as it is no longer regarded as the sole responsibility of individual professors or, at the most, of the department or faculty, but has become rather the focus of institutional and national policies (also refer to Enders 2005).

But there are more shifts involved. At a large EU conference in April 2004, a working group on the future of doctoral education and training summarized the following trends that could be noted all over Europe:

- from national to international;
- from curiosity driven to result oriented (i.e., growing importance of relevance and impact);
- from individual to team;
- from narrow and discipline guided to multidisciplinary research;
- from small laboratories to larger research institutes and programs (i.e., critical mass);
- from fragments to programs;
- from purely academic to also professional; and
- from national in scope to competitiveness, job creation, and sustainable development on a broader scale.

It still remains to be seen whether doctoral education and training in Germany will eventually be shaped according to the Anglo-American PhD model. However, since there is still a majority of doctoral candidates being trained the traditional way, we can assume that not one way of getting a doctoral degree will prevail, but rather that the forms of doctoral education and training will multiply and that there will be several different forms and ways of getting a doctoral degree in parallel.

BIBLIOGRAPHY

Bartelse, Jeroen. 1999. *Concentrating the Minds: The Institutionalisation of the Graduate School Innovation in Dutch and German Higher Education*. Enschede: CHEPS and Utrecht: Lemma.

Berning, Ewald, and Susanne Falk. 2005. "Das Promotionswesen im Umbruch" (Changes in the Shape of the Doctorate). In *Beiträge zur Hochschulforschung* (Contributions to Higher Education Research) Vol. 27, No. 1: 48–72.

Bourner, Tim, Rachel Bowden, and Stuart Laing. 2000. "Professional Doctorates: The Development of Researching Professionals." In *New Directions in Professional Higher Education*, edited by T. Bourner, T. Katz, and D. Watson, 214–55. Buckingham: SRHE and Open University Press.

Centre for Higher Education Policy Studies (CHEPS). 2002. *Science, Training and Career: Changing Modes of Knowledge Production and Labour Markets.* Proceedings of an International Workshop organised by the Centre for Higher Education Policy Studies, University of Twente, October 2002. http://www.utwente.nl/cheps/documenten/engreportproceedings1 (accessed on 16 July 2007).

Commission of the European Communities. 2003a. *Communication from the Commission: The Role of Universities in the Europe of Knowledge.* Brussels (COM (2003) 58 final).

Commission of the European Communities. 2003b. *Communication for the Commission to the Council and the European Parliament: Researchers in the European Research Area: One Profession, Multiple Careers.* Brussels (COM (2003) 436 final).

DAAD (German Academic Exchange Service). 2004. *50 Select International Postgraduate Programmes at Universities in Germany.* Bonn: DAAD.

Enders, Jürgen. 1996. *Die wissenschaftlichen Mitarbeiter. Ausbildung, Beschäftigung und Karriere der Nachwuchswissenschaftler und Mittelbauangehörigen an den Universitäten* (The Academic Assistants: Training, Employment, and Career of Junior Researchers and Middle Level Research and Teaching Staff at Universities). Frankfurt/M., New York: Campus.

Enders, Jürgen. 2005. "Brauchen die Universitäten in Deutschland ein neues Paradigma der Nachwuchsausbildung?" (Do German Universities Need a New Paradigm for Training Future Researchers?) In *Beiträge zur Hochschulforschung* (Contributions to Higher Education Research), Vol. 27, No. 1: 34–47.

Enders, Jürgen, and Lutz Bornmann. 2001. *Karriere mit Doktortitel? Ausbildung, Berufsverlauf und Berufserfolg von Promovierten* (Careers of Doctoral Degree Holders: Education, Careers, and Professional Success of Doctoral Degree Holders). Frankfurt/M., New York: Campus.

Hochschulrektorenkonferenz (HRK). 2003. *Zur Organisation des Promotionsstudiums* (About the Organisation of Doctoral Studies). Entschließung des 199. Plenums vom 17./18. February. http://www.hrk.de/de/beschluesse/109_253.php (accessed 16 July 2007).

Hüfner, Klaus. 2004. "Doctoral Degrees in Germany." In *Doctoral Studies and Qualifications in Europe and the United States: Status and Prospects*, edited by Jan Sadlak, 51–61. Bucarest: UNESCO-CEPES.

Hüttl, Reinhard F. 2005. "Kernelemente für eine Neugestaltung der Promotionslandschaft" (Core Elements for a New Structure of Doctoral Education). In *Hochschule Innovativ,* No. 14: 12–13.

Kehm, Barbara M. 1999. *Higher Education in Germany: Developments, Problems and Perspectives.* Bucharest: UNESCO CEPES and Wittenberg: Institute for Higher Education Research.

Kehm, Barbara M. 2004 and 2005a. "Developing Doctoral Degrees and Qualifications in Europe: Good Practice and Issues of Concern." In *Doctoral Studies and Qualifications in Europe and the United States: Status and Prospects,* edited by Jan Sadlak, 279–98. Bucharest: UNESCO-CEPES. Reprinted under the same title in *Beiträge zur Hochschulforschung* (Contributions to Higher Education Research), Vol. 27, No. 1: 10–33.

Kehm, Barbara M. 2005b. "Promovieren in Europa: Strukturen und Konzepte im Vergleich" (Getting a Doctoral Degree in Europe: A Comparison of Structures and Concepts). In *Hochschule Innovativ,* No. 14: 2–3

Kupfer, Antonia, and Johannes Moes. 2003. *Promovieren in Europa. Ein internationaler Vergleich von Promotionsbedingungen* (Getting a Doctoral Degree in Europe: An International Comparison of Conditions). Frankfurt/M: GEW and Hans Böckler Foundation.

OECD. 2002. *Science, Technology and Industry Outlook.* Paris: OECD.

Prömel, Hans Jürgen. 2005. "Promovieren an der Humboldt-Universität" (Getting a Doctoral Degree at Humboldt University). *In Hochschule Innovativ,* No. 14: 6.

Sadlak, Jan, ed. 2004. *Doctoral Studies and Qualifications in Europe and the United States: Status and Prospects.* Bucharest: UNESCO-CEPES.

Scott, David, Andrew Brown, Ingrid Lunt, and Lucy Thorne. 2004. *Professional Doctorates: Integrating Professional and Academic Knowledge.* Buckingham: SRHE and Open University Press.

Senger, Ulrike. 2003. *Internationale Doktorandenstudien. Ein Modell für die Internationalisierung der Doktorandenausbildung an deutschen Hochschulen und Forschungseinrichtungen* (*International Doctoral Studies: A Model for the Internationalisation of Doctoral Education at German Universities and Research Institutes*). Bielefeld: Bertelsmann.

Statistisches Bundesamt. 2003. *Bildung und Kultur. Prüfungen an Hochschulen* (*Education and Culture: Examinations at Higher Education Institutions*). Fachserie 11, Reihe 4.2. Wiesbaden.

Wissenschaftsrat. 1995. *Empfehlungen zur Neustrukturierung der Doktorandenausbildung und-förderung* (*Recommendations for a New Structure of Doctoral Education and Financial Support of Doctoral Students*). Köln.

Wissenschaftsrat. 2002. *Empfehlungen zur Doktorandenausbildung* (*Recommendations for the Education and Training of Doctoral Students*). Drucksache 5459/02. Saarbrücken. http://www.wissenschaftsrat.de/texte/5459–02.pdf (accessed 18 July 2007).

2 • UNITED KINGDOM

HOWARD GREEN

INTRODUCTION

In 1996 the UK Council for Graduate Education (UKCGE) noted that "doctoral education was frequently regarded as a cottage industry, a prestigious yet somehow fringe activity in higher education" (UKCGE 1996). This paper outlines the key changes that have taken place since that time, identifying some of the major drivers for change and finally highlighting some current issues, as yet unresolved. In so doing it suggests that the movement from a cottage industry to one that provides excellence in an increasingly mass production environment continues to challenge universities and their regulators in the UK and that there remains much to be done.

It is recognised that since devolved responsibilities for higher education were given to Scotland and to a lesser extent Wales, there have been divergences in the way in which higher education has developed, in particular with regard to funding. Specific attention is not given to these differences; they are noted only for comparative purposes where appropriate. It is acknowledged that generalisation about doctoral education in the UK is increasingly difficult because of these developments.

FORCES OF CHANGE

The doctorate has changed, and continues to change, in response to the many pressures that come in all directions and which are often idiosyncratic and unstructured. This section examines some of these influences and points to the kinds of responses that are observable in the overall system. These will be developed subsequently. Overall these influences are often ill-coordinated and are leading to a rather incremental and disjointed approach to change. What follows is itself rather random; the influences are neither necessarily in order of importance or in any chronological sequence.

The importance of research and the PhD to the sustainability of the national economy is of great significance to governments that fund universities and students to undertake doctoral study. Discussion of the role of doctoral study and its value to society is not new. In the late 1960s a working group of the Committee for Manpower Resources for Science and Technology observed:

> This Committee's recommendations are that the scale of support for postgraduate training leading to academic research should be reviewed, that research grant support involving manpower should in general rise in step with the growth of university staff in the three fields, that industry and the schools should take all possible steps to attract graduates of high quality; that further attention should be given to meeting demand in industry and the schools, by redeployment, and the possibility should be examined of developing more long-term quantitative assessments of the balance of distribution of qualified manpower, in order to assist long term plans for collaborative response of education and industry.—Committee on Manpower Resources for Science and Technology, 1996

An earlier report had made the following point:

> However education should take the initiative e.g., examining the PhD and trying to orientate it towards the requirements of industry; while industry should vigorously recruit people qualified in science, engineering and technology.—Committee on Manpower Resources for Science and Technology, 1968

In the early 1990s the desire to make research and the doctorate in particular more relevant to the needs of the national economy intensified. Several national stakeholders began to question the nature and purpose of the PhD. Pressures for change were driven by three key concerns: (1) an apparent loss of international standing of the British PhD, (2) lack of personal and professional skills, and (3) disappointing "time to completion" and completion rates.

The 1993 white paper, *Realising Our Potential,* formalised the debate about research and research training arguing that "the Government welcomes the growth in postgraduate courses. It is concerned, however, that the traditional PhD does not always match up to the needs of a career outside research in academia or in an industrial research laboratory" (DTI 1993, 57). The white paper highlighted the perceived nature of the concerns about the PhD when it stated that "a period spent in PhD training represents a substantial investment of public funds and it is important to ensure that it represents good value for money for the taxpayer as well as the individual concerned" (DTI 1993, 57). It went on to argue that there is a role for preparatory matters in research training when it suggested that "for most students who have undertaken a first degree, the Master's qualification will provide an opportunity to acquire extra knowledge and skills, either in preparation for a period of research training leading to a PhD or for employment" (DTI 1993, 61).

Through the offices of the Office of Science and Technology (OST), government steered a policy towards much more fundamental training in research methods and generic skills which led to a fundamental shift in the way in which PhDs are perceived and delivered. Specific details of these are discussed below. In 1994 the OST published a paper building on the proposals of the white paper. It argued that those trained to postgraduate level should have skills better matched to the needs of potential employers, including those outside the academic world and that this should include elements of non-science specific training including at the very least communication skills and human, material and financial resource management (OST 1994).

The OST outlined a recommended structure for a new one-year Research Masters (MRes) degree, which would include both taught and research components. This degree was intended as a foundation either for a doctorate or for a research career in industry or the public sector. The OST proposed:

- a significant research component (60 percent of the 42–week postgraduate year);
- the provision of a grounding in research techniques relevant to a range of disciplines as well as the development of specialist knowledge; and
- the inclusion of modules intended to broaden the students' experience and to equip them with transferable skills in management, communication, commercial understanding, the exploitation of research, and team working.

The key driver of change in the late 1990s came from Harris's review of postgraduate education in the mid 1990s. Harris covered both Postgraduate Taught (PGT) and Postgraduate Research (PGR). The impetus for this review came from concerns about quality, concerns about growing numbers and perhaps fundamentally, concerns about the cost of provision, cross subsidy and value for money. The review's analysis and conclusions on

PGR began a chain reaction that is reflected in the majority of what we currently observe. Key elements included:

- the development of a code of practice;
- selective funding of universities delivering research degrees according to key attributes;
- far greater attention to the supervisory process; and
- the inclusion of research training in the research degree ME.

The UK doctorate has prided itself on being a quality product for many years and indeed the work of the Quality Assurance Agency (QAA) has been fundamental in enhancing the quality of the doctorate experience. Much of the drive for quality improvement has come via the QAA and its Code of Practice (The Code for Postgraduate Research Programs was recently revised and is now a comprehensive framework document for quality practice). Whilst there is little other than anecdotal evidence of poor quality in the Doctoral experience, nevertheless there is a view that to maintain international competitiveness, quality must be a constant driver.

Comparison between the two editions of the Code in the context of research training and employability highlights the growing emphasis on this aspect of doctoral work. However, the Code highlights one of the key problems associated with the increasing emphasis on training—that of explicitly giving credit to the work undertaken when it says "Institutions may also wish to implement some form of recognition of the acquisition of transferable skills in parallel with, or as part of, the academic assessment of the student's progress" (QAA 2004, 22).

Employability seems to be a word used increasingly across higher education in the UK and is certainly applicable to the doctoral sector. Although demands for more employable research students date back more than two decades, the 1993 white paper highlighted this issue. It observed that many PhDs did not have the appropriate skills to work in industry (more the science base) and needed to have enhanced generic skills.

Value for money represents a significant driver for change in the UK as Governments increasingly recognise the costs of training doctoral students (e.g., JM Consulting 2005). Through the respective funding councils Government continues to press for more effective doctoral training, better completion rates and higher quality students engaging in doctoral work. Several white papers from the seminal *Realising Our Potential* to the most recent *Investing in Innovation* have emphasised this requirement.

Often expressed in terms other than value for money or return on investment, such as high completion rates, the underlying issue is value for money.

International forces are a key element of change in the doctorate particularly as a significant number of doctoral students, particularly in the sciences are classed as overseas, as seen below. The demands of overseas sponsors have been particularly important in shaping the awards themselves, and the development of the so-called "New Route" PhD can be interpreted as a direct response to international demands. This award, which is normally a four-year award, includes more taught elements than in the traditional PhD.

It is perhaps noteworthy that the demands of Europe are less significant. Whilst the UK is a signatory of the Bologna Accord it pays little more than lip service to its demands of 3 + 2 + 3. In part this is because the only significant element that is not directly compliant with the Accord is the Masters element (the UK having one year postgraduate masters as opposed to the European two years). As far as the doctorate is concerned, the UK three-year model with apparently excellent completion rates is seen as a model of excellence.

It is perhaps noteworthy that absent from the drivers of change is any significant concern for the labour market and workforce planning. Whilst there has been a slow realisation than only a minority of doctorates will obtain academic appointment, there has been little discussion, other than by the British Academy, that academic placement is important. In the context of academic employers little is said of the demand for doctorates and indeed there remains an open market with universities themselves dictating the level of provision. From time to time there have been questions raised by various disciplines and research councils about the numbers coming forward for doctoral study—but these have been more in terms of narrow sectoral interests such as the problems of recruiting economists or engineers, rather than systematic analysis of need at a national level.

Important Consequences of the Forces for Change

This review began with the quote from the UKCGE report that discussed the cottage industry nature of the doctoral process. This has certainly changed as a result of the more systematic regulatory environment that has been provided by the QAA. The new, revised, Code of Practice (QAA 2004), discussed subsequently will further enhance the quality of doctoral education. The key to success of the Code will of course be in its implementation and the manner in which audit teams interpret and monitor at institutional level. It will be vital that the selection and training of auditors reflects the need to enhance further the quality of doctoral provision.

Of particular interest will be the way in which universities respond to the demands of the Code. As noted elsewhere (Green and Powell 2004) the increased complexity of the Code may create problems for many of those universities that have relatively small numbers of research students—probably over 50 percent of the total number of universities—and cause them to reconsider the financial viability of delivering doctorates at all.

Section 1: postgraduate research master's was the first section of the Code to be published (January 1999). Given the relatively small population of postgraduate research students it is noteworthy that it was "first" in this way. It might be asked whether this reflected a concern by the QAA regarding the need to improve the quality assurance of PGR. It is also notable that while the rest of the Code covers all aspects of taught provision, including postgraduate taught provision, it was felt necessary and appropriate to have a separate code for all aspects of PGR.

The revised Code launched in September 2004 is a longer, more thorough document that responds to the views of the Better Regulation Review Group (BRRG). The guidance sections of the first edition of the Code are replaced by explanations for each precept. The QAA emphasizes that the Code does not require compliance but rather provides a compendium of good practices. Notwithstanding the reference to the BRRG the Code remains heavily prescribed and for some necessarily so. The UKCGE response to the draft noted that: "the current draft is considerably more prescriptive, longer, and more complex than the previous version with a total of thirty precepts as opposed to twenty-five in the previous version. The general tone of the draft is also more imperative with should being replaced by will, suggesting that the precepts are standards for compliance rather than pointers to good practice" (UKCGE, http://www.ukcge.ac.uk).

Underlying this discussion is a belief that the delivery of postgraduate research programs requires special measures to ensure that it delivers the Government agenda. The discussion also highlights the sensitivities of academics towards the research degree process and that of senior mangers towards regulation. In many cases both groups are blind to the difficulties that research students experience during their research studies and the need for a rigorous approach to the delivery of research awards.

The Institutional Audit is a second element of the QAA's work that can influence the doctoral process in institutions. The process of institutional audit was introduced in 2002–2003 and developed out of the continuation audit process. In theory and as far as doctoral work is concerned, both processes examine how institutions are responding to the Code of Practice. However there is very little to suggest that the audits undertaken so far have paid serious attention to the research degree process. (See for example Metcalfe et al. 2003, Annex F QAA Audit reports). If continuation institutional audit is to have an impact on the improvement of doctoral research processes, considerably more time and effort will be required during audit by auditors with significant experience of the research degree process and the revised Code of Practice.

DOCTORAL AWARDS

The doctoral award as employed within the UK Higher Education sector is varied in its manifestations. Indeed this diversity and an understanding of diverse structures and their purpose represent major current concerns for doctoral education in the UK. Students can work towards doctoral awards with different nomenclatures—involving different levels of entry qualification, modes, and kinds of study. The broad categories of doctoral study in the UK can be summarized as follows:

- PhD;
- Taught Doctorate;
- Doctor of Medicine;
- Higher Doctorates;
- PhD by Published Work;
- Professional Doctorate; and
- Practice-Based Doctorate.

It is arguable that with the exception of the Doctor of Medicine and the Higher Doctorate, this categorization is often more apparent than real and that the within category variance is greater than that between categories across institutions, all of which have their own regulations and requirements.

The pressure to move beyond the situation described above towards the kind of diversity that now exists came initially from the increasing intellectual demands of industrial and commercial contexts. As the complexity of the workplace increased and the need for highly qualified postgraduates developed the demand grew for more doctoral level work. However, the raison d'etre of the PhD came under challenge. It was no longer the case that the Doctorate acted as a route into a career in academia; instead it became a qualification for work in diverse intellectual settings. The criticism was leveled that the PhD was too narrowly "academic" and that the kinds of knowledge and skills displayed by successful PhD candidates were not readily usable in the workplace contexts they sought to enter. Pressure came from the areas such as engineering and chemistry for doctoral level study that was more applied and more relevant to the work expected of successful candidates as they entered the appropriate professions. These criticisms and pressures set the scene for the broadening of doctoral study from the PhD alone to a range of doctoral studies.

The Purpose of the Doctorate

Notions of purpose vary from: (1) training for an academic career, (2) training for a research career in academia, (3) training for research in the economy at large, (4) curiosity-driven work in its own right and for its own sake, and (5) high level training within a professional context.

The notion of the Doctorate as an apprenticeship for academia is predicated on two assumptions. First, that all academics need a Doctorate in order to practice their profession, and second, that the Doctorate provides the appropriate level of experiential learning to equip the individuals for academic life. In assessing the appropriateness of the Doctorate for those wishing to enter academia, it may be useful to examine roles that academics are required to fulfill. Not necessarily in order of importance, these may be identified as: research, teaching, and "other" (where "other" will include administration, management, consultancy, exploitation of IPR, counselling, etc.). The proportion of each of these activities will vary across institutions and through the career of any individual academic. Whilst the Research Assessment Exercises (RAEs) have focused attention on the research element of the portfolio of activities, significant numbers of staff undertake little or no formal RAE funded research. Even "Russell Group" (a grouping of prestigious universities) institutions such as Bristol University have over 40 percent of staff without Doctorates.

Significant numbers of successful doctoral candidates follow careers in industry and the professions in a range of capacities. The demands may relate specifically to research. Although the UK's performance in research and development is not at the top of the international league, UK industry still takes large numbers of doctorates into research posts. The pharmaceutical and petrochemical industries are good examples. Here the benefits of the Doctorate may relate to specific technical knowledge or laboratory competences. It was from these types of employers however that concerns about Doctorate capability arose in the 1990s. Such concerns have lead to greater emphasis on a broad range of skills in addition to those associated with research itself. In short, some employers were complain-

TABLE 2.1. Number of awards awarded in 2002–2003

Subject	*Doctorates*	*First degrees*	*All awards*
Medicine and dentistry	1360	6175	9875
Subject allied to medicine	885	23665	63145
Biological sciences	2375	23725	32730
Veterinary science	70	560	760
Agriculture and related subjects	230	2150	4560
Physical sciences	2180	12480	19225
Mathematical sciences	370	5100	6895
Computer science	375	18240	33560
Engineering and technology	2020	19455	33420
Architecture, building, and planning	175	6555	12470
Social studies	1245	25315	47285
Law	255	11745	24515
Business and administrative studies	555	40310	85345
Mass communications and documentation	65	7415	11870
Languages	900	20025	28305
Historical and philosophical studies	855	13285	19355
Creative arts and design	310	26465	36295
Education	620	9730	53760
Combined	25	9990	34415

SOURCE: HESA 2004

ing that successful doctoral candidates knew "an awful lot about an awful little" and were lacking in skills of, for example, communication and team working. These concerns were a key element in the development of the MR programs (OST 1994) and the funding initially of the OST Graduate Schools and subsequently the development of the UK Grad program.

Data is not available within the UK on the number of employees in the professions with doctorates and hence it is not possible to identify clearly the importance of the Doctorate to those professions. It is possible however to make certain inferences from the data on the number of doctorates awarded in a number of subjects that are predominantly professional in nature, as illustrated in table 2.1. In terms of the number of awards made, the Doctorate appears to be of limited importance to many of the professionally related disciplines. For many, the postgraduate diploma or masters is the passport to the profession. This does perhaps highlight the need for innovation and the importance of the professional doctorate.

Who Can Deliver Doctoral Awards?

The issue of who can deliver research degree programs has recently come under review from two perspectives, first the decisions about university status and second, the impact of the new approaches to funding. They appear to have divergent effects.

As a general rule all universities are licensed to have doctoral programs within their award portfolio. Institutions of higher education, which are not universities—such as the university colleges or specialist institutions—are able to run doctoral programs, but in association with a university which acts as the awarding body. In this case the final award is from the awarding university, not that delivering the program. Recently there has been a change in the requirements to achieve university status that hence gives them the authority to award doctorates. In practice most of the university colleges will eventually gain university status and hence become eligible to award doctorates.

Government has been eager to encourage the concentration of doctoral education in a smaller number of institutions. This policy of concentration was raised in the Higher Education white paper (The Future of Higher Education, DFES 2003). The paper compared the current picture to that of the US in which it was suggested doctoral programs were highly concentrated. The white paper concludes:

> we will ask HEFCE to set high minimum standards for the training of PhD students which must be met before higher education institutions can draw down funding for PhD places, though they could still fund PhD places from their own resources if they wished to do so. This may lead to larger graduate schools in fewer HEIs, as some institutions decide not to offer PhD places, and others are in a position to play to their strengths in PhD training by expanding their postgraduate provision. In time, this might play into a model where postgraduate degree awarding powers are restricted to successful research consortia.—Para 2.26

Much of the comment about the delivery of doctoral programs had its origins in the Roberts Review of science, engineering, and technology, which found that it may be the case that the delivery of doctorates is best undertaken in large groups where economies of scale can be achieved in the provision of expensive equipment and the scientific laboratories. It does appear less clear in the case of Social Science, the Arts, and Humanities, where such economies are less obvious.

The relationship between the research degree awarding powers and university status is of particular interest as it develops the argument in the white paper that institutions can retain their title university—without research degree awarding powers. The argument is complex and goes to the very heart of university—in the UK at least, where such powers have always been the distinguishing feature between the true university and those institutions—the university colleges and former polytechnics, masquerading as such. It is noteworthy that pre-1992 when the Council for National Academic Awards was the guardian of standards for the polytechnics, a significant number of polytechnics were awarded research degree awarding powers by the CNAA. Several however did not apply for such powers and were automatically awarded them in the 1992 changes.

Up to the 2004 the criteria for university title included the following:

- At least 300 FTE HE students in five of eleven stated subject categories;
- At least 4,000 FTE HE students;
- At least 3,000 FTE students on degree courses;
- AND at least sixty current research degree registrations and more than thirty doctor of Philosophy conferments (no time period stated) (DFES 2004).

In July 2004, the Minister of State for Life Long Learning and Higher Education, Alan Johnson, announced that Government had relaxed the research degree requirement and awards the title of university on the basis of taught degree awarding powers (written Ministerial Statement, 16 July 2004). As a consequence many institutions which had until that point been barred from even applying for that status until they had achieved the required number of enrolments and conferments could now do so. The announcement also opened the door for applications from corporate organisations to apply for the title university. So far none appear to have done so. The link between the university and the Doctorate was duly severed.

The second key element in the equation relates more to an ability to have programs in terms of the overall capacity to deliver, in relation to the QAA Code of Practice and in the funding rather than in the constitutional right to so do. We saw in the distribution of doctorates awarded a concentration of awards in a small minority of institutions. Implicit in the use of the Code of Practice is a culling of institutions that have the capability to deliver doctoral programs. This has largely backfired, as there is little relationship between critical mass of doctoral students or the research assessment rating and the ability to comply with the Code!

The key message concerning who delivers however is related to funding—and who is funded to deliver. Here there is a clear message coming from the funding agencies that only departments that are rated 4 and above in the Research Assessment Exercise (RAE) will in the future be funded for doctoral programs. However, institutions will continue to offer doctoral programs—even at a loss for reasons of mission, status, and profile enhancement.

TRENDS IN DOCTORAL EDUCATION

The growth in the postgraduate population has created a sector that is out of all recognition to that of the 1960s when the Robbins Report, the first major study of Higher Education in the UK, noted a population in 1961–62 of 19,400 full-time and 6,300 part-time students. By 1994–95, at the time of the Harris report, there were 128,300 full-time and 187,100 part-time postgraduate students. The relative position of postgraduate student numbers similarly changed during this period. In 1979, 13 percent of the total student population were postgraduate (100,900 postgraduate in a total population of 787,000), yet in 1994–95 the comparable figure was 21 percent (315,400 out of a population of 1,528,600). By the end of the millennium, the total population of postgraduates was 151,330 full-time and 257,290 part-time (HESA 2001).

Similarly, structural changes were observed in the mode of programs with a growth in the number of part-time students, and equalisation of the gender balance and, more recently, a significant growth in the numbers of overseas students. In 1992–93, there were 25,100 international postgraduate students in HEIs in the UK, 8 percent from the EU, 92 percent from the rest of the world. By 1997–98 this figure had risen to 81,000, of which now 33 percent were from the EU and 67 percent from the rest of the world, theoretically at least making a major impact on the funding of programs. The global market, and in particular the UK's position in that market, has been a key factor in the discussion of quality (Spagnold 1994).

As far as doctoral awards are concerned, the importance of this growth is further emphasised with 14,875 doctorates awarded by 129 HEIs in 2003. Table 2.2 illustrates the trend since the mid '90s.

The distribution of the awards is highly skewed across universities as is clearly seen in table 2.3. Five universities, the Universities of Cambridge, Oxford, Birmingham, Manchester, and University College London, all located in England, accounted for 25 percent of the total awards in 2000.

This concentration is further emphasised by the figures for the constituent nations of the UK as in table 2.4.

These figures do not of course take into account the number or size of the HEIs in each of the nations nor the total number of students from each of the nations who are being awarded doctorates because of transnational movement, and hence should be interpreted with some care. Nevertheless they do clearly demonstrate the dominance of English universities in the UK doctoral education market.

The figures also conceal the variety of awards themselves. Whilst the PhD may remain the most important of the doctoral awards, the last ten years has seen the development of awards such as the Professional Doctorate, Practice Based Doctorate, PhD by Published Work, New Route PhD, and others. Interestingly, there is no national data that allows differentiation of these new awards in total numbers, as HESA combines them all into the broad category, namely *Doctorate.*

Table 2.5 illustrates the importance today of the part-time mode in doctoral programs to all institutions. The data does conceal some students who originally started their study full time who have subsequently changed mode at the end of their three year grant and who are frequently referred to as "writing up." In many cases these students are the outcasts of research council funds.

Finally, table 2.6 highlights the age distribution of UK first year students. Whilst the young postgraduate age 21–24 is still the dominant group, the table shows the far broader age distribution now characteristic of doctoral education, a distribution which has major challenges for institutions in terms of student needs and demands.

Table 2.1 above presented the data for the overall discipline distribution of doctorates awarded. The dominance of the physical, biological, and medical sciences, as well as engineering and technology, is clearly evident. This disciplinary mix and the traditions associated with these disciplines helps explain some of the debates about the doctorate, including the need for generic skills development(—is it assumed that science graduates are less able to communicate?), completion rates and the notion of the writing up period (is it assumed that actually writing up is not part of the research degree process no longer based in the lab and hence there is no need for funding), the notion of critical mass, (whilst the science doctorate may involve team working in the lab, this

TABLE 2.2. Total number of doctorates awarded by UK HEIs, 1996–2002

Year	*Total*	*Annual Growth (%)*
1996	10,800	
1997	11,860	9.8
1998	12,660	6.7
1999	13,140	3.8
2000	13,670	4.0
2001	14,115	3.2
2002	14,210	0.6
2003	14,875	0.95

SOURCE: HESA 2004, Table 12

TABLE 2.3. The distribution of doctorates awarded by Institution (2000)

Quartile	*Number of Universities*
Upper	5
Second	9
Third	18
Lower	97

SOURCE: Millicope 2001

TABLE 2.4. National distribution of doctorates awarded 2002–2003

England	12,270
Wales	605
Scotland	1,605
Northern Ireland	390
Total	14,875

SOURCE: HESA 2004, Table 12

TABLE 2.5. PGR Students Mode of Study 2002–2003

	Full time	*Part time*	*Total*
Old universities	49,600	44,370	93,970
Post-1992 Universities/Colleges/ Institutes	5,670	8,970	14,640
Total	55,270	53,340	108,610

SOURCE: HESA 2004, Table 9C

TABLE 2.6. Age structure: First year UK students 2002–2003

	Postgraduate Research Student	
Age	*FT*	*PT*
Under 21	50	5
21–24	6,250	600
25–29	1,755	925
30 plus	2,115	3,980
Total	10,170	5,510

SOURCE: HESA 2004, Table 1D & 1H

does not apply to all disciplines) and so on. Too often, the science model of the doctorate dominates thinking to the detriment of intellectual creativity and change.

The Prime Minister's initiative towards overseas students that focuses specifically on longer-term relationship building has had a major influence on the position of the British Higher Education and the British Doctorate in particular.

The demand for doctoral research programs has risen considerably over the past ten years, illustrating the attractive nature of the British PhD although there is some evidence that this has now levelled off. Although much of the growth in overseas student demand has been funded by private sources, estimated to represent 60 percent, the British Council report (British Council 2004) observed that 40 percent of the 39,000 postgraduate research students were funded, in part or in full, from UK sources including institutional scholarships and fee waivers. The

FIGURE 2.1. First year doctoral research students by domicile and mode, 1995–96 to 2001–02

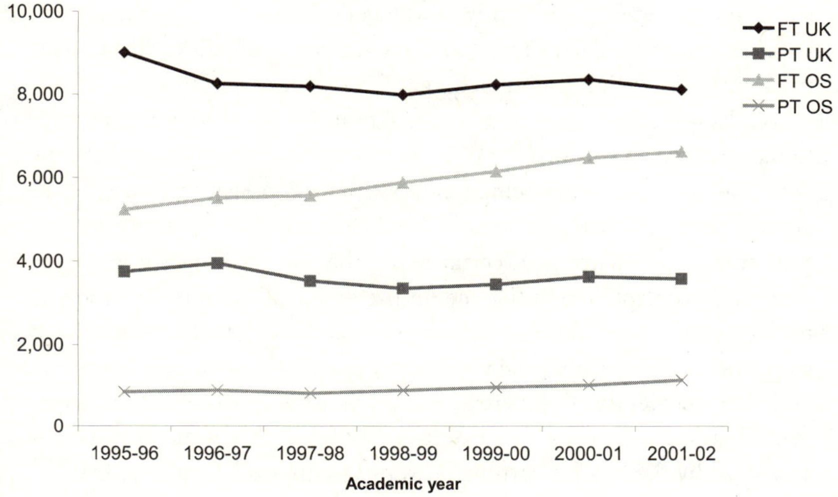

SOURCE: Sastry 2004

remaining 15 percent are funded through home government or employer scholarships.

There are several reasons for this rate of change that relate to nature of the award and the doctoral process itself. From the pre-Harris days of the early 1990s there has been a significant change in the way the doctorate is delivered and quality is assured, as noted above. The QAA's Code of Practice for Postgraduate Research Awards and the associated institutional audit of process are major factors in reassuring international students and sponsors of the quality of the doctorate.

The language of delivery is also significant, particularly in the sciences where English is now the common international language of the scientific community. Clearly the UK is not the only English language speaking country offering doctorates, with Australia, Canada, and the US competing for students. Whilst the US has the greatest proportion of its international students studying at postgraduate level, the UK is catching up and if, as the British Council forecasts, the postgraduate proportions for international students in the UK increase significantly over time, it could overtake the US to have the largest proportion of postgraduate students. Research undertaken in the English language is increasingly observed in non-English speaking countries. The Nordic countries, Germany, and Holland undertake much of their research in English. Additionally language is perhaps less important in the Social Sciences, Arts, and Humanities.

Expected time to completion is a further significant factor in attracting overseas students to the UK. Recent evidence suggests that overseas students complete in significantly shorter periods than in many other countries. This is particularly important for overseas candidates who are paying significant tuition fees and charges for accommodation.

Whilst it is suggested that there are significant advantages for international students to study in the UK, the growth relative to the overall student body is increasingly being treated with care. A lack of coordination among government regulations and policies can have a major effect on the student experience and recruitment. The recent changes in the right to work have had some influence on the financial situation of students from overseas. Regulations now allow overseas students to take unrestricted paid work without additional visa requirements. There is some anecdotal evidence however that this increased opportunity is directing students away from their research work to the detriment of time to completion. This is acerbated by the relative earning power of many students in the UK relative to their home country. Some it seems use the additional earnings to support families back home. Recent changes in visa renewal policies have also impacted on the budget of many students and hence may impact future recruitment.

The traditional view concerning the recruitment of overseas students has in part revolved around income to institutions. As the number of students from the UK willing and able to enter PGR programs, particularly in the Sciences, Engineering, and Technology has been problematic, institutions have been keen to use the overseas student as a lucrative source of income. Interestingly, recent work by the Policy Research Institute (Sastry 2005), building on the costing work of JM Consulting, has shown that over the life of a doctoral program even overseas students fail to cover the full costs of provision. Assuming the Sastry analysis to be correct, then impact on institutions, and potential future recruitment behaviours will depend on the significance of overseas students to the overall student mix. Table 2.7 illustrates the case for postgraduate students as a whole.

It was noted earlier when discussing the purpose of the doctorate that there was a variety of potential destinations for those who earn doctorates. The first destination figures presented in table 2.8 illustrate the wide range of employment destinations—and the limited importance of academic employment. It always seems to come as a surprise to the academic community that this is the case.

A recent study by UKGRAD has re-emphasized this pattern.

TABLE 2.7. Proportion of PG students in ten institutions

	Overseas PG as percent of student body	*All overseas student fees as percent of revenue*
London School of Economics	42.2	33.6
Cranfield	31.9	3.5
Essex	22.6	17.2
UMIST	18.3	11.6
Surrey	16.9	10.7
Oxford	16.1	4.5
Cambridge	15.4	5.4
Imperial	14.7	6.7
Institute of Education	13.7	3.6
UCL	13.6	7.1
England	6.2	7.5

SOURCE: Sastry 2004

TABLE 2.8. First destination of Research Council funded PhD graduates

	1994	*1996*	*1998*	*2000*
Total number of leavers	3,166	3,201	3,735	3,262
Of which destination unknown	1,057	621	938	766
Known destinations	2,109	2,580	2,797	2,496
Of which:	%			%
Permanent academic appointment	5	5	5	5
Fixed term academic appointment	29	21	26	25
Further training (excluding teaching)	5	4	4	4
School teaching or teacher training	3	2	2	2
Private sector, industry or commerce	22	33	29	24
Government or other public sector	5	5	6	5
Other employment	4	2	4	4
Not employed	19	18	15	18
Overseas	10	9	10	13

SOURCE: OST: Set Statistics Table 5.13

PRESSURES TO COMPLETE

Attention was focused on the length of doctoral training programs, submission rates and time to completion in the early 1980s with the events leading to the publication of the Winfield report (1987). (See table 2.9.)

The table also highlights the variation between the different disciplinary groupings represented by the Research Councils. Although not high by today's standards, NERC and SERC (now EPSRC) have much larger numbers of students completing within four years.

The sanctions policy implemented before Winfield, but subsequently endorsed by his report, has been paralleled by a significant improvement in submission rates for Research Council funded candidates. Whether this is a case of correlation or causality may be disputed. Those working in the sector in the early 1980s will certainly recall the increased attention given to submission by institutional and departmental managers. The pattern of submission today shows a very different picture as is highlighted in table 2.10.

Rates show considerable variability across institutions and disciplines. This is reflected in the AHRB figures; for example, where the institutional range is from 100 percent to 0 percent in terms of four-year submission. At the disciplinary level, Music, Art History, and the Classics continue to have relatively low four-year submission rates, whilst much higher rates are observed for Law, Theology, and Archaeology.

In 2004 HEFCE completed a study into doctoral submission and completion rates across the sector (HEFCE 2005). The study incorporated all degrees that are examined predominantly through research, thus including the Professional Doctorates and the so-called New Route PhD as well as the traditional MPhil/PhD. This work presents a picture that was far from the optimistic one coming from the Research Councils and AHRB. It emphasised the importance of funding, age, mode of study, discipline, and institution in any explanation of time to completion. The study revealed that after seven years of study 71 percent of full-time students had completed (82 percent had completed or were still active). In terms of part-time numbers, 34 percent students had completed (62 percent had completed or were still active); 38 percent were no longer active and within that group 4 percent (of the overall number) had left with an MPhil.

The main conclusions of the study may be summarised as follows.

- Completion rates for full-time students were more consistent than for part-timers.

TABLE 2.9. Submission rates: 1976–1980 starters

	Less than 4 years				*Less than 5 years*			
Year	*ESRC*	*DES/BA*	*NERC*	*SERC*	*ESRC*	*DES/BA*	*NERC*	*SERC*
1976	11	15	50		23	29	69	
1977	12	16	53	48	25	27	71	
1978	15		47	48	26		62	
1979	17	11	53	48	29	24	76	
1980	18		49	50	24			

SOURCE: Winfield 1987

TABLE 2.10. Submission rates: 1990–1997:
Percent submission within four years

Start date	*BBSRC*	*EPSRC*	*ESRC*	*MRC*	*NERC*	*PPARC*	*AHRB*
1990	70	67	73	64	73	82	45
1992	72	67	75	67	72	81	54
1994	85	72	76	72	73	81	57
1996	86	71	76	75	78	84	70
1997	90	75	81	75	88	85	71

SOURCE: OST/AHRB

- Completion rates were improved if funding was received from the Funding Councils.
- Discipline areas were a factor in terms of completion rates for full-time students (less so for part-timers).
- Research Council students tended to complete more quickly than non Research Council students.
- Overseas students tended to complete more quickly than home students.
- Sex was a minor effect (women's completion rates being lower than men's).
- Similarly age was a minor effect (older students were less likely to complete or took longer to complete.) (Early 20's had an 80 percent completion rate; early 30's had a 60 percent completion rate.)
- There was a slight advantage in terms of completion time if the student's previous qualification was a first class degree.

- Institution type (Pre- or Post-1992) had no discernable effect.
- Discipline area had a significant impact with natural/medical sciences completing much more quickly than humanities and social sciences ("vocational subjects" fell between the two).
- Critical mass of research group was not a factor, i.e., there was no indication that students in small units were disadvantaged in comparison to students in larger units.
- The overall average times for completion of doctoral programs were: 60 percent completed in four years and 70 percent in five years.

This work will undoubtedly raise questions about performance across the sector and give rise to questions within institutions about activity supported without funding.

ORGANIZATION AND SUPERVISION

One of the significant changes in the last ten years in the management and the organisation of doctoral programs has been the establishment of graduate schools. It is particularly fortunate that there have been two surveys of graduate schools that document both their initial development in the early years of the 1990s and their maturation in 2004 (UKCGE 1995; Woodward et al. 2004). In 1995 a significant number of universities had established graduate schools: thirty-three universities and one college of higher education had done so with a further twenty-three universities having definite plans to establish such systems. Graduate schools were less common in the new (post-1992) universities, one sixth of which had them, and in the colleges of higher education, one tenth of which had them. By 2003–04 the graduate school had become the dominant model for the organisation of graduate education across the sector. Two thirds of the universities who responded to the UKCGE survey now had graduate schools while six other universities were considering establishing one.

Beneath the headline figures given above there is a range of models of what constitutes a graduate school and what role it performs. The model adopted depends, in part at least, on the size of the university and the number of doctoral students it has. In cases where there are a large number of doctoral students, graduate schools tend to be at faculty or departmental level. In universities with relatively few doctoral students the graduate school will tend to be at university level. Also, the resources, facilities, and responsibilities of graduate schools vary widely between the different models adopted. Many have dedicated accommodation for their staff with associated teaching and learning space for other staff and students. Many are responsible for research training programs and in some cases for the training of supervisors. Particularly in the university-wide graduate school, quality assurance and student monitoring, the management and support for higher degree committees and institutional returns to the various agencies are often vested in the graduate school.

While this focus on the management and organisation of doctoral programs in graduate schools is a very welcome addition to the internal structure of universities and may bring associated improvements in the quality of delivery of doctoral programs, it is not without its tensions. Perhaps most important of these is the severing of any existing links between research students and the broader student population and the potential disenfranchising of departments and faculties from the research degree process in general.

So far there has been little discussion of development of discipline based graduate schools at either the institutional or regional level, as has been the case in countries such as Finland. It does seem likely however that in view of pressure to concentrate the delivery of doctoral programs in groupings with adequate critical mass, such developments will take place in the future.

Supervision and supervisory practice have received increasing attention in the literature and from regulatory and sponsor organisations. The report from the Wellcome Trust (2001) is one of the few analyses of the views of supervisors themselves. Bound up in the discussion of the nature and purpose of the PhD is the nature of supervision. Is it a matter of researching—linked to the notion of the PhD being a piece of original research or is it a matter of teaching—reflecting the view of the PhD as being the training of advanced researchers? Such a dichotomy is clearly too simplistic. It does however challenge us to clarify the role and nature of doctoral supervision. In the QAA Code there is recognition, in Precept 5, that part of the research degree process is one of learning as well as of undertaking research.

> Precept 5: Institutions will only accept research students into an environment that provides support for doing and learning about research and where high quality research is occurring.—QAA 2004, 8

The code then goes on to describe the characteristics of such a research environment concluding that:

> Such a learning environment will also enable research students to make judgements requiring creativity and critical independent thought, accepting that

> uncertainty is a feature of the conduct of research programs. This environment should enable students to grapple with challenges that develop intellectual maturity and encourage a high level of reflection on the student's own learning about research as well as on research outcomes.—QAA 2004, 8

> In appointing supervisors, institutions need to be aware of and guided by the overall workload of the individual, including teaching, research, administration and other responsibilities, for example, external examining duties and other professional commitments, such as consultancy or clinical responsibilities.—QAA 2004, 17

The need to train supervisors has been recognised by policymakers and funders in the UK for over ten years. As early as Winfield (1987) it was noted that supervisors were attending seminars and workshops for training purposes. This theme is developed in the Social and Economic Research Council (SERC) discussion paper on research supervision that notes, "in order to become effective and productive managers, supervisors must *acquire* discipline related skills, core research skills and management" (SERC 1992). More recently the pressures to rethink the role of the supervisor, as well as increased emphasis on the training of supervisors and the importance of supervision come from a range of sources that may conveniently be referred to as those pushing institutional change and those pulling or encouraging institutions to change their practices. The push factors come from a series of initiatives and reports over the past ten years or so, each of which has, in one way or another, exerted pressure on institutions to pay more attention to supervisor behaviors. The Harris Report (1996), itself a landmark in postgraduate education in the UK, initially identified the need for more careful supervision and indeed for the training of supervisors. Harris identified the key attributes necessary for the successful delivery of research degree programs and identified supervisor training. The Research Councils have begun to recognise the importance of the supervisory process to successful completion of award (in this they are led, arguably, by ESRC). This has become formalised within the 2001 training guidelines from the ESRC in which it is stated:

> The ESRC will expect to see a statement about the provision of professional development opportunities for supervisors in applications for recognition. It follows that the ESRC will expect outlets to have formal systems in place for monitoring the performance of supervisors, for identifying the training and development needs of supervisors and for ensuring that these are

> met.—ESRC Training Guidelines 3rd Edition 2001, C3.2 Training and monitoring of supervisors and supervision arrangements

The Policy Paper, *Improving Standards in Research Degree Programs* produced by the UK Funding Councils (HEFCE 2003, table 1, section 4a) states that in connection with threshold standards for research degree supervision, "All new supervisors [are] to undertake mandatory institutionally specified training."

The revised QAA Code of Practice is less specific than the HEFCE publication noted above but is also potentially more demanding on supervisor training. Precept 11 states that "Institutions will appoint supervisors who have the appropriate skills and subject knowledge to support, encourage and monitor research students effectively" (QAA 2004). Whilst not using the word "training" explicitly therefore, under the revised Code *all* supervisors will be expected to engage in development of various kinds to equip them to supervise. The explanation beneath this Precept goes on to refer to development activities, "to assure . . . competence in the role," "to demonstrate . . . continuing professional development," ". . . . in updating knowledge and skills" and ". . . sharing good practice" (QAA 2004). The Code then identifies the new supervisor who will "participate in specified development activities arranged through their institution, to assure their competence in the role."

EXAMINING

The approach to examination of the doctorate is a further element of the process that has received attention recently, in part because of empirical research that has confirmed the anecdotal evidence of examining as a less than structured affair (Tinkler and Jackson 2004; Underwood 1999). There is evidence in the literature about a lack of clarity with regard to the purpose of the viva (a) from an institutional perspective (Powell and McCauley 2002) and (b) in terms of the perceptions of the various participants (Tinkler and Jackson 2004). For example, the viva may be interpreted as an examination in the broadest sense of the term (and here questioning may extend beyond the work presented in the thesis itself to encompass issues of the candidate's knowledge of related subject matter) or as merely a matter of verification of authenticity. Indeed, many oral examinations seem (to examiners and students alike) to become effectively opportunities to fine-tune the written work of the candidate in order that it reaches a notional standard that is acceptable for scrutiny by peers in the relevant intellectual community. Tinkler and Jackson (2004, 16) list nine main distinct "roles" that were cited by respondents in relation to the purpose of the viva; no one role was mentioned by more than 40 percent of respondents.

The UK national qualifications framework (QAA 2001) describes doctoral level work as that which makes a significant contribution to knowledge and which is original. Institutions interpret this description in the way in which they set out criteria (a description of a level clearly differs from the assessment criteria that need to be attained to meet that level). Some use "contribution to knowledge and to the application of that knowledge"; some include the notion of "publishability." This last indicator is usually expressed in a somewhat imprecise way. However, in some disciplines the pressure to publish is more explicit; for example, BPS/UCOSDA (1995) suggest that a doctoral submission should be equivalent to at least two articles in refereed journals.

In all of the above there is little evidence that attempts have been made in a systematic way to describe the benchmarking of doctorateness, though Shaw and Green (2001) use the QAA Framework (2001) to explore the possibilities of doing just that. In their work they identify the elements of the doctoral outcomes from the QAA's doctoral learning outcomes and develop a series of performance standards against which these can be assessed. In this way they demonstrate how each of these elements may form the basis for criteria in the assessment process. Whilst not concluding with a definitive framework of criteria, they do demonstrate some of the strengths and weaknesses of such an approach.

The viva has come under scrutiny in terms of the way it is conducted with considerable anecdotal evidence about the inadequacies of the process and the power of the external examiner. The QAA Code pays specific attention to the way in which examiners are appointed and the viva is conducted, suggesting that the practice of appointing an independent chair for each viva is an approach worthy of consideration. Whilst this is used increasingly, it poses problems for institutions that have large volumes of doctorates in terms of both cost and availability of suitable staff.

FUNDING

The current arrangements (December 2004) for the funding of universities for research students are complex, and as with all funding regimes open to manipulation. Funding arrangements are bound up in the structure of the dual support system of research funding, which itself has been the subject of review in the recent past. Following the Gareth Roberts' review of the RAE (Roberts 2003), some changes will be made in the next RAE in 2008, but in principle the current arrangements hold true. Put simply, the dual support system provides universities that reach a particular level (according to the RAE) a funding stream often referred to as QR, reflecting the quality of the research. The precise level of funding is determined by:

- The quality rating. This rating is on a scale of 1–5 plus 5*. In principle only departments with a rating of 4 or above receive QR funding.
- The number of staff rated in each department, the volume measure. The more staff the greater the funding. Research students contribute to this volume.
- The academic subject under consideration (see below).

The basic philosophy of this side of the model is to provide universities with a level of funds to maintain staff and infrastructure at an adequate level to undertake research.

The other funding stream of the dual funding model comes from those agencies that fund specific projects. These agencies include the Research Councils, the Research Charities, Government Departments, and Commercial Organisations and Companies.

And although universities are moving to a full cost recovery approach to research funding, the principle of the dual support approach will for the present be retained for research.

The costs to universities for the delivery of doctoral programs are funded through a dual support structure similar to that for research projects and scholarship. In the case of doctoral programs, the Funding Councils provide one element and students, frequently through a sponsor, provide the other through their payment of fees. Following the Roberts Review an additional element of £850 on average for the period 2004–05 has been added to support the delivery of research training for Research Council funded students only (Loeffler 2004). A similar approach has been adopted for 2004–05 by the Arts and Humanities Research Council (AHRC), which currently contributes £450 per year for its research students. The AHRC will join the "Roberts" allocation from 2005–06, following its changed status to Research Council.

In addition to funds from the Funding Councils, universities also charge fees for the period of research. Fees vary between universities and across academic subject categories. In some cases fees reflect market conditions and can be substantially above levels advised by the Department for

Education and Skills (DfES). A considerable level of university discretion appears to apply in the setting of fees with an increasing blurring of the line between full cost (usually overseas) and home/EU students. Similar variation applies to the charging of bench fees.

The fourth element of the funding stream for research students comes from tuition fees and associated bench fees (such latter fees present, in some cases, a substantial additional cost to research in science and engineering to cover items such as materials and chemicals). The broad structure of full-time fees is set by the DfES and as usual is subdivided into three broad categories: Home and EU, Overseas and Channel Islands. With some variability between disciplines there is broad parity of fees charged within the broad framework provided by DfES and little evidence that universities are exploiting the market by either significant variability between subjects within cost centres or between universities with different market positions for research. As we will note below, some universities even waive the fees for some students and hence, theoretically at least, we have a doctoral research degree process in some universities for which the university receives a negative fee!

Table 2.11 highlights several key facts about doctoral funding in the UK that reveal a lot about the way in which training is approached. The role of the Research Council funding has been declining over the period from 46.5 percent to 33.3 percent of doctoral student fees. On the other hand the self-financing of fees, whilst only 15.4 percent in 2001–02 has increased by 85.8 percent during the period. Private industry, an insignificant funder at 4.6 percent of the total, has become increasingly *insignificant* with a reduction of 19.6 percent during the period.

Table 2.12 highlights the importance of self-financing for part-time doctoral students, who total approximately 46 percent of students over the period. While not making such a significant contribution to the total number, both university and government department funding have increased significantly, 37 percent and 66 percent respectively, over the period. Notwithstanding the positive statements about the access agenda and the need to encourage more part-time research students, the Research Councils make only a minimal contribution.

In December 2004 the English Funding Council announced that it was to change the payment to institutions and that a single payment—a supervision fee—would be paid to institutions for research students in departments rated four or above in the RAE 2001 (plus a small number of other departments receiving capability funding) (see HEFCE 2004).

TABLE 2.11. Major source of tuition fees: UK domiciled full-time first year doctoral students in science, engineering, and technology

Source	*1995/6*	*1997/8*	*1999/0*	*2001/2*
Universities	813	896	800	950
Local Government	118	73	50	215
Govt. Dept.	397	342	340	325
Research Councils	2343	2136	2340	1780
Other UK Public	18	17		5
Self Financing	444	426	540	825
Charities	149	122	160	165
Private Industry	311	342	290	250
EC	9	5		5
Other Overseas	37	28	140	115
Others/Unknown	390	306	630	700
Total	5029	4693	5280	5340

SOURCE: OST SET Statistics Table 5.7

TABLE 2.12. Major source of tuition fees: UK domiciled part-time first year doctoral students in science, engineering, and technology

Source	*1995/6*	*1997/8*	*1999/0*	*2001/2*
Universities	186	219	310	255
Local Government	10	1	20	20
Govt. Dept.	99	58	150	165
Research Councils	13	13	20	5
Other UK Public	2	1	0	0
Self Financing	782	730	820	915
Charities	14	6	10	10
Private Industry	285	333	260	300
EC	1	0	0	0
Other Overseas	0	1	20	20
Others/Unknown	283	159	260	305
Total	1675	1521	1850	1995

SOURCE: OST SET Statistics Table 5.7

One implication of this new approach is to withdraw progressively funding from over 5,000 departments across the sector.

Stipend is the term used here for the maintenance grant paid to doctoral students for the period of their research. The word is used interchangeably with bursary and scholarship. It is expected that the stipend will cover all the domestic costs including accommodation, subsistence and transport. The level of the stipend has come under scrutiny in recent years, linked to difficulties in attracting good quality candidates to research programs and the possible difficulties in completion as students are obliged to take part-time employment to complement the stipend. The Research Councils for example note an increase in unfilled studentships, both Masters and Doctoral, from 300 in 1996–97 to 618 in 1998–99, an increase from approximately 4.5 percent to 11 percent of the studentships available. EPSRC had particular problems in the period with 25 percent of Masters and nearly 30 percent of MRes places unfilled in 1998–99 (Research Fortnight 1999a; Research Fortnight 1999b; Hinde 1999).

The attractiveness of the stipend has been the subject of several reviews. This has been true particularly in the case of science and engineering and in some of the social science areas, notably economics (Hodges 1999). Roberts (2002) demonstrated that the level of the stipend fell by 4.5 percent in real terms between 1971–72 and 1991–92; while during the same period starting salaries for graduates with an upper second first degree rose by more than 42 percent. Despite the recent increases, from £6,800 in 2001 to £9,000 in 2003–04, stipends represent little advantage over the UK national *minimum* wage. The Roberts recommendation that the stipend should be increased to £13,000 based on comparisons with mean net graduate salaries is a welcome recognition of the lamentable approach to PhD stipends and one which the 2003–04 and 2005–06 spending reviews agreed to fund. The analysis does not however include an international comparison, a major omission in the increasingly global market for high quality graduate students. Such an analysis reveals that the UK continues to lag behind many of our competitors (including English language speaking competitors). Whatever the relativities it will be important to ensure that the stipend is both nationally and internationally competitive if the UK is serious in its demands to recruit the most able students into its PhD programs.

The Roberts conclusions, however, are based on average conditions and do not consider variability across discipline, even within science. The Roberts report also neglects some of the more subtle aspects of funding such as national insurance contributions and maternity and paternity entitlement during and after the research period. While there is some evidence that starting salaries are higher both within and outside the academy for those with a doctorate, the evidence is not overwhelming enough to compensate for low stipends (see for example the British Academy discussion, British Academy 2001, 35; Conlon and Chevalier 2002).

STUDENT ISSUES

The representative student organisation in the UK is the National Postgraduate Committee (NPC). It received charitable status in 2002 and has been in existence for over ten years. It is made up of postgraduate student representatives from educational institutions with postgraduate students. The NPC aims to promote the interests of postgraduates studying in the UK, while remaining politically non-aligned. The Committee holds an annual conference and publishes various guidelines and codes of practice as well as the Journal of Graduate Studies.

The NPC has been influential in the past in developing a range of resources for both students and institutions. More recently it has been involved in the development of the QAA Code of Practice. It does not however have the significance that the National Union of Students (NUS) has more generally or the lobbying influence of student bodies in other countries. It does however provide a basis on which to systematically identify an agenda of issues of concern to students. What follows is anecdotal rather than the result of survey or review.

The status of research students continues to attract attention. Currently, a research student may have the status of a student or a member of staff. In the former case, the student will be funded on a grant or bursary and be subject to institutional regulation for students. On the other hand, as a member of staff, research assistant, GTA or lecturer, the terms of engagement and the associated regulations will be completely different. So, in a science research laboratory of eight doctoral candidates, each may have different conditions; the student on a stipend from a Research Council and well funded, the student who is self funding, the student who is institutionally poorly funded, a part-time student with no funding, a research assistant on a short term contract, a research fellow on a permanent contract and a member of the lecturing staff undertaking a PhD part-time, and an overseas student funded generously by their sponsor government.

The quality of supervision is a matter of concern to students: NPC frequently has questioned the quality and commitment of supervisors and supervisory practice. A glance at the NPC web site will highlight this by the several stories from disillusioned students. Whilst each individual case of poor supervision is a tragedy for the student, there does not appear to be other than anecdotal evidence of endemic supervisory problems. Indeed the welcome survey for example indicates that the vast majority of students are content with their lot. Nevertheless the improvement of supervisory practice is highlighted in the Code as we have seen.

CONCLUSION

At the opening of the paper it was observed that whilst the "cottage industry" is no more there remain major challenges for doctoral education in the UK. The final section lists some pertinent current issues.

The European challenge is probably just beginning as the third cycle enters the arena. As noted earlier the UK has taken a less than enthusiastic attitude towards the Bologna model. The recent referenda about the constitution may well encourage other nations within Europe to change and adopt a similar approach. It is clear that with a system that is internally so diverse, it will be a major challenge to take the "bananas and custard" approach, one of defined uniformity, to the doctorate.

Currently the UK Doctorate has a competitive advantage in the European and World market. First because, particularly in the sciences, English is the dominant international academic language; second because of the rigorous quality assurance processes that are in place; and third because of the timely completion rates as far as Research Council students are concerned at least. However, these competitive advantages may diminish certainly in Europe as the EU model introduces common standards for quality, delivery and completions in the move towards 2010, and increasingly individual universities across Europe teach and research in English. The recent HEFCE analysis of completion rates will not be helpful in this context.

The purpose of the Doctorate is key to its future. The future number of doctorates in the UK is largely unplanned and left instead to the vagaries of market forces. The question of the supply of doctoral candidates has recently come to the fore with the closure of some science departments and hence a potential long-term reduction in research capacity in some subjects. While not wanting to enter detailed discussion of funding, recruitment, and national needs it is useful to note how some international competitors are realising their needs.

Currently there is little relationship between the supply of PhD places at universities and the demand for the services of doctoral candidates once their studies have been successfully completed. If unemployment rates of PhDs in the UK are an indicator, then demand does appear to be particularly buoyant. However, at some point there will be a need to examine in systematic manner how many doctorates are needed rather than simply leave it to the individual decisions of individual universities.

The diversity of awards with the general title of doctorate creates a serious level of confusion in the market for suppliers, consumers, and their sponsors. This confusion raises the question as to whether or not there has been a fundamental shift of differentiation in the Doctorate in which divergent processes and outcomes have been developed to address changing needs. It is suggested that the answer to this question must be no. What has been evident is a tinkering at the margins to satisfy particular needs without a fundamental review of purpose. The writer has argued elsewhere that there is a serious need for the development of a model that allows a level of coherence without uniformity. In a system however in which the autonomy of institutions is paramount, it will be interesting to see where this discussion is finally resolved. (Green and Powell 2005)

The development of electronic submission and storage has major potential for the development of the Doctorate and the bringing together of the various doctoral forms as it allows us to focus on a single form of submission for the diversity of disciplines and their traditions. The UK is lagging behind the US and Australia and New Zealand in this regard. Whist there are currently pilot schemes being developed, there is no single model being developed and the British Library, the former repository of all UK theses, is moving slowly on the implementation of change.

The interactive potential of electronic submission will for example permit both musician and chemist to demonstrate their competences in performance and experiment respectively and will potentially offer an entirely new approach to the presentation and testing of evidence. Electronic submission will also, of course, enable wider and quicker access to research findings that form part of doctoral submissions. This increased accessibility will bring benefits both in terms of spreading the knowledge base and in increasing the transparency of standards of doctoral work across international borders

The Personal Development Plan (PDP) required of UK universities for all award bearing provision, including doctorates, follows the Dearing Report recommendation (1997) that HEIs should develop:

- a transcript recording student achievement which should follow a common format devised by universities collectively through their representative bodies; and
- a means by which students can monitor, build and reflect upon their personal development.

The QAA has subsequently developed policy and practice which requires universities to put in place Personal Development Plan (PDP) initiatives to ensure that students:

- become more effective independent and self confident self directed learners;
- understand how they are learning and relate their learning to a wider context;
- improve their general skills for study and career management;
- articulate their personal goals and evaluate progress towards achievement; and
- encourage a positive attitude to learning throughout life.

Perhaps PDP will begin to address the many concerns over employability and capacity development in research students. What it has done is to lump doctorates within the overall portfolio of HE provision, along with both undergraduate and postgraduate taught programs and in so doing possibly ground it in the world of learning.

The current structure of funding for both universities and students is complex at best and confusing at worst; the complexity and confusion lead to degrees of games playing. The HEFCE costing review and the move towards the recovery of full economic costs will have significant impacts on universities and the availability of doctoral programs. One outcome will surely be a more critical review of the Doctorate and its place in the higher education system. The system proposed for future funding of doctoral work (HEFCE 2004) reinforces the current concentration of doctoral programs in the more research-intensive universities.

There is within the UK the possibility of a two-tier system of delivery developing with regard to doctoral education. This matters if it means that the experience of doctoral study for those in the lower tier is less than for those in the higher and if the final doctoral outcomes (both "contribution to knowledge" and candidate) are in any way diminished. This question is particularly relevant to the way in which both students and institutions fund the Doctorate and the resources and opportunities that are made available. Institutions are increasingly aware of the costs of delivery, as are students of the costs to maintain themselves, part and full-time. Can one be confident however that these matters are fully examined when doctoral students are offered places and consequently many will be under-funded?

Many of the issues discussed above are concerned with aspects of the doctorate, its organisation, funding and delivery—all very important matters to be considered. What continues to be absent from the discussion is the doctorate itself and its purpose. Why do institutions offer it as an award? Why do students want to follow doctoral programs? Why do employers wish to employ candidates with doctorates? Why does Government wish to fund the delivery of doctoral programs? These remain as matters for discussion. Perhaps worryingly—place a group which represents each of those perspectives together and ask the question and there will be as many answers as people in the group. The key question must be "does this matter?" The answer must be: it does.

LIST OF ABBREVIATIONS

The following list is provided for information and includes the majority of abbreviations found in the literature on British Doctoral education.

ACS	Academic Cost Centre
AHRB	Arts and Humanities Research Board
AMusD	Doctor of Musical Arts
BBSRC	Biotechnology and Biological Sciences Research Council
BPS/UCOSDA	British Psychological Society and Universities and Colleges' Staff Development Unit
BRRG	Better Regulation Review Group
CBI	Confederation of British Industry
CEQ	Course Experience Questionnaire
CNAA	Council for National Academic Awards
CQFW	Credit and Qualifications Framework, Wales
CRAC	Careers Research and Advisory Centre
CVCP	Committee of Vice Chancellors and Principals now Universities UK (UUK)
CDP	Committee of Directors of Polytechnics
DArt	Doctor of Art
DBA	Doctorate in Business Administration
DBA	Diploma in Business Administration
DClinPsy	Doctor of Clinical Psychology
DD	Doctor of Divinity

DES	Department for Education and Science
DfES	Department for Education and Skills
DLitt	Doctor of Letters
DMus	Doctor of Music
DNurse	Doctor of Nursing
DPhil	Doctor of Philosophy
DProf	Professional Doctorate
DSc	Doctor of Science
DSocSc	Doctor of Social Sciences
DTA	Doctoral Training Accounts
DTI	Department of Trade and Industry
EdD	Doctor of Education
EngD	Doctor of Engineering
EPSRC	Engineering & Physical Sciences Research Council
ESRC	Economic and Social Research Council
EU	European Union
FHEQ	Framework of Higher Education Qualifications
FT	Full-time
GTA	Graduate Teaching Associate
HEFCE	Higher Education Funding Council for England
HEFCW	Higher Education Funding Council for Wales
HEI	Higher Education Institution
HEIF	Higher Education Innovation Fund
HEQC	Higher Education Qualifications Council
HESA	Higher Education Statistics Agency
HMSO	Her Majesty's Stationary Office
ILT	Institute of Learning Teaching
IP	Intellectual Property
IPR	Intellectual Property Rights
JISC	Joint Information Systems Committee
LEA	Local Education Authority
LLD	Doctor of Law

MA	Master of Arts
MD	Doctor of Medicine
MPhil	Master of Philosophy
MRC	Medical Research Council
MRes	Masters by Research
MSc	Master of Science
NERC	Natural Environment Research Council
NICATS	The Northern Ireland Credit Accumulation and Transfer
NPC	National Postgraduate Committee
NUCCAT	Northern Universities Consortium for Credit Accumulation and Transfer
OECD	Organisation for Economic Co-operation and Development
OST	Office of Science and Technology
PgCert	Postgraduate Certificate
PgDip	Postgraduate Diploma
PGR	Postgraduate Research
PGT	Postgraduate Taught
PhD	Doctor of Philosophy
PI	Performance Indicator
PPARC	Particle Physics and Astronomy Research Council
PREQ	Postgraduate Research Experience Questionnaire
PT	Part-time
QAA	Quality Assurance Agency for Higher Education
QR	Quality Research
RAE	Research Assessment Exercise
RDA	Regional Development Agency
SEEC	Southern England Consortium for Credit Accumulation and Transfer
SERC	Science and Engineering Research Council (now EPSRC)

SHEFC	Scottish Higher Education Funding Council
TAPPS	Training and Accreditation me for Postgraduate Supervisors
THES	The Times Higher Education Supplement
UKCGE	UK Council for Graduate Education
UoA	Units of Assessment

ACKNOWLEDGMENT

I would like to acknowledge the contribution of Professor Stuart Powell in commenting on this review and permitting me to use material freely from *Doctoral Studies in Contemporary Higher Education* published by The Open University Press in July 2005.

BIBLIOGRAPHY

British Academy. 2001. Review of Graduate Studies in the Humanities and Social Sciences. Main report. London: British Academy.

British Council. 2004. *Vision 2020: Forecasting International Student Mobility.*

BPS/UCOSDA (British Psychological Society and Universities and Colleges' Staff Development Unit). 1995. *Guidelines for Assessment of the PhD in Psychology and Related Disciplines.* Sheffield: OCOSDA.

Conlon, G., and A. Chevalier. 2002. *Rates of Return to Qualifications: A Summary of Recent Evidence.* London: The Council for Industry and Higher Education (CIHE).

Dearing, R. 1997. *Higher Education in the Learning Society.* London: National Committee of Inquiry into Higher Education.

Department for Education and Skills (DfES). 2003. *The Future of Higher Education.* White Paper, Cm. 5735, HMSO. London: DfES.

DTI. 1993. *Realising Our Potential: A Strategy for Science, Engineering and Technology.* White Paper, Cmnd. 2250, HMSO. London: DTI.

Economic and Social Research Council (ESRC). 2001. *Postgraduate Training Guidelines,* 3rd ed., http://www.esrc.ac.uk.

Green, D. H. and S. D. Powell. 2004. "The High Price of Good Quality." *The Independent Education,* 13 October.

Green, D. H. and S. D. Powell. 2005. *Doctoral Study in Contemporary Higher Education.* London: SRHE and Open University Press.

Harris, M. 1996. *Review of Postgraduate Education.* Higher Education Funding Council for England, Committee of Vice-Chancellors and Principals Standing Conference of Principals HEFCE, ref: M14/.

Higher Education Funding Council for England (HEFCE). 2001. *Review of Research: Report on Consultation.* http://www.hefce.ac.uk/pubs/hefce/2001/0117.htm (accessed 12 September 2004).

Higher Education Funding Council of England (HEFCE). 2003a. *Improving*

Standards in Postgraduate Research Degree me. Informal Consultation. HEFCE 2003/01. London: HEFCE.

Higher Education Funding Council of England (HEFCE). 2004. *Funding for Research Degree mes (RDPs).* www.hefce.ac.uk/research/postgrad/rdpfund.htm (accessed 20 January 2005).

Higher Education Funding Council for England (HEFCE). 2005. "PhD Research Degrees: Entry and Completion." HEFCE 2005/2. http://www.hefce.ac.uk (accessed 12 January 2005).

Higher Education Statistics Agency (HESA). 2001. *Students in Higher Education Institutions, 1999/2000.* Cheltenham: HESA.

Higher Education Statistics Agency (HESA). 2004a. *Students in Higher Education Intuitions,* 2002/3, Table 9C. Cheltenham: HESA.

Hinde, J. 1999. "Science Fails to Fill PhDs." *Times Higher Educational Supplement* (THES), 26 February.

Hodges, L. 1999. "Economists Fall for the Lure of Lucre." *The Independent Higher Education,* 10 June.

J M Consulting Ltd. 2005. "Costs of Training and Supervising Postgraduate Research Students." A Report to HEFCE by JM Consulting Ltd., February 2005. http://www.hefce.ac.uk/pubs/rdreports/2005/ (accessed 4 February 2005).

Loeffler, T. 2004. *Skills Training Funding for Research Council Funded PhD Students and Postdoctoral Researchers.* Research Councils UK Training Group, March.

Metcalfe, J., Q. Thompson, and D. H. Green. 2002. "Improving Standards in Research Degree mes." A Report to the Funding Councils of England, Scotland, and Wales. http://www.hefce.ac.uk/pubs/rdreports/2002/.

Millichope, R. 2001. "Doctorates Awarded from United Kingdom Higher Education Institutions." *Statistics Focus,* Vol. 3, Issue 2.

Office of Science and Technology (OST). 1994. *Consultative Document: A New Structure for Postgraduate Research Trainings, Supported by Research Councils.* London: Cabinet Office.

Powell, S. D. and C. McCauley. 2002. "Research Degree Examining—Common Principles and Divergent Practices." *Quality Assurance in Education, (Special Edition "Standards and the Doctoral Award",* 10(2): 104–16

Quality Assurance Agency QAA. 2001. "National Qualifications Framework." http//www.qaa.ac.uk/crntwork/nqf/ewni2001/contents.htm (accessed 27 August 2004).

Quality Assurance Agency (QAA). 2004. *Code of Practice for the Assurance of Academic Quality and Standards in Higher Education: Section 1: Postgraduate Research mes,* 2nd ed. Gloucester: Quality Assurance Agency.

Research Fortnight. 1999a. "Alarm Bells Ring over Vacant Studentships." *Research Fortnight,* Vol. 5, No. 9.

Research Fortnight. 1999b. "Universities Choose Conditions for PhDs." *Research Fortnight,* Vol. 6, No. 2.

Roberts, G. 2002. *Set for Success: The Supply of People with Science, Technology, Engineering and Mathematical Skills.* HM Treasury. www.hm-treasury.gov.uk (accessed 20 October 2004).

Roberts, G. 2003. *Review of the Research Assessment Exercise. Report for the Funding*

Bodies, HEFCE Issues for Consultation May 2003. http://www.ra-review.ac.uk/reports/roberts/roberts_summary.doc (accessed 20 January 2005).

Sastry, T. 2004. *Postgraduate Education in the United Kingdom.* Oxford: Higher Education Policy Institute.

Sastry, T. 2005. *Postgraduate Research Degree mes in English Universities—Costs and Revenue.* Oxford: Higher Education Policy Institute.

Science and Engineering Research Council (SERC). 1992. *Research Student and Supervisor: An Approach to Good Supervisory Practice,* 2nd ed. Swindon: SERC.

Shaw, M. and H. Green. 2001. "Benchmarking the PhD—A Tentative Beginning." *Quality Assurance in Education* 10(2): 116–24.

Spagnold, F. 1994. "Students Abroad Sponsored by the Government." *Infoscapes,* Vol. 2, No. 1: 10–17

Tinkler, P. and C. Jackson. 2004. *The Doctoral Examination Process: A Handbook for Students, Examiners and Supervisors.* Buckingham: Open University Press.

UK Council for Graduate Education (UKCGE). 1995. *Graduate Schools Survey.* Warwick: UKCGE. http://www.ukcge.ac.uk/report_downloads.html (accessed 20 January 2005).

UK Council for Graduate Education. 1996. *Quality and Standards of Postgraduate Research Degrees.* Warwick: UKCGE. http://www.ukcge.ac.uk/report_downloads.html (accessed 20 January 2005).

Underwood, S. 1999. *What is a PhD? Towards a Discussion Paper.* Lancaster: Higher Education Development Centre.

Wellcome Trust. 2001. *Review of the Wellcome Trust PhD: The Supervisor Perspective.* London: Wellcome Trust.

Winfield, G. 1987. *The Social Science PhD: The ESRC Inquiry on Submission Rates.* London: ESRC.

Woodward, D., P. Denicolo, S. Hayward, and E. Long. 2004. Review of Graduate Schools Survey. Lichfield: UKCGE. http://www.ukcge.ac.uk/filesup/Graduateschools.pdf (accessed 20 January 2005).

3 • NORDIC COUNTRIES

HANS KRISTJÁN GUÐMUNDSSON

INTRODUCTION

This chapter presents a short overview of doctoral education in the Nordic countries: Denmark, Finland, Iceland, Norway, and Sweden, with specific attention to the situation in Iceland. A quick reference is given to the developments related to the Bologna process. Some statistics on doctoral education and doctoral degrees in the Nordic countries are shown with some additional material relating to the Baltic countries. The facts and data shown are compiled from different sources, and the reader is referred to those for a closer study. The progress of the Bologna process can be quickly reviewed in the latest national reports,[1] and an excellent overview of thirteen countries is given in the UNESCO-CEPES report of 2004,[2] which also includes a comparative study by Dr. Barbara M. Kehm including Sweden and Norway among several other countries.[3] The statistics shown and some of the analysis are taken from the Nordic-Baltic statistics data base on doctoral education and degrees, NORBAL, covering the Nordic and the Baltic countries.[4] The reader is also referred to earlier reports issued by NorFA, the Nordic Academy for Advanced Study, accessible through the web sites of the Nordic Research Board: www.nordforsk.org.[5] These web sites also illustrate the cross-border activities in research training under the auspices of the Nordic Council of Ministers.

NORDIC DEVELOPMENTS IN RESEARCH TRAINING

For the last decades, the forms for doctoral studies as part of the higher education system in the Nordic countries have undergone radical changes, at different times and to a different degree in each country. The systems have everywhere been subject to several revisions, and in all the countries recent revisions and amendments of laws are bringing the systems into an organized, programmed form of doctoral education, and departing from the "classical" master-disciple system. The aim has been to increase the number of highly qualified researchers in a shortened timeframe and to assure that these researchers are prepared not only for academic positions but also for other parts of society. Already in the late sixties, Sweden created a four year doctorate combining courses and thesis work in a single program.

The Nordic countries have for a long time cooperated closely and have in many practical contexts been a common area for work and study with an extensive direct cooperation among higher education institutions. Cooperation among educational institutions and nations started with parliamentary cooperation through the Nordic Council and continued under the auspices of the Nordic Council of Ministers in the seventies. The early programs involved inter-Nordic mobility grants and research training courses planned and given in cross border cooperation between Nordic universities and researchers, the courses normally being accepted in the students' study plans. In 1991 the Nordic Academy of Advanced Study, NorFA, was established to oversee and develop research training cooperation. The mobility grants and the courses continued, and networking grants were created, developing later into Nordic Graduate School pilot programs. These activities are, as of 2005, continuing within the new organization NordForsk (the Nordic Research Board), which has incorporated NorFA. These Nordic activities are designed to fit needs of the national systems. The latest developments, thematic graduate schools, were modeled mainly on the graduate schools established in Finland, but also partly on Danish and Swedish models. These Nordic schools are run as time limited thematic projects, preferably inter- and multidisciplinary, involving research groups at several different universities. The graduate school network model is organized with an administrative leader and a common program involving both senior and young researchers, supervisors, and doctoral students, establishing a critical mass not possible to obtain with each of the groups involved. In this Nordic pilot model, central Nordic financing is given to cover the administrative and cooperation costs, such as meetings, courses, mobility, etc. The degrees are earned within each participating university, unless an agreement on joint degrees is reached. Obviously such a simple cross border cooperative program model would be a helpful and even necessary step towards further integration requiring legislative changes.

Since the Bologna declaration in June 1999, a lot of work has been put into the development of the European Higher Education Area, EHEA. The Bologna process is quickly changing the scene of higher education in Europe and seems to be an effective driving force for change. The latest development in the process is based on the ministerial conference held in Berlin 2004, where definite ties were made to the European Research Area, ERA, by including doctoral education as a third cycle, following the previously agreed two cycle degree system, the bachelor's and the master's degrees. Doctoral education has always been a fundamental concern in the development of the ERA, because doctoral education is partly a source for human capital for research but is also an extremely important part of the research itself.

At the Bergen ministerial conference in May 2005 the ministers declared: "We note that the efforts to introduce structural change and improve the quality of teaching should not detract from the effort to strengthen research and innovation. We therefore emphasize the importance of research and research training in maintaining and improving the quality and enhancing the competitiveness and attractiveness of the EHEA. With a view to achieving better results we recognize the need to improve the synergy between the higher education sector and other research sectors throughout our countries and between the EHEA and the European Research Area . . ."

The Ministers also declared that: "The core component of doctoral training is the advancement of knowledge through original research . . ."; they considered "participants in third cycle programs both as students and as early stage researchers . . ." and urged "universities to ensure that their doctoral programs promote interdisciplinary training and the development of transferable skills, thus meeting the needs of the wider employment market." The ministers furthermore asked for a report "on the further development of the basic principles for doctoral programs, to be presented to Ministers in 2007" and stated that "Overregulation of doctoral programs should be avoided."

As a basis for the development of doctoral education in Europe these various developments give important guidelines that emphasize the research component of doctoral education, the quality of the thesis work, and the status of doctoral students as researchers, while at the same time underline the importance of developing skills for a wider market (core competences of the doctor).

All the Nordic countries are working towards the Bologna "three cycle system," the first two cycles being more or less in place, while the third cycle—doctoral education—is being developed. The status of this development can be seen in the national reports to the Bergen ministerial conference in May 2005.[6]

Table 3.1 is a comparative overview of the higher education system in the Nordic countries is taken from the NORBAL data base[7] with some

TABLE 3.1 An overview of the higher education system in the Nordic countries

Land	Years of study as formally defined									
	1	2	3	4	5	6	7	8	9	10
	Basic education					Research education				
Denmark	BA – 3 yrs			Candidate – 2 yrs		PhD – 3 yrs				
	BA – 4 yrs				PhD – 4 yrs					
Finland	Candidate – 3 yrs			Master – 2 yrs		Licentiate – 2 yrs				
						Doctoral degree – 3-4 yrs				
Iceland	BA – 3 yrs			Master – 2 yrs		PhD – 3-4 yrs				
Norway	BA – 3 yrs			Master – 2 yrs		PhD – 3-4 yrs				
Sweden	Basic education – 3 yrs			Licentiate – 2 yrs						
				Doctoral degree – 3-4 yrs						

SOURCE: NORBAL

minor correction and with the understanding that this review does not necessarily reflect the most recent changes. The table does not include the traditional doctoral degrees still existing in Denmark, Iceland, and Norway.

STATISTICS ON AWARDED DOCTORAL DEGREES AND DOCTORAL STUDENTS IN THE NORDIC COUNTRIES

The following overview and statistical aspects are taken from the NORBAL data base,[8] and the reader is invited to consult the database directly for further details and yearly updates. NORBAL is a statistical data base established at *NIFU STEP* and commissioned by The Nordic Academy for Advanced

Study (NorFA), which has been incorporated in the new Nordic Research Board (NordForsk), established 1 January 2005. The database comprises data on awarded doctoral degrees and active doctoral students in the Nordic and Baltic countries. In NORBAL statistics are presented that show a time series on the number of awarded doctoral degrees. The statistical summary also shows the distribution of doctorates according to gender and fields of science, and their ages at the time of dissertation or doctoral exam. NORBAL also presents statistics on active doctoral students in the individual countries—including gender and field distributions.

NORBAL covers all years from 1990 inclusive to the extent that data are available. In Finland and Sweden there is also the licentiate degree, a degree containing a component of research training although on a lower level than the doctoral degree. NORBAL also includes statistics on the licentiate degree. In the paragraphs that follow some issues relating to the trends seen in the statistics and the time series are highlighted. Tables and diagrammes are regularly updated and can be accessed through through the NORBAL web site.

In 2002,[9] 5,470 persons were awarded a doctoral degree in the Nordic countries. This is close to a doubling in ten years. Around 42,400 doctoral students were registered in 2002. The total population of the Nordic countries was 24.3 million in 2002. About two-fifths of the total number of doctoral degrees in the region in 2002 were awarded in Sweden, one-fifth in Finland, and one-fifth in Denmark. As a percentage of the population size, the number of awarded doctorate degrees has increased in all the Nordic countries. Sweden and Finland have the highest number of degrees per capita. These two countries also display the highest increase among the Nordic countries.

Women accounted for 43.1 percent of doctoral degrees awarded in 2002. This marks a considerable increase since 1990, when the proportion was around 26 percent. The female percentage was highest in Finland, being 49 percent in 2002.

High Average Age

As for the age of the new doctors, in Finland, Iceland, Norway, and Sweden candidates are approximately thirty-seven to thirty-eight-years-old when defending their thesis, in Denmark thirty-four years. The average age at the time of dissertation or award is thus relatively high, and has remained quite stable after 1990. However, the average age varies considerably between the various fields of science in which the doctoral degree has been awarded. In the humanities and the social sciences the average age is generally higher than in the natural sciences and technology. There are variations, however, between the countries.

Increasing Number of Doctoral Students

The number of doctoral students has increased considerably between 1990 and 2002. The increase was particularly high in Finland but more moderate in Sweden and Norway. As noted previously, the female percentage of doctoral students also increased. In 2002 women accounted for about 50 percent of doctoral students in Finland and in Iceland. In Sweden the female percentage was about 45 and in Denmark and Norway above 40. However, the female percentage varies among the fields of science. Finland has by far the highest number of doctoral students per capita. The increase in Finland has been very strong during the last few years. Denmark and Norway have the lowest ratio among the Nordic countries.

ICELAND

Iceland is a small country with population just below 300,000. It is thus always difficult to include Iceland in comparative studies and small fluctuation in numbers can register as huge percentage-wise. Iceland, however, has one of the strongest economies in the world and a particularly strong scientific community. The quality of life is high and the country is generally prosperous having moved in less than a hundred years from being a poor developing country to a highly developed modern society. It normally scores very high on the OECD scales of research, innovation and entrepreneurial indicators. The main keys to this development are no doubt the internationalization of the society and its economy and clever and sustainable utilization of natural resources such as geothermal and hydropower and not the least of the biosystems in the ocean. This is in turn resting on a base of knowledge and skills gained through international openness and high mobility of students and workforce. It can sound like a paradox and it is interesting to look at how such a small country can build up a strong scientific community and a knowledge based industry at the forefront of science without offering research training within its universities. It is also interesting to look at how the development of research training at home will influence the future.

An Internationally Strong Research Community Built Without Domestic PhD Programmes

In earlier years Iceland offered practically no PhD programmes at the universities. The very few awarded doctoral degrees at the University of

Iceland through the years have been of the classical type being a result of an individual's at times lifelong research work. Students have instead been encouraged after their bachelor's and/or master's degrees to take a doctoral degree at universities abroad. Apart from possible grants and fellowships awarded by the receiving university, the Icelandic student loan fund has made this generally possible, offering favorable loans that can cover not only costs of living but also tuition fees. This has been a tremendously valuable source of knowledge and created a unique resource of human capital when these people return with their doctorates and equivalent degrees awarded at the best institutions in the world—in Europe, USA, Japan, etc. Some only return after having gained postdoctoral and further academic and research experience. This has created a stimulating and fertile "multicultural" research environment in Iceland which has in many fields put the country at the forefront of science, for example in geosciences, life and health sciences, and in technology sectors like the energy sector, especially the geothermal technology, as well as fishing and fish processing technology. Iceland is now a top spender on research in relation to the GNP at the level of 3 percent of which somewhat above a third is publicly financed. It should not be forgotten, however, that the absolute figures are small in international comparison, the total expenditure as measured for the year 2003 being around 24 billion ISK (310 million EUR; 375 million USD) supporting around 3,000 full time equivalents of man-year research work.[10] Success rates in the competitive programs of the European Union and several grants given by the NSF and the NIH in the USA show that research work in Iceland is excellent and internationally competitive, and Icelandic scientists score high in the Science Citation Index. It is interesting to note in this context that close to 20 percent of the expenditure on research is financed from sources outside Iceland largely on a competitive basis.

Toward Less Mobility?

The (out of necessity) extreme mobility of Icelandic researchers and research students and not the least their willingness to return with knowledge and skills gained abroad, combined with a seemingly inherent entrepreneurial spirit, has created a unique capacity in a small society. However, we are now facing interesting developments when shaping the future research environment. The research groups are small and there is both a demand and a need to create PhD programs at home so as to enhance the capacity of the most active groups, research students being an extremely valuable workforce in academic research. At the same time high-quality research environments have emerged with high quality supervisor potential able to give doctoral students support of the quality needed for an internationally recognized PhD. The pressure from the students is high as they obviously find it easier to take their PhD at home than going abroad. We may therefore be seeing a trend towards less mobility in the doctoral education of Icelanders. Due to the smallness of the society it is very difficult to create the critical mass needed and to offer the variety of other elements necessary for a complete and internationally competitive doctoral program. Facing a present rapid growth of registered doctoral students at home, we have an immediate task on our hands to assure the quality of the doctoral education offered, avoiding the creation of "second rate" programs which would undermine the future potential for research and innovation. "Home-based" internationalization including creation and participation in international multi- or bi-national graduate school programs, agreements with foreign universities on joint programs and joint degrees will have to be further developed and enhanced with priority given to our strongest fields. The University of Iceland, now being the host institution for almost all the doctoral students registered in Iceland, is very much aware of this and guidelines are in place for doctoral programs offered in several fields of study the doctoral programs being in harmony with the Bologna model of three to four years mostly based on a two years master's degree program. The course basis is around 15 percent. The legal basis for the University does not hinder engagement in either joint degrees or programs.

Statistics on Doctoral Degrees and Doctoral Education in Iceland

Of the nine higher education institutions in Iceland only two presently offer doctoral programs, almost all at the University of Iceland being by far the largest institution, the Pedagogical University of Iceland being the other. Looking back a few years, around forty Icelanders have finished a PhD every year, the largest number being forty-eight in the year 2002. In 2003, thirty-five Icelanders finished their PhD; thirty-seven did so in 2004. These are total numbers including degrees taken at home and abroad around the world. In 2004 five women and five men graduated from the University of Iceland, others (twenty-seven) graduated from universities around the world. The distribution between countries is somewhat uneven showing that 40 percent of the doctoral students go to the USA and about 20 percent to the Nordic countries. The average age of the PhDs graduating from the University of Iceland was thirty-five years in 2003 and thirty-eight years in 2004.

Table 3.2 shows in absolute numbers the doctoral degrees of Icelanders

TABLE 3.2

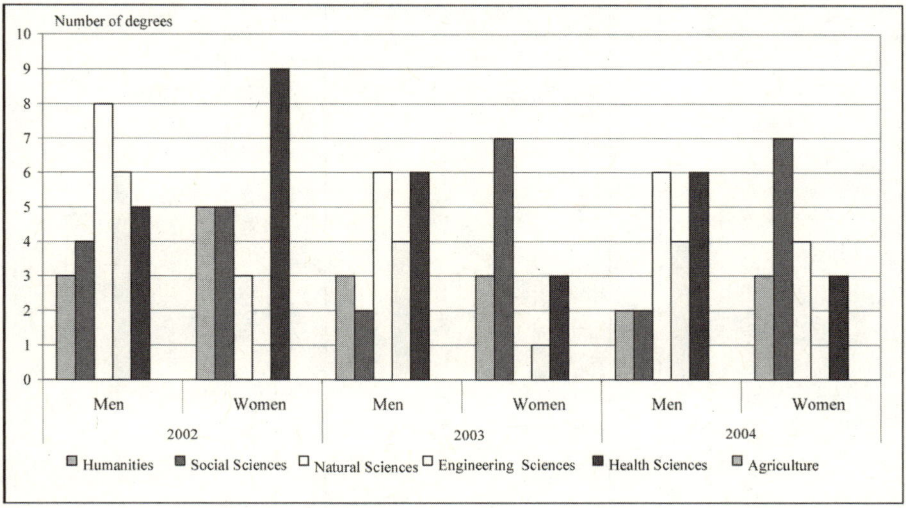

SOURCE: RANNIS, unpublished

taken in the period of 2002 to 2004. The degrees are presented according to sex and fields. Reservation is made for the accuracy of the statistics on PhD degrees awarded at universities outside Iceland as they are based on voluntary information given by the individuals and the figures are most likely underestimated.

An interesting picture emerges when the development in the number of doctoral students registered at Icelandic universities is considered. Table 3.3 shows this development—almost all students being registered at the University of Iceland. The table shows a steep and general increase in registrations, from seven in 1995 to 144 in 2004, reflecting both the increased interest of the students and the increased offer of doctoral programs. It also shows the distribution on fields and sex.

It is interesting to note that of the 144 doctoral students in 2004 women account for 60 percent. It is also seen that majority of the women are studying within social and health sciences while the men tend to register in natural sciences. There is no information available on whether this high number of doctoral students at home will affect the number of students abroad or whether we will be seeing increased output in the coming years. It is, however, very likely that fewer students will take their whole doctoral education abroad and leaves the universities in Iceland with the challenging tasks to offer high quality doctoral programmes of a high international standard. This also creates some pressure on the government to increase funding.[11]

TABLE 3.3 Number of doctoral students registered at universities in Iceland

				Total						
Field	*1995*	*1996*	*1997*	*1998*	*1999*	*2000*	*2001*	*2002*	*2003*	*2004*
Humanities	1	3	7	10	12	12	15	14	20	22
Social Sciences			2	3	1	4	9	15	26	37
Natural Sciences					5	11	17	17	30	36
Engineering Sciences					1	1	2	3	4	5
Health Sciences	6	6	5	8	16	24	26	31	34	44
Agricultural Sciences								0	0	0
All fields of study	7	9	14	21	35	52	69	80	114	144
				Women						
Field	*1995*	*1996*	*1997*	*1998*	*1999*	*2000*	*2001*	*2002*	*2003*	*2004*
Humanities	0	2	2	4	5	5	7	10	13	16
Social Sciences			1	1	1	1	5	6	14	22

Natural Sciences					1	4	8	7	15	17
Engineering Sciences							1	1	2	2
Health Sciences	3	5	2	4	7	10	12	17	21	28
Agricultural Sciences									0	0
All fields of study	3	7	5	9	14	20	33	41	65	85

Men										
Field	*1995*	*1996*	*1997*	*1998*	*1999*	*2000*	*2001*	*2002*	*2003*	*2004*
Humanities	1	1	5	6	7	7	8	4	7	6
Social Sciences			1	2		3	4	9	12	15
Natural Sciences					4	7	9	10	15	19
Engineering Sciences					1	1	1	2	2	3
Health Sciences	3	1	3	4	9	14	14	14	13	16
Agricultural Sciences									0	0
All fields of study	4	2	9	12	21	32	36	39	49	59

Statistics from the University of Iceland and Iceland University of Education.

Iceland in the Bologna Process

Higher education institutions and doctoral education come under the jurisdiction of the Minister for Education Science and Culture. The Bologna process is followed actively, a national Bologna follow-up group is active and a special committee on quality in the education sector was set up in 2004. A three-year-action plan (2005–2007) was created to evaluate higher education institutions. The issue of developing doctoral education is a central one in the general research policy agenda. The Science and Technology Policy Council, chaired by the Prime Minister, have in their policy declaration, confirmed by the government, emphasized the importance of research training at the doctoral level in strengthening the research at university level. It was also stated that the fund for research training needed revision and strengthening.

CONCLUDING REMARKS

In this paper a descriptive overview has been given on doctoral education in the Nordic countries, Denmark, Finland, Iceland, Norway, and Sweden. In all the countries the doctoral education has been reformed recently involving a clear trend towards programmed training, and all the countries are participating in the Bologna process for the creation of the EHEA, The European Higher Education Area. A specific treatment is given on the situation for Iceland which is an interesting case of a small country developing over the years a strong scientific community without offering its own doctoral education. However, this strong knowledge society has developed a need and a demand for domestic doctoral training, which in fact is under rapid development at the universities as registration numbers soar. The question is raised how the domestic programs will develop in competition and in cooperation on the international arena to guarantee the continued high quality of the Icelandic research environment.

NOTES

1. The national reports can be found at the Bologna-Bergen web site: http://www.bologna-bergen2005.no/.

2. Jan Sadlak, ed., *Doctoral Studies and Qualifications in Europe and the United States: Status and Prospects* (Bucharest: UNESCO-CEPES: 2004).

3. B. M. Kehm, "Developing Doctoral Degrees and Qualifications in Europe: Good Practice and Issues of Concern—A Comparative Analysis," in Doctoral Studies and Qualifications in Europe and the United States: Status and Prospects, ed. Jan Sadlak (Bucharest: UNESCO-CEPES, 2004), 279–98.

4. NORBAL can be assessed through the web site: http://english.nifustep.no/norbal__1/eng/startpage.

5. See for example: http://www.nordforsk.org/_img/Quality_in_research_2.pdf on Quality in Research Training; http://www.nordforsk.org/_img/ACF104.pdf, Nordic Research Training: Common Objectives for International Quality; and http://www.nordforsk.org/_img/ACF106.pdf, Barriers to Mobility in Research training in the Nordic Countries.

6. The national reports can be found at the Bologna-Bergen web site: http://www.bologna-bergen2005.no/.

7. http://www.nifustep.no/norbal__1/eng/startpage.

8. http://www.nifustep.no/norbal__1/eng/startpage.

9. The statistics given in this paper refer to the year 2002. For the latest information the reader is referred to the NORBAL database for updated statistics. As an example for the year 2005 the total number of awardees is more than 6,000 of whom 48 percent were women. Also at the end of 2005 around 58,000 students were registered in the Nordic Countries.

10. In the year 2005 the total expenditure measures more than 28 billon ISK.

11. Statistics for 2006 show that the number of PhD students registered in Icelandic Higher Education Institutions has risen to 232 in total. Preliminary information furthermore indicates that the total number of doctoral degrees obtained at home and abroad is similar to those of previous years. However, the number of degrees awarded abroad has decreased both in absolute and relative terms (RANNIS).

BIBLIOGRAPHY

Bologna-Bergen web site: http://www.bologna-bergen2005.no/.

Kehm, B. M. "Developing Doctoral Degrees and Qualifications in Europe: Good Practice and Issues of Concern—A Comparative Analysis." In *Doctoral Studies and Qualifications in Europe and the United States: Status and Prospects*, edited by Jan Sadlak, 279–98. Bucharest: UNESCO-CEPES.

NORBAL web site: http://www.english.nifustep.no/norbal__1/eng/startpage.

NordForsk web site: http://www.nordforsk.org.

Sadlak, Jan, ed. 2004. *Doctoral Studies and Qualifications in Europe and the United States: Status and Prospects.* Bucharest: UNESCO-CEPES.

4 • THE EUROPEAN UNIVERSITY INSTITUTE

ANDREAS C. FRIJDAL

INTRODUCTION

The European University Institute (EUI) in Florence, Italy, was created as an institution exclusively dedicated to doctoral education thirty years ago. It provides doctoral training in the social sciences, such as economics, history, law, and social and political science. Although it is located in Florence, it has the legal structure of an inter-governmental organization funded by the European Union member states, currently nineteen. A contract with the remaining six EU member states is being negotiated so that there should soon be twenty-five Contracting States at the EUI. The Institute's objective for 2006 is six hundred doctoral research students, one hundred postdocs, and over fifty full-time professors supported by one hundred and fifty administrative and technical staff, all working in various historical buildings on the hills of Fiesole just north of Florence, Italy.

This paper describes developments in the European University Institute since its founding. Due to its unique European character, the EUI caters to all European countries. In order to structure the changes which mostly marked and are relevant for the debate at the EUI I have taken two reference points, which were major strategic reviews that took place in the early 1990s, and I refer mostly to the report then published called *Beyond Maintenance*.[1] The second strategic review, *Enlarging and Enhancing*,[2] took place around 2000, which dealt also the with European Union enlargement. But we will start with a general appreciation of the Bologna declaration and its effects on doctoral education.

THE BOLOGNA DECLARATION AND EUROPEAN DOCTORAL EDUCATION

The main objectives of the declaration of 1999 are as follows:

- adoption of a system of easily readable and comparable degrees;
- adoption of a system essentially based on two cycles (under-graduate and graduate);
- establishment of a system of credits;
- promotion of mobility;
- promotion of European co-operation in quality assurance; and
- promotion of the European dimension in higher education

The first objective is to reach, by 2010, a generally accepted uniform 3 + 2 + 3 year model including a credit transfer system in the entire European area. Today we see that a large number of countries have approached the issue by introducing the first three-year structures, or a variation on that, for the first degree. It is generally recognized that one of the main motivations behind the objectives of the Bologna Declaration was to reduce the duration of the first post-secondary degree to a controllable number of years. In some European countries—especially in Germany and the Nordic countries—it took more than five years to obtain the first degree, whilst in the UK and Ireland it took only three to four years, in France/Belgium and the Netherlands four to five years. In some other European countries, the length of time of the first degree was almost uncontrollable, as in the case of Italy. The EUI is particularly well placed to compare the different outcomes of the system; one has only to observe the age at which various nationalities start their doctoral work at the EUI.

The second objective was to combat the very high dropout rate in some systems. In the beginning of 2000, two-thirds of students in Italy did not reach the first degree. Since this paper deals with the doctoral aspect, it needs to be observed that the doctoral discussion in the Bologna Declaration entered the debate only at a very late stage. It was really only in 2005 when the first declaration, at the instigation of the European University Association, stated how the doctoral component of the Bologna Declaration should be interpreted. Very little has been done in most countries, and the structures in most European countries still stick to the original models as they existed before the Bologna Declaration.

The 3 + 2 + 3 model in a number of countries was called the BAMA (BA/MA model, bachelor's and master's). Also the fact that the doctoral part was only three years shows that there was no clear idea how long it took in most European countries to finish a thesis. Although the ideas about the first degree and the doctoral degree have now crystallized, very little is known in the debate about the MA degree: each country has its own interpretation and this is particularly true for the research masters. In our intake the majority of the masters are one-year degrees. Furthermore, in some countries such as the UK, the postgraduate market is extremely lucrative for one-year taught MAs. Last but not least, let us not forget that in some countries the doctoral component is hardly more than 5–10 percent of PGE. After having reduced the length of the first degree, the major ongoing discussion remains: what are the components of the masters and how does it link to the doctorate and whether there might be a selection between these phases of the 3 + 2 + 3 model.

It is striking that the Bologna Declaration stipulates three years for the doctoral program. This must be the result of sheer ignorance. In reality doctoral studies, as in the US, take much longer in Europe. Hardly any statistical evidence is available to underpin this three-year proposal. Countries that made the effort to collect data about the length of doctoral education (such as the UK, the Netherlands, Belgium, and Sweden) have accepted from the statistical facts that it is not realistic to believe that a doctorate can be done in less than four years. Indeed it is remarkable to observe that those national studies that do exist clearly showed that completion rates were very low and times-to-degree were very long. It is not accidental that the Swedish report is called "Four years," not "for years"!

To further enter into the specific question of the conference organizers, the Bologna Declaration indeed has had a globalizing effect. It is widely recognized that the Bologna model is emulating the Anglo-Saxon approach to university education. Does this globalization have a national flavour? Yes, it needs to be added here that a number of countries, whilst having signed the Bologna Declaration, still tend to give it an interpretation of their own. For example, in the Netherlands the first degree allows for four to five years (3 + 2) and the doctorate four years (3 + 1). In Belgium the first degree now is four years; it will become 3 + 1.

THE CHANGING DOCTORAL LANDSCAPE

During the 1990s further changes took place at an increasing speed that can be characterized by five distinctive aspects:

1. Growth
2. Diversification
3. Substitution
4. Professionalization
5. Competition

Although in the 1970s the literature in the United States predicted a decline in postgraduate education—and also in Europe based on demographic assumptions—a considerable growth took place in both the United States and in Europe. In the US the number of doctorates went from 33,000 per year to over 45,000. In Europe some countries had a more than tenfold development in the wider postgraduate educational sector and Europe is now producing 70,000 PhDs per year. In reality the postgraduate education sector grew much more if one looks beyond the doctoral education sector. Where doctoral education was the core activity in the postgraduate education market twenty-five years ago, today it only represents 10 percent of the market. So if one extrapolates the real growth in doctoral education as representing only 10 percent of the market one can get an idea of the explosion of postgraduate activities in the US and in Europe. This development is mainly caused by the exponential creation of new degrees for a non-academic market.

As mentioned earlier, by introducing the Bologna model governments have tried to limit the time spent on the first degree, but obviously this will result in a large spill-over into a newly created postgraduate education sector of curricular content that was formerly covered by traditional longer first degree education. This substitution effect will lead to an increased demand for mid-level postgraduate education training of a professional or academic character.

Doctoral education in the past was very much a type of "in-house" training and a start in a career for a professorial job, particularly in the social sciences and humanities. Most of those who started an academic career twenty-five years ago were appointed in assistant, or assistant professor jobs that made them a university employee. On average in the first six to ten years one dedicated part of one's time working under the wings of a supervisor but at the same time started to teach, to organize practice, and to carry out some research alongside the normal doctoral work. There were no or very few structured courses or structured training programs. After the first ten years, generally a doctorate was delivered that provided the requisites for the first appointment as assistant/associate professor.

In the mid-eighties this tradition was abolished in a number of European countries and a number of appropriate structures for doctoral education, following the American model of graduate schools in various formats (Ecole Doctorale, Graduate School, Graduiertenkolleg, Onderzoekscholen) were created. In some countries the legal position of the doctorandus changed fundamentally: from a normal university employee position one became a grant holder.

Dramatic changes in the labour market in the late nineties resulted in decreasing interest for doctoral training positions, especially in areas such as economics. Universities are in competition with each other for the best graduate students. For example, the London School of Economics created a policy to stimulate the undergraduates to continue at the LSE. A British paper's headline recently read, "Warwick offers cash bonus to keep graduates at the University," and the Max Planck Society offers special grants to attract foreign students to come to Germany, etc. The US still attracts several thousand doctoral students per year. Other countries such as the Netherlands have provided new funds to increase PhD numbers and also provide attractive four-year grants.

THE EUROPEAN UNIVERSITY INSTITUTE 1990–2005

After fifteen years of existence the EUI had reached the following situation as summarised by the report: forty full-time professors, three hundred doctoral/research students, and forty postdoc fellows. The committee set up by the High Council (Board of Governors) stated that the changes in the Institute's environment in terms of higher education systems of member states and the upheavals in Eastern Europe offer an occasion to ask what the Institute's future should look like over the coming decades. Highlighting the major issues from the above-mentioned reports will provide insight concerning this changing European landscape. It must be added that a pilot role was also being played by the ESRC in the UK. That body was obliged, under pressure of the government, to review their postgraduate training practices.

The First Strategic Review 1992: Beyond Maintenance

The major problems observed by the early 1990s review group can be summarized as follows. Completion rates were too low, time-to-degree was too long, there was an insufficiently clear profile/character of the European University Institute, and the governance structure of the Institute was no longer suitable since its establishment in 1976.

This issue might be more relevant to the EUI than to other graduate schools, but nevertheless in this case it had to do with the typically European debate about subsidiarity: a European initiative should not double what is already ongoing in the various national universities. A distinct profile of the Institute, which for many meant a kind of European-ness, then became rather difficult to define. There was also a debate about whether there should be a policy component, dealing with issues related to the European agenda. A lot of resistance existed at that particular time within the Institute itself as regards policy research, but this was a more generic and widespread issue in academia at the end of the eighties in Europe. Policy research had a kind of negative stigma; it was considered to be linked too much to contract research money, also referred to as "soft money," and Europe was not yet considered to be an academic topic of interest—for many wrong reasons, of course.

Rather than emphasize this debate, the Institute in an additional effort decided to create a special Centre, called the Robert Schuman Centre for Advanced Studies, which would get its own professors and attract people who would work in the various disciplines at the Institute but would be more interested in policy issues. The development of the Centre became an immense success and with this the EUI built up its reputation as being active in the foremost areas of discussion in the European agenda. At the same time, the quality of the research carried out in the Robert Schuman Centre also made the whole issue whether it would be second rate disappear. Simultaneously there was a strong development of the profile of research carried out within the departments, which was of direct relevance to the European agenda. A lot of comparative work was done both in the political and social science department and in the Law department, which actually developed over the years as the cradle of European law. The relevance of a clear profile was immediately reflected in a redistribution of the applications to the different departments; those with a clear profile saw their share increasing significantly.

The completion rates in the early nineties were only around 40 percent (up from 25 percent in the mid-eighties), but still considered too low by the review group. Also, time-to-degree was too long. The review group therefore wanted to set the objective for the end of the decade at 75 percent, with a medium time-to-degree of five years. In order to achieve this, the structured first year was introduced, very much modelled on the first year in an American graduate school: a curriculum was developed with the necessary research skills and advanced training in the field, so that the young researcher acquired the proper tools for the future. Supervision was also considered a major issue, and the spirit of the moment is best illustrated by the following phrase from the report, ". . . the teaching should not only be done by excellent professors, but it should also be excellent." As a result the EUI introduced a two-fold system of seminars/teaching and supervision assessment. Since its introduction this was a permanent topic of fierce debate. The main questions became the anonymity of the assessor and the low response rate and validation of the result. This debate continues and needs further reflection.

Because of growth the decision-making body, which until then had been the Academic Council, had become too large and, meeting once a month, no longer responded well to the management needs of the Institute. It was decided to create an executive council, composed of the heads of departments, the director of the Schuman Centre, the President, and the Secretary-General, who together would be responsible for the daily running of the Institute on a more frequent, fortnightly basis. This, combined with an increased responsibility of the heads of department, with a longer-term appointment of up to three years, improved the decision-making process significantly.

Last but not least, in order to realize all objectives the Institute should have a real growth of its budget of roughly 25 percent for its next decade. This translated into a real budgetary growth of 2.3 percent each year. This was maintained for the first seven to eight years, until the Budget Committee stopped allowing any real growth at the end of the year under the pressure of complying with the Maastricht budgetary guidelines (deficits maximum 3 percent of the GDP) in the Member States.

The Second Strategic Review 2000: Enhancing and Enlarging—The Future EUI

Earlier than foreseen the Institute reached the main objective of the *Beyond Maintenance* report. The Robert Schuman Centre for Advanced Studies (RSCAS) developed into a very successful research centre of advanced studies, with a large postdoctoral component, and the TTD was reduced to 4.1 year with a completion rate of 76 percent. Due to a number of significant changes in the PGE landscape, as mentioned above, the High Council called for a new strategic plan. The first of the recommendations was to further develop the mission of the EUI to be a top ranking doctoral program and centre of excellence for European research. Other issues addressed in this review included consequences of new developments such as the generalised introduction of doctoral schools, the Bologna declarations and the approaching accession of ten new members to the European Union.

Recommendations Made By the Second Report, Enhancing and Enlarging—The Future EUI (2001)

Although the objective of the *Beyond Maintenance* report had been reached (75 percent completion rate in five years) the report found that—the medium time to degree not being an average—it allowed people to exceed far beyond four years. Also, some people were leaving in the last year of study due to a lack of funding, and therefore a solution had to be found to further increase the efficiency of the doctoral programs. The solution was fourth-year funding, which should significantly speed up the completion of the thesis. Indeed, while the funding stopped after three years and only occasional three to six month grants were available for a limited number of people for writing up the thesis, a significant number of researchers were obliged to take up all kinds of small jobs, which in this crucial phase of writing the thesis is not an optimal solution. This was also recognized in England where the research councils fund a 1 + 3 scheme. This proposal encountered very stiff opposition from some of the member states but was finally introduced in the 2004–2005 academic year.

A further step was taken by introducing a maximum time to be spent on the PhD. After closely analyzing all data of completion at the EUI (we have a complete data set on all our research students from day one) we realized that the attrition rate after five years increases dramatically. Therefore a maximum time for defending the thesis of five years was introduced, which is now operational at the EUI. Not only do employment reasons influence attrition, but also a declining interest in the subject. Decisions to switch interest or supervisor also contribute to significantly unpredictable outcomes.

Deadlines are crucial ingredients in getting jobs done. In doctoral research a four to five year time horizon is fatal for most young researchers. Breaking down the whole process into a realistic set of short-term objectives contributes to increased completion. As a result, the structure of the four years was further fine-tuned in the sense that after each year, a clear objective in writing and in research was defined, and only when those conditions were fulfilled, passage to the next year would follow. For example, at the end of the first year a number of papers, written exams and a final "June-paper" allow an exam committee to decide on passage to second year. At the end of the second year, one quarter of the thesis in research and writing needs to be accomplished. Finally, the funding of the fourth year is conditional on the progress at the end of the third year: two-thirds of the thesis work, in writing (condition 1) plus the supervisor's statement that there is sufficient evidence that the thesis will be finished (in first draft) in a further six months. If, after three years + six months a first draft of the thesis is submitted, then the remaining six months are paid.

Furthermore, if the thirty-six months deadline for delivering two-thirds is not met by the end of the third year, no first installment is paid at the start of the fourth year. So if someone finishes in thirty-seven months, s/he loses the entire chance of receiving the first installment of the fourth-year payment. On the other hand, if the person reaches the thirty-six month objective, which we consider a very important criterion and is paid the first installment, but if the first draft is delayed up to the forty-second, forty-third, or forty-fourth month s/he might still get funding but it will be reduced as a penalty for exceeding the time limit.

One of the major challenges confronting the Institute was the enlargement of the European Union itself. In May 2004 the EU was enlarged by adding ten additional member states, which meant that the Union's population increased by 350 to 475 million inhabitants. Estimates made by the Institute showed that this would lead to an increase of about 40 percent in students in the years to come. This immediately revealed a number of financial problems. Firstly, because the GDPs in the new member states are significantly lower than the current member states, in the range from 1:10 to 1:4. From the general negotiations with the member states it resulted that the maximum increase of contribution that the Institute would receive from these member states was at that time only 4.6 percent, compared to a potential 40 percent increase in the number of students—clearly a huge discrepancy. Therefore the issue of the size and growth of the Institute came on the agenda. I will dedicate a separate section to this later on.

It was clear that with the changes in the European doctoral landscape postdoctoral training had become more and more important, not only because of the fact that the doctoral training was much shorter compared to the seventies, but also because the character of the training had moved away from the "master-disciple" model and young doctors did not have the same kind of experience as twenty years before. At the same time a fast development of the postdoctoral scene took place in the US, which increased its number of post-doctoral positions far beyond 50,000, according to some estimates. Europe was nowhere near, and as a result, a huge flux of excellent young academics went to the US. In order to reverse that trend, keep some of the good people, offer alternatives in Europe and attract good non-European scholars, the Institute decided to set a new trend and increased its existing postdoctoral program to approximately one hundred postdocs.

Confronted with the issue of how many researchers from the new member states the EUI should host, the issues of growth and optimal size came on the agenda. The various components of the Institute were consulted and there was a clear reaction from the researcher body at the Institute who stated: don't grow too big, because we are afraid of losing the special atmosphere that exists in the various departments. In order to analyze what would be a possible optimal size in a department and in graduate schools we analyzed the available statistics, discovering an interesting phenomenon in the NSF data published 1996. According to these data there is an optimal size for a graduate school. In other words, there is a convergence about the number of people in graduate schools, as shown in table 4.1.

Observing the size of top graduate schools in the US, it became clear that department size converged to approximately one hundred and fifty students. Based on this evidence, the EUI then decided that its total size should be limited to six hundred, with about one hundred and fifty students in each of the departments.

How was the Institute going to deal with an increase that seemed to be mandated by the enlargement of the UE, if there were already over five hundred students at that time? As mentioned earlier, there were two ways for approaching the problem. First of all, the introduction of the fourth-year grant and conditional funding should significantly increase the program's efficiency. Indeed following the reasoning of Bowen and Rudenstine[3] as to student year cost, we wished to reduce the number of years invested in each doctorate and to use this type of calculation to establish the allocations of funding to the various departments.

$$\text{SYC} = \frac{\Sigma \textit{ Student Years Invested}}{\text{Number of PhDs Earned}}$$

As a result two years ago, a component of output funding was introduced in order to stimulate the departments to further encourage their students to finish within the optimal time of four years. At that particular moment there was a large number of sixth, seventh, and sometimes even eighth-year students who were still using the infrastructure up to their defence date. Using the carrot of the fourth year grant to stimulate completion within four years, we introduced a proverbial "stick" in the form of a five-year time limit. These two elements are expected to reduce the number of students participating in the program enough to free up positions for additional students from the new member states.

TABLE 4.1 Concentrating the minds: Quality (ranking) and size (number of students)

Quarter	*Econ*	*Soc*	*Pol*	*Hist*	*Biochem*	*Phys*	*Math*	*Chem*
1	112	80	112	151	84	150	93	180
2	68	65	68	67	45	74	51	88
3	48	43	47	56	28	51	37	53
4	48	31	47	30	18	27	22	31
Mean	70	55	69	76	44	75	50	88
Corr.	-0,91	-0,99	-0,91	-0,92	-0,96	-0,95	-0,96	-0,95

SOURCE: "Research Doctorate Programs in the United States, Continuity and Change," NRC, Washington D.C. 1995.

TABLE 4.2

Political Science students		*Sociology students*		*History students*	
Harvard	172	Chicago	155	Yale	188
UCLA	143	Madison-Wisconsin	221	UCLA	206
Yale	69	Berkeley	109	Princeton	68
Michigan	173	Michigan	163	Harvard	146
Stanford	89	UCLA	139	Columbia	334

SOURCE: "Research Doctorate Programs in the United States, Continuity and Change," (Washington, DC: NRC, 1995).

Introduction of a Code of Supervision and the Dean of Studies

To complete the existing doctoral regulations a code of conduct for supervision was introduced. Furthermore to look after all the above points a Dean of Studies was appointed, a most important element in the assurance that the rules governing doctoral study are indeed implemented and observed.

CONCLUSIONS

1. Doctoral education in Europe has gone through significant growth during the last decades. The number of doctorates produced each year has doubled to reach approximately 70,000.

2. This growth has been accompanied by very different structural developments, depending on which country one examines. In some countries, such as the UK, parts of the Netherlands, and in some cases France and Germany, doctoral or graduate schools have developed in a structured way, and these have improved the quality and the efficiency of doctoral education. In other countries, the increase in numbers has unfortunately not been paralleled by improvements in the structure of doctoral education.

3. Significant improvement could be made by making doctoral education far more student-oriented and user-friendly and by breaking with the old tradition where doctoral education was defined by the master-pupil relation (such as still found in Germany, Doktervater relation) which is genuinely recognized to be a sub-optimal solution for large-scale doctoral education. Is this an exclusively European illness?

4. Governance structures within universities and lack of political will do not contribute when it comes to creating the kind of graduate schools and doctoral programs that have enough critical mass that can result in very high-quality research training, as seen in some of the top schools in the United States.

5. In view of the Barcelona objectives and the Lisbon agenda, it is desirable that European universities address their governance issues and approach implementation in the last phase of the Bologna agenda in such a way that Europe can become more competitive and eliminate prejudices as regards elitist training or selection procedures in order to concentrate the best candidates in good doctoral programs. It is sad to observe that the majority of universities in Europe do not have the possibility of selecting their student intake while on the other hand this is possible for training in conservatories and hotel schools.

NOTES

1. "A Strategic Plan for the European University Institute," November 1991, IUE 340/91 (CS 15).

2. "The Future EUI," November 2001, IUE 271/01 (CS 6).

3. William G. Bowen and Neil Rudenstine, *In Pursuit of the PhD* (Princeton, NJ: Princeton University Press, 1992), 163.

BIBLIOGRAPHY

Bowen, William G., and Neil L. Rudenstine. 1992. *In Pursuit of the PhD*. Princeton, NJ: Princeton University Press.

European University Institute. 1991. *Beyond Maintenance: A Strategic Plan for the European University Institute.* Florence, 3 December, IUE 340/91 (CS 15).

European University Institute. 2001. *Enhancing and Enlarging: The Future EUI.* Florence, 6 November, IUE 271/01 (CS 6).

National Research Council. 1995. *Research-Doctorate Programs in the United States: Continuity and Change.* Washington, DC: National Academy Press.

Palayret, Jean-Marie. 1997. "A Great School in the Service of a Great Idea: The Creation and Development of the European University Institute in Florence." *EUI Review* (Summer): 1–3.

5 • THE BOLOGNA PROCESS

JEROEN BARTELSE AND JEROEN HUISMAN

INTRODUCTION

The Bologna process is a European-wide, intergovernmental endeavor to create a coherent and cohesive higher education zone. Two objectives were set at the start of this process in 1999: the adoption of a system of comparable degrees and the adoption of two main cycles of higher education—the bachelor's degree and the master's degree. At this point in the process, forty-five countries have joined the process. In the last two ministerial conferences on the Bologna conference, those in Berlin (Berlin Communique 2002) and Bergen (Bergen Communique 2005), the third cycle of higher education, the doctoral degree, was addressed, and in London (2007) progress will be evaluated again. The incorporation of the third cycle in the Bologna process seems to forecast a period during which doctoral education will feature high on European science and education agendas. Current policy debates on doctoral education in Europe will be addressed in this chapter. For a good understanding of these debates it is worthwhile to put them into historical perspective.

THE ROOTS OF EUROPEAN DOCTORAL EDUCATION

The predecessor of the modern doctorate has its roots in the universities of Bologna and Paris of the twelfth century (Noble 1994). One could argue that—despite institutional differences from university to university—higher education across Europe was at that time "united" in terms of its subordination to a common religion, a common language (Latin), a uniform program of study and a uniform system of examinations. With the emergence of the nation states—throughout the seventeenth, eighteenth, and nineteenth centuries—however, national governments left their imprints on the development of higher education, including doctoral education (Neave 2001). Add to this the different educational philosophies that emerged in the eighteenth and nineteenth centuries and influenced higher education systems since then, and a much more varied pattern of higher education and training emerges. Within this variety, two European models of doctoral education can be distinguished (Bartelse 1999). The medieval model is based on the idea that the doctoral degree was a sign of the highest intellectual competence and authorized one to teach at any European university. The process of acquiring the doctorate differed among faculties and universities and could be either structured or rather informal. The Humboldtian model involved the student much more in research. Written theses were required to obtain the degree, and the doctorate was broadened to other disciplines (not only signifying a competence in philosophy). Furthermore, the Humboldtian doctorate was not so much a sign of high competence, but more an acknowledgement that the holder possessed the capabilities to be an independent scholarly investigator (Noble 1994). The two models clearly differ from the American model. Although many of the roots of the American higher education system can be traced back to Europe (notably Germany and England), there are clear differences in the American doctoral tradition. While acknowledging the variety within the higher education system, in the US, the doctoral education process was much more structured into postgraduate programs often located in graduate schools.

Distinguishing among these models is helpful for understanding some of the general patterns of doctoral education, but it is also important to keep in mind the variety of national higher education systems. The educational philosophies of Von Humboldt and Newman, for example, have had different effects on higher education systems. Structural features of national educational and research systems play a role in the differences among doctoral programs as well: the location of much—if not most—of nationally funded research outside universities (as in France, Germany, and many Central and Eastern European countries) has a considerable impact on the structuring of the doctoral education process. Second, although a particular doctoral model may be dominant in a nation, within countries there can still be considerable variation in the structuring of the doctoral process. To take the United Kingdom as an example, five different practices can be distinguished (Hoddell, Street, and Wildblood 2002; UK Council for Graduate Education 2002): the traditional doctorate (a mixture of the medieval and Humboldt models described above), the doctorate by published work, the taught doctorate (bearing similarities to the American model), the practice-based doctorate and the professional doctorate.

The variety across countries within Europe and even within countries, in combination with different disciplinary traditions, makes it difficult to develop national level policies, let alone European level policies, that meet the needs and wishes of specific countries, institutions and disciplines. Furthermore, the location of the doctoral process at the crossroads of education and research has not made it easier to develop adequate policies. Often in national policy-making the doctoral process has been a neglected child (if not an orphan), or the parents (those responsible for higher education and those responsible for research and development) fought their territorial wars over the heads of their offspring. Because doctoral education takes place in such a variety of ways and in the context of such complex and different approaches to national research policy, doctoral education seems to be resistant to change, and not necessarily because of a lack of willingness of those involved. At the same time, doctoral education is one of the few institutionalized academic practices that are more or less under the authority of the professoriate. Doctoral education therefore embodies some of the oldest and most honored traditions developed since the beginning of universities in the Middle Ages. These traditions are still visible in the rituals connected to defense and graduation ceremonies across Europe. It would therefore be accurate to state that given the variety of European higher education systems and the institutionalized character of the doctorate, the doctoral process has been an issue of concern in national policies but change so far has not been marked.

POLICY DEBATES ON DOCTORAL EDUCATION IN EUROPE

Three broad policy issues dominate European debates about doctoral education (see e.g., National Science Foundation 1998; OECD 1987, 1991, 1995; Sadlak 2004). We summarize these here.

1. Role and Function of the Doctorate

Traditionally, the core function of the doctoral education is to raise up the next generation of scientific researchers. From this perspective doctoral training is a process in which the candidate acquires the skills and competences to carry out independent and original scientific research. This function of the doctorate is gradually being adapted. As the economic and social fabric of European societies is increasingly knowledge related, it is crucial to have a highly educated work force. Doctoral degree holders are considered to play a vital role in this work force—and not only in academia. European governments are actively stimulating an increase in the number of doctorates primarily for this reason. The argument supporting this policy change is that the function of the doctorate, being the ultimate phase of university education, is to educate people that have the competencies to work in highly complex and knowledge intensive environments. This places more emphasis on transferable skills to be acquired in structured programs and course modules.

These shifting functions bring along interesting challenges to doctoral programs regarding their educational concept, the nature of the dissertation and the relationship between the supervisor and the candidate. In a way, they bring us to the question of how to organize and structure doctoral training for larger numbers of doctoral students—perhaps even for "mass" doctoral education.

2. Quality Assurance

The general issue of quality assurance consists of three interrelated elements: transparency, the demands of the labor market, and the doctoral training process. Partly because of the professors' dominant role in the doctoral process, quality assurance is perceived to lack sufficient transparency. Academic quality itself is not so pressing a concern. The involvement of peer reviewers when it comes to judging the final product provides a guarantee that quality is maintained. Furthermore, there is a commonsense understanding among academics that the dissertation should be original, should contribute significantly to the existing stock of knowledge and should prove the ability of the student as an independent researcher. Certainly, academic experts may differ in their views on the achievements of individual students (given the rather unspecified nature of the requirements), but overall there are few reasons to doubt the internal quality assurance process. There is however an increasing demand to make degree requirements more explicit and transparent.

Additionally, employers outside universities often complain that PhDs are lacking skills necessary to succeed in industry and government. The complaints differ by labor market sector, but generally employers from business and industry judge the PhD holder to lack communication and synthesizing skills and to be over-specialized. These concerns are not to be downplayed, for across Europe a substantial number of graduates cannot pursue careers within academic settings. A third element of quality assurance is the focus on the output (the quality of the dissertation) and a lack of attention to the process. One aspect of the process is the educational component, which only in the recent decade has become more prominent in Europe. Governments and higher education institutions themselves have developed structural solutions to this problem, for instance by setting up graduate schools—intra-university and interuniversity—which mandate a considerable number of taught classes for PhD students. A second problematic aspect of the process is the long time to degree in combination with high dropout rates. To some extent, relatively high dropout rates can be acceptable in light of the high demands on the candidates and the rather unpredictable nature of the work towards the PhD (i.e., refining and adding to knowledge). On the other hand, however, it cannot be denied that inadequate selection procedures, insufficient supervision, a lack of planning and organization of the process, ill-defined research projects and unfavorable labor conditions (salary)—elements certainly under some control of the universities and the government—in general are detrimental to the successful completion of the PhD (see e.g., Booth and Satchell 1995; Rudd 1985; Van Ours and Ridder 2003; and Visser and Moed 2005 for European research on time to degree and drop out). The quality assurance issue therefore boils down to increasing attention to transparency (setting objectives and specifying competences) and satisfying the demands of the non-academic labor market.

3. Academic Careers

As will be clear from the above, the PhD process is not an end itself, but should be considered as a means: the preparation of independent scholars and preparation for work outside academe. While the process is not without problems, life after graduation can also be problematic. Here again, this general issue of the uncertainty of continuing an academic career can be broken down into components: the lack of available posts, the hierarchical and inflexible nature of the academic profession, the salary conditions and gender bias (see e.g., Huisman, De Weert, and Bartelse 2002). The first problem is the lack of university posts. Surveys among PhD students across Europe indicate that a majority of these would like to continue their careers within a university setting. At the same time, destination after graduation data indicates that only a minority find jobs in such settings. There are considerable differences among countries and disciplines, but the general pattern is that there are more candidates than positions. A second issue is that the academic rank structure is quite inflexible. Departmental structures tend to be based on a relatively standardized personnel allocation model (of a combination of x professors, y readers, and z lecturers). Such a structure functions as a funnel for those aspiring to a "higher" position, and the structure is certainly not geared towards allocating posts on the basis of quality. It must be stressed that some countries have more flexible personnel allocation and promotion policies (e.g., in the United Kingdom, promotion to higher ranks takes place on the basis of quality and is hardly driven by structural limitations). However, taking into account that it is very difficult for recently graduated PhDs to acquire either a temporary or tenured position at a university and the relatively high level of job insecurity (Enders and Teichler 1997, 350–51), the situation obviously is problematic and calls for action at different levels. Universities should communicate realistic information on career patterns, and students should be prepared for a broader range of careers than solely a continuation in an academic environment. PhD students should be realistic as well in terms of their expectations and should be willing to have a broader perspective on the labor market. At the government and university agencies level, the current inflexible job structure should be reconsidered.

A third problem is related to salary. Comparative research indicates that university salaries are lagging behind the private sector (see e.g., Huisman and Bartelse 1999). These findings are confirmed by more recent national-level inquiries. The situation is complicated by the fact that in many countries, salaries for PhDs are generally low. When students are dependent on bursaries or scholarships, other problems loom: a low income in combination with the potential for a low pension at retirement. Academics have generally chosen their careers for reasons other than money. The ability to work in relative autonomy is a dominant motivation across the world. Consequently, the relatively low salaries in combination with job insecurity and long working weeks (Enders and Teichler 1997) do not discourage candidates.

A fourth and final problem is gender imbalance. While the percentage of women starting a career is on the increase (at the master's level women have quite often surpassed men in many European countries, in some countries this also is the case at the PhD level), the percentage of women in higher ranks is still very low. Targeted actions of governments and universities, such as the Aspasia program in the Netherlands and the Athena project in the United Kingdom (Huisman et al. 2002), are examples of efforts to contribute to establishing balance. However, these programs are often considered but a drop in the ocean. One of the reasons for the limited success is the relatively small amount of funding in the programs mentioned. Other reasons are more institutionalized: the lack of part-time positions, particularly at higher levels, a masculine university culture, and gender bias in academic review procedures.

As will be clear from the three policy issues set out above, the challenges are multifaceted, interrelated, and difficult to solve by only one actor. It seems that these problems need to be tackled by a combined effort of all involved: governments, universities (and their representing agencies), PhD and other postgraduate students' organizations, and employer organizations. An unanswered question, so far, is to what extent the supranational level can add to solving these problems: does the Bologna process shed new light on these issues and/or provide solutions?

THE THIRD CYCLE IN THE BOLOGNA PROCESS

As mentioned at the outset, doctoral education was addressed at two Bologna summits, those of Berlin (2003) and Bergen (2005). In the Berlin communiqué, a new action line was introduced aiming at establishing closer links between the European Higher Education Area (EHEA) and the European Research Area (ERA). The full section on this action line reads as following:

> Conscious of the need to promote closer links between the EHEA and the ERA in a Europe of Knowledge, and of the importance of research as an integral part of higher education across Europe, Ministers consider it necessary to go beyond the present focus on two main cycles of higher education to include the doctoral level as the third cycle in the Bologna Process. They emphasize the importance of research and research training and the promotion of interdisciplinarity in maintaining and improving the quality of higher education and in enhancing the competitiveness of European higher education. Ministers call for increased mobility at the doctoral and postdoctoral level and encourage the institutions concerned to increase their cooperation in doctoral studies and the training of young researchers.

The Bergen Communiqué (2005, 4) contains the following section on the third cycle: "Considering the need for structured doctoral programs and the need for transparent supervision and assessment, we note that the normal workload of the third cycle in most countries would correspond to 3–4 years full time. We urge universities to ensure that their doctoral programs promote interdisciplinary training and the development of transferable skills, thus meeting the needs of the wider employment market. We need to achieve an overall increase in the number of doctoral candidates taking up research careers within the EHEA." In the communiqué, the Bologna follow-up group is asked to prepare a report on the further development of basic principles for doctoral programs, to be presented at the next ministers' conference in London in 2007.

At face value the Berlin and Bergen texts regarding the third cycle are disappointing. They hardly address the issues set out in the sections above. However, the lessons we learn from the Bologna process indicate that we should not underestimate the impact of the content of the communiqués. Indeed, the communiqués are primarily political statements, which are carefully formulated to take into account the large variety of national perspectives and opinions. By definition, the texts are abstract. Concrete or provocative sections would jeopardize the legitimacy of the document. However, if an issue is addressed in an action line, it often sets in motion an avalanche of seminars, committees, and conferences on the topic. The bulk of the real progress in the Bologna process takes place in meetings. They are in fact the driving force of the Bologna process. Hence, the mere fact that doctoral education is addressed in the Bologna accords may lead to profound changes in the European doctoral landscape—as it did in many countries in the first and second cycle.

Since the Berlin conference, a series of so-called Bologna seminars have been devoted to doctoral education. Much of this work that has been carried out under the auspices of the European University Association (EUA), the main representative of higher education institutions awarding doctoral degrees in Europe. The EUA organized two conferences on the theme in Maastricht (2004) and Salzburg (2005). In addition, the EUA launched a project that brought together forty-two universities from twenty-two different countries to exchange issues and challenges related to the future development of doctoral studies. The report of this project offers rich insights into the practice of doctoral training across institutions in Europe. The main findings of the project reflect the problems and challenges that doctoral training has grappled with in the past decades. A number of "good" and "innovative" practices illustrate the dynamics that gradually penetrate doctoral systems. The report says about these reforms: "It should be emphasized that reforms of doctoral education are proceeding at varied paces and, in some countries, the debate on reform is only at the beginning. While the reform of the first two cycles is well underway across Europe, the transformation of doctoral education presents a different order of challenge" (EUA 2006, 7).

The project's main findings, together with the discussions at the conferences mentioned above, led to the identification of ten basic principles of doctoral education (EUA 2005, 2).

1. The core component of doctoral training is the advancement of knowledge through original research. At the same time it is recognized that

doctoral training must increasingly meet the needs of an employment market that is wider than academia.

2. Embedding in institutional strategies and policies: universities as institutions need to assume responsibility for ensuring that the doctoral programs and research training they offer are designed to meet new challenges and include appropriate professional career development opportunities.

3. The importance of diversity: the rich diversity of doctoral programs in Europe—including joint doctorates—is a strength that has to be underpinned by quality and sound practice.

4. Doctoral candidates as early stage researchers: should be recognized as professionals—with commensurate rights—who make a key contribution to the creation of new knowledge.

5. The crucial role of supervision and assessment: in respect of individual doctoral candidates, arrangements for supervision and assessment should be based on a transparent contractual framework of shared responsibilities between doctoral candidates, supervisors, and the institution (and where appropriate including other partners).

6. Achieving critical mass: doctoral programs should seek to achieve critical mass and should draw on different types of innovative practices being introduced in universities across Europe, bearing in mind that different solutions may be appropriate to different contexts and in particular across larger and smaller European countries. These range from graduate schools in major universities to international, national, and regional collaboration between universities.

7. Duration: doctoral programs should operate within an appropriate time duration (three to four years full-time as a rule).

8. The promotion of innovative structures: to meet the challenge of interdisciplinary training and the development of transferable skills.

9. Increasing mobility: doctoral programs should seek to offer geographical as well as interdisciplinary and intersectoral mobility and international collaboration within an integrated framework of cooperation between universities and other partners.

10. Ensuring appropriate funding: the development of quality doctoral programs and the successful completion by doctoral candidates requires appropriate and sustainable funding.

THE EU AGENDA

The current attention to doctoral education in the Bologna process cannot by separated from the agenda and policies of the European Commission. Although the European Union includes only twenty-five member states (against the forty-five members of the Bologna process), the cooperation on education, research, and innovation among these member states has an impact on the pace and progress of the Bologna process.

The agreements made among the member states at the Lisbon summit in 2000 form a landmark in the ambitions of the EU to stimulate cooperation in the area of research and higher education. At this summit, government leaders set the objective to build Europe as the most dynamic and competitive knowledge based economy. Higher education and research have an important role to play if a leading position is to be achieved in a competitive global economy. Europe needs more highly educated people and researchers to be employed in various sectors of society. Doctoral education is the primary source of researchers, and this topic is gracing the agenda of the European Commission more prominently than before.

The European Commission addressed doctoral education in two "communications" (European Commission 2003). The publication from 2003, "Researchers in the European Research Area: one profession, multiple careers," is the most comprehensive. This publication discusses the recruitment and careers of researchers as well as the training of researchers. The communication pleads for the development of competencies and skills of doctoral candidates that take a broader labor market perspective into account. Also, recommendations are put forward to structure doctoral education, to improve supervision, and to adequately finance doctoral programs and doctoral candidates.

In the 2002 publication, which was prepared by the STRATA-ETAN expert group, scenarios were sketched of the challenges for research training. This publication is outspoken regarding the need to change the "traditional" PhD: "preparing postgraduate students . . . could imply more involvement of the research apprentice in collaborative projects with 'non-academic' patterns and also more direct involvement of 'non-academic' partners in the training of researchers" (European Commission 2002, 51).

POLICY AND PRACTICE

We observe that the issues and challenges identified are now incorporated in the agendas of universities and national and supra-national governments. The Bologna (and Lisbon) processes have had a catalyzing effect in this respect. They set the agenda of the governments and higher education institutions in the countries involved. However, an agenda is not yet a concrete policy, let alone real change. In this respect, our assessment of "progress" is mixed. On the one hand we do not yet see break-through policies in European countries in the area of doctoral education. Doctoral education remains caught between two worlds: education and research. The challenges to doctoral education are already long standing (and so are the potential responses). In this respect, current policy documents echo messages that were sent out a decade ago (Frijdal and Bartelse 1996; OECD 1995). Consequently, the collective pace of change is slow and the analyses seem to follow well-trodden paths and to neglect promising innovations, e.g., in the area of professional doctorates (Huisman and Naidoo 2006).

On the other hand, the Bologna and Lisbon processes stir the European debate on doctoral education. And this debate is no longer restricted to the realm of higher education researchers and those involved in doctoral training. Indeed, Europe seems to have rediscovered the full potential of the third cycle in higher education. Moreover, the agenda-setting activities at the supra-national level have invited responses from the institutional level: institutional leaders and policy-makers have discovered the importance of the third cycle. Projects like the EUA study are good examples of discussions of innovative practices, problems, and barriers at the institutional level. In this sense, the practice-oriented, micro- and meso-level, bottom-up initiatives complement the macro-level awareness-raising activities. Network based activities, driven by the primacy of problem solving, could form the basis for real change. Given the sensitive nature of the doctoral phase—recall that we portrayed it as one of the few remaining academic practices almost under full control of the academic professoriate—such an approach has much more potential than a top-down policy approach. Still, it should be acknowledged that change may still be piecemeal and slow.

We should not expect the third cycle to go through the same process as the first and second cycle. In the first and second cycle remarkable change has taken place in many European countries. (Admittedly, there are examples of slow movers as well.) The third cycle remains essentially different from the other two cycles, because its core component is research. There is a challenge for higher education researchers to join both the macro-level policy discussions and the practice-based networks. Both audiences would profit from in-depth studies on doctoral education, both quantitative and qualitative, particularly of a comparative nature. An important imperative is to go beyond the descriptive mode and to keep an eye open for creative solutions to long-existing problems.

BIBLIOGRAPHY

Bartelse, Jeroen. 1999. *Concentrating the Minds: The Institutionalisation of the Graduate School Innovation in Dutch and German Higher Education.* Utrecht: Uitgeverij Lemma BV.

Bergen Communique. 2005. "The European Higher Education Area—Achieving the Goals." Bergen: Bergen Communique.

Berlin Communique. 2002. "Realising the European Higher Education Area." Berlin: Berlin Communique.

Booth, Alison L., and Stephen E. Satchell. 1995. "The Hazards of Doing a PhD: An Analysis of Completion and Withdrawal Rates of British PhD Students in the 1980s." *Journal of the Royal Statistical Society* 158(2): 297–318.

Enders, Jurgen, and Ulrich Teichler. 1997. "A Victim of Their Own Success? Employment and Working Conditions of Academic Staff in Comparative Perspective." *Higher Education* 34: 347–72.

European Commission. 2003. *Researchers in the European Research Area: One Profession, Multiple Careers.* Brussels: European Commission.

European University Association. 2006. *Doctoral Programmes for the European Knowledge Society: Report on the EUA Doctoral Programmes Project 2004–2005.* Brussel: European University Association.

Frijdal, A., and J. Bartelse, eds. 1996. *The Future of Postgraduate Education in Europe.* Brussels: European Commission.

Hoddell, S., D. Street, and H. Wildblood. 2002. "Doctorates—Converging or Diverging Patterns of Provision." *Quality Assurance in Education* 10(2): 61–70.

Huisman, J., and J. A. Bartelse. 1999. *Academic Careers: A Comparative Perspective.* The Hague: Advisory Council for Science and Technology Policy.

Huisman, J., E. De Weert, and J. Bartelse. 2002. "Academic Careers in Europe: The Declining Desirability of the Faculty Position." *Journal of Higher Education* 73(1): 141–60.

Huisman, J., and R. Naidoo. 2006. "The Professional Doctorate: From Anglo-Saxon to European Challenges." *Higher Education Management and Policy* 18(2): 57–69.

National Science Foundation. 1998. *Graduate Education Reform in Europe, Asia, and the Americas and International Mobility of Scientists and Engineers.* Washington: National Science Foundation.

Neave, G. 2001. "The European dimension in higher education: An excursion into the modern use of historical analogues." In *Higher Education and the Nation State: The International Dimension of Higher Education,* edited by J. Huisman, P. Maassen, and G. Neave, 13–76. Amsterdam/London: Pergamon.

Netherlands Association of Universities. 2004. *Hora Est.* Utrecht: VSNU.

Noble, K. A. 1994. *Changing Doctoral Degrees: An International Perspective.* Buckingham: SRHE and Open University Press.

OECD. 1987. *Post-graduate Education in the 1980s.* Paris: OECD.

OECD. 1991. *Postgraduate Education Today: Changing Structures for a Changing Europe.* Paris: OECD.

OECD. 1995. *Research Training: Present and Future.* Paris: OECD.

Rudd, E. 1985. *A New Look at Postgraduate Failure.* Guildford: NFER and Nelson.

Sadlak, Jan. 2004. *Doctoral Studies and Qualifications in Europe and the United States: Status and Prospects*. Bucharest: UNESCO-CEPES.

UK Council for Graduate Education. 2002. *Professional Doctorates*. Dudley: UKCGE.

Van Ours, J. C., and G. Ridder. 2003. "Fast Track or Failure: A Study of the Graduation and Dropout Rates of PhD Students in Economics." *Economics of Education Review* 22: 157–66.

Visser, M. S., and H. F. Moed. 2005. *Quantitative Analysis of PhD Degrees Granted at Flemish Universities (1991–2002)*. Brussels: Flemish Council for Science Policy.

· II ·

DOCTORAL EDUCATION IN AFRICA, SOUTH AMERICA, AND MEXICO

6 • SOUTH AFRICA

AHMED BAWA

South Africa's higher education system has its roots in the nation's colonial and Apartheid past. This has shaped a deeply fragmented legacy upon which the building blocks of the new system must draw. In this presentation on the state of PhD studies in post-Apartheid South Africa, reference must be made to this legacy and its impact on the way that new thinking around doctoral studies has evolved.

In the run-up to the first elections in 1994 a host of studies were initiated by what was then the national liberation movement relating to science and higher education systems (see Cloete 2002). The purpose of this was to position the government-in-waiting to develop a program of action on which it was to enter the elections and then to provide the basis for a substantial policy development process in the post-election period. These studies revealed many interesting and challenging issues of which, for the purpose of this paper, a few are listed here.

FRAGMENTATION OF THE HIGHER EDUCATION SYSTEM

The higher education system was seen to be fragmented in various ways. First of all there was the traditional split between "mind" and "hand" represented by the silos around the "universities," "technikons," and "technical colleges." These different forms of institutions represented different systems of education, so that the disarticulation between the systems was profound. There was little if any teaching or research collaboration amongst these kinds of institutions, and there was very little opportunity for a coherent program of student transfer between them. This disarticulation was accompanied by a substantial level of non-differentiation amongst institutions in each of the three sectors. But more importantly, this disarticulation led to an incoherent approach to high-level human resource development. Thus we had the situation in which universities running substantial access programs had no systemic approaches for developing the capacities of technical, further education and training colleges to prepare students. But the colonial origins of the system also meant that the system was significantly inverted in terms of enrollments, with there being more students in universities than in technikons and in the further education and training colleges. This resulted in poor levels of efficiency and effectiveness.

But the higher education system was fragmented in another way. Following in Apartheid's imagination, the universities and technikons could be classified in another way into two broad categories: the historically white institutions and the historically black ones. The former were created in the image of the universities of Europe and were always conceived of as having a high-level research function that shaped their imagination and their ethos. (Bawa and Mouton 2002) Needless to say they were funded in a way that would support such a high-level research function. Until the mid-1980s, these historically white institutions were predominantly white in terms of their student bodies as well as in the professoriate. The historically black institutions, on the other hand, like their counterparts in what Mahmood Mamdani has called "middle Africa"—Africa south of the Sahara and north of the Limpopo—were conceived of primarily as producers of civil servants, professionals to serve the local populations and certainly not as institutions driven by the desire to produce new knowledge. They were funded and evaluated in these terms. The technikons and historically black institutions, while they had doctoral programs on their books and did indeed offer them, were extremely ineffective and inefficient at graduate education. (Bunting 2002) The advent of taught masters programs breathed some life into the enterprise.

The third form of fragmentation that pervaded the system was that between the universities and the science councils, such as the Council for Scientific and Industrial Research, which might be regarded as being similar in concept to the national laboratories in the United States. In a science system as small as that of South Africa's this kind of disarticulation comes at high cost. For instance, the fragmentation of highly qualified researchers in different science sectors reduces the capacity of the system to generate high-level scientifically trained human resources. And perhaps as importantly, the lack of formal mechanisms for articulation between the different science sectors provides the basis for deeply entrenched research silos to develop on the one hand and for significant mission creep on the other hand.

DISARTICULATION

One of the findings of pre-1994 studies and surveys related to the massively high levels of disarticulation that existed between the universities and broad needs of society (NCHE 1996). Needless to say these "broad needs of society" were not simply those defined by the Apartheid regime, a set of needs that pertained to the "Europeanised" elite in an "Europeanised" environment. Hence we had the situation that whilst the South African higher education and science systems could produce the world's first heart transplant, it fails (even today) to help the nation deal with the basic diseases of poverty and deprivation such as cholera, tuberculosis, and the onslaught of HIV/AIDS. Such disarticulation pervaded all forms of the nation's science and higher education systems.

This disarticulation had another very important diagnostic indicator. For the level of scientific output the level of industrial innovation was extraordinarily low, and the key measure of this is the failure of the system to give rise to larger numbers of small high-tech industries/companies on the one hand and the failure of South African large industry to break into global markets except in a small number of sectors (NACI 2003). Another representation of this is the poverty of the system's outputs in terms of patents.

RACE AND GENDER IMBALANCES

The system described above could only produce a science system that was deeply imbalanced in terms of South Africa's race profiles. This was due not only to the fact that the historically black institutions were deemed to be producers of human resources for the local civil service, but also due to the abject failure of the township and rural school systems which severely affect the ability of universities to address the race imbalances in a significant way. But there were other more structural issues that militated against addressing this issue. The first is that there were few if any employment opportunities for black science specialists—taking into account various legislative frameworks such as the Job Reservations Act.

The numbers are bleak. About 80 percent of South Africa's science human resource base is white and about 80 percent of people in academic training are white. Approximately 90 percent of the scientific output of the country is by white scientists. If South Africa's science system is to grow and compete, as indeed the government hopes, then there is no alternative but to increase the number of scientists, engineers, etc., primarily in the black community. The gender imbalances follow very much the international trends. Hence in the natural sciences the representation of women in the engineering, mathematical, and physical sciences remains very low. But the level of participation of women in the biological and medical sciences is significantly higher.

THE NEW HIGHER EDUCATION LANDSCAPE

The policy process that unfolded through the establishment in 1995 of the National Commission on Higher Education led to a new Higher Education Act that sought to create a new system—reflective both of the negotiated final report of the Commission and the construction of a post-Apartheid system.

Many changes have been imposed on the system. For the purposes of this paper we describe just two of these changes. The first is the considerable change in the nature of the institutional landscape. The universities and "technikons" were constituted into a single system bound together by a National Qualifications Framework, a common funding formula and a common quality system led by the Higher Education Quality Committee of the Council on Higher Education—a statutory body defined by the Higher Education Act with the mandate of advising the Minister of Education. It has a Board that is independent of the government. The institutional landscape has now entered a fairly dramatic stage with the announcement in 2004 by the Minister of Education of a set of institutional mergers. The other major change has been in the way that the national budget investment in higher education is distributed in terms of the subsidy elements. But we shall return to this later.

The Nature of South Africa's Degree System

The South African higher education system is based upon twelve years of school beginning at age six and progressing to age seventeen. Students obtaining a certain level of pass with fixed course selections qualify for entrance into university. Admission into undergraduate programs may require specific coursework.

The bachelor's degree may be a three-year or four-year program. The latter are usually professional qualifications such as Engineering, Accounting, and Law, while the former relate to general qualifications such as the Bachelor of Arts, Bachelor of Science, Bachelor of Social Science, Bachelor of Commerce, etc. The bachelor's degrees usually require a fairly substantial level of specialization in two majors. Thus a person graduating with a major in Physics would for instance have a second major in Mathematics.

About 15 percent of the students graduating with the general bachelor's qualifications take an additional year to complete an Honors degree, which is regarded as a postgraduate qualification. So there are Bachelor of Arts Honors, Bachelor of Science Honors, etc. These are intense specialization courses, and though they usually have a project component, the emphasis is mainly on the coursework. Usually the nature of the Honors program is aligned with the research agendas of the departments offering it. Thus it is highly unlikely that a Physics Department that does not have any research interests in the area of "the physics of renewable energy" will offer such a course.

The Honors qualification is generally required for entry to a masters program, though there are three exceptions to this rule. First, students who graduate with one of the four-year professional qualifications may proceed directly into a masters program in that area of study. Second, there are some masters programs that have been approved by the National Department of Education that are regarded as (and are funded as) two-year programs. These are allowed to take students directly from a bachelor's degree onto a two-year set of courses and research activity. Third, students who may not have the necessary entry requirements but who have other forms of substantial experience may apply to the institution for the application of special discretion for entry. Most universities have such a facility.

There are several kinds of masters programs. Except for the two-year program described in the last paragraph, all of them are nominally one year in length for the purpose of subsidy allocation. Most students, however, take longer than a year to complete the degree. Many departments at universities offer master's degrees that are "pure" research—meaning that there aren't any formal coursework requirements. It is necessary to recollect that such a program will sit upon an intensive Honors program. Of course in the case that the supervisor determines that a student requires some additional coursework he/she might require the student to take the course. These are often referred to as "Research Masters programs."

The "Coursework Masters programs" refer to, as the name implies, programs of study that lead to a master's degree that have both a coursework component and a research component. The size of the research component varies. The National Department of Education requires the research component to total at least 50 percent of the credits for the qualification to result in the full subsidy per FTE. This is of course a mechanism to prevent the outright proliferation of the coursework masters programs that have small research profiles. This implies of course that there has been an exceptionally large expansion of offerings of this nature in recent years—

mainly as a means to respond to immediate market needs and as a means to attract fee-paying students and subsidy allocations. Some of the more established research institutions require at least a 50 percent research component for entry into PhD study.

THE NATURE OF DOCTORAL STUDY

Doctoral study in South Africa is pinned on a program of study leading to a PhD, although there are other historical doctoral programs in place. This is nominally a three-year research-based program. Though there are no formal coursework requirements on the basis that each program is necessarily built upon masters and honours qualifications, many doctoral programs do now expect students to take courses. While the National Qualifications Framework and the South Africa Qualifications Authority establish the broad requirements in terms of the accreditation and funding schemes, the Senates of institutions determine the philosophy, nature, supervisory policies, the establishment of student-supervisor contracts, etc. Most doctoral study programs continue to be concentrated in the disciplines, but there is also an expansion of programs in interdisciplinary spheres, such as Development Studies, Culture and Media Studies, Environment and Development, etc. As may be expected, the proliferation of these programs brings structural tensions into play in the ways in which universities organise themselves.

In the professional areas there is an ongoing discussion about the need for, the efficacy of, and the wisdom of creating PhD-equivalent qualifications that are seen to be more practice oriented and which serve the professions in a way that it is assumed that PhDs can't. These discussions are ongoing in areas such as medicine (MD, Doctor of Clinical Medicine), Psychology (DPsych), Law (JD), Education (EdD), etc. There has been neither a serious challenge from within universities to these qualifications nor any perceived interest in the Department of Education for these to be recognised and funded. The reason that it is important to raise this issue is that in a system that is small these kinds of realignments might cause significant instability and with often unexpected and potentially dangerous outcomes for the ultimate balance of the system.

An allied issue that has implications for this discussion is the transformation in the funding of science by the Department of Science and Technology and the Department of Trade and Industry (see HSRC 2005). One way of addressing the disarticulation of the higher education and the rest of the science system from the development of a culture of social/cultural, technological, and industrial innovation was to use funding to encourage the system to create a culture of innovation. This kind of funding also pushed the graduate programs towards interdisciplinary and Mode 2–type research. Similar approaches were adopted by the National Research Foundation (the South African counterpart of the National Science Foundation) and other research funding agencies. The impact of this kind of research funding is yet to be measured, although early studies indicate that these drivers are indeed significantly shifting the research profile of higher education institutions.

THE STATE OF SOUTH AFRICA'S RESEARCH COMMUNITY

A recent set of studies indicates a number of serious issues related to the state of South Africa's research community and national human resource development. The PhD is seen as the central programmatic mechanism to grow the scientific community and yet it is increasingly clear that there are significant problems with the state of PhD education and therefore the development of the next generation of South Africa's researchers. This has enormous implications for the medium-to long-term sustainability of the system.

At a recent meeting convened by the Ministers and Departments of Science and Technology and of Education, several important and potentially devastating issues were highlighted. The meeting was convened to discuss the development of human resources necessary to prepare South Africa to be a globally competitive player as a knowledge-producing nation (see HSRC 2005). In very broad brush-strokes the following issues provided the basis for this meeting. We repeat some of these below.

Surveys carried out by the Department of Science and Technology for 2000–2003 indicate a 4 percent loss in the number of permanent academics with doctorates at SA universities during this period. This is reflective of tensions between the challenges of building a long-term sustainable system and the needs for the eradication of race and gender imbalances in the system. This is also an indication of the failure of the higher education system to remain competitive as an employer of choice for strong researchers. This latter is a reflection of two kinds of brain drain: an internal one and an external one. Analysis shows that a PhD is now held by 82 percent of professors, 67 percent of associate professors, 38 percent of senior lecturers, and 13 percent of lecturers. In terms of actual numbers the numbers of academics at universities with PhDs declined from 4,469 (40.9 percent of total academic staff) in 2000 to 4,134 in 2003 (37.4 percent).

This phenomenon is reflected in the size and shape of the national public research workforce. Table 6.1 (taken from HSRC 2005) provides some sense of this. Between 1991 and 2001–02 there has been a 6,700 FTE decline in what is referred to as the public research and development—a shocking 42 percent decline. This has happened during a time when there have been clear and unambiguous policies and financial commitments to bolster the capacity of the nation to grow into a knowledge-based society and economy. It has happened at a time when the funding of science has begun to grow!

The internal brain drain is therefore clearly not into other public sector research and development activities but into other forms of employment. And while studies indicate that the external brain drain is substantial, the impact of this on the system is not yet fully understood. Thus exactly at the time it is necessary to increase the production/development of new researchers, the capacity to do so at SA universities is in dramatic decline.

In fact the situation is more serious than it may seem from this set of data. This data does not reflect the progressive aging of the SA research workforce. One measure of this is that while in 1990 18 percent of all articles produced by SA scientists were published by authors who were fifty-years-old or older, the comparable percentage for 2002 is 48 percent. This appears to be a devastating set of figures, especially in the context that as the government and private sectors increase their R&D spending, it is highly unlikely that there will be the capacity for scientists to use these new resources. A survey carried out by the Human Sciences Research Council in 2003 (Kraak 2003) predicted a shortage of more than 6,500 academics over the next five years.

How is this seen and experienced? On the one hand there is the inability of universities to make high-level appointments in most disciplines. This is now clear and unambiguous, and there is a growing fear that there is not enough time for the SA higher education system to replenish its stock simply through the local development of a new generation of researchers. Another measure is that SA's scientific output based on ISI has had a steady decline in the production of publications from 0.7 percent of world share in 1987 to 0.49 percent in 2000. And in fact if one takes into account non-ISI publications, the total rate of publication has been fairly stagnant over the last ten years. This is the case even though SA's R&D budget increased from 0.76 percent of GDP in 2001–02 to 0.81 percent in 2003–04. The target is to increase this percentage to 1.0 percent of GDP by 2008. There is deep concern, of course, within government circles whether the currently constituted scientific community will permit the effective, productive and efficient uptake of this substantial increase in funding.

TABLE 6.1 R&D Workforce (1991–2001/2) full-time equivalents

Sector	*Categories*	*1991*	*2001/2*
Higher Education	Researchers	5,984	3,424
	Technicians	289	217
	Support Staff	260	231
	Total	6,533	4,042
Government (incl. Science Councils)	Researchers	3,629	2,134
	Technicians	2,384	1,344
	Support Staff	3,437	1,842
	Total	9,450	5,171
All Sectors	Grand Total	15,983	9,213

SOURCES: SA science and technology indicators, 1991; R&D Survey 2001/2

How to Address This Issue

The discussion has to take into account the local conditions and contexts. What are the key relevant ones?

- The first is that the growth in South Africa's economy in recent years is predicated on the emergence of knowledge-based, high-tech industries. And whilst much of the research and development is done in industry, which in turn draws heavily on work done in international laboratories, there is a growing concern about the lack of synergy/connection/articulation between the research activities of universities and science councils. In 2003–04 the business-sector spending on research and development is 55.5 percent of the overall national spending. Thus there are powerful economic arguments for the development of a strong national research base.
- On the other hand there is a substantial failure in the production of high-level human resources in the areas that are relevant to the reconstructive needs of this dramatically bipolar society. For instance, while this is a science system that manages to produce the highest level of human transplant technology, we have rampant infectious disease problems for which we do not produce sufficient specialists in infectious diseases or epidemiology.
- This of course explains why it is that, in the face of enormous other national challenges like housing, health, education, water reticula-

tion, etc., the national state wishes to and insists on making a major investment in research and development. Thus there is the commitment to increase this spending to 1 percent (from 0.81 percent) of GDP over the next three years. This has enormous implications for the production of high-level human resources during this next period. Early assessments indicated that some 7,000 new researchers are required by 2008 to create a research community that will be able to make maximal use of the increase.

- The overwhelming race imbalances in the national system mean that it is not possible to think about this and other higher education challenges without addressing the issue of broadening/redressing the representation of the different race groups and to move towards an equitable distribution. And of course the racialization of South African society means that we continue to have a dysfunctional school system in the poor (and hence predominantly black) areas of the country. It should be remarked here that approximately 90 percent of the research output is carried out by white scientists and researchers—this in a country where about 80 percent of the population is black. Attempts to address this through a laissez-faire process have failed, and more directed, purposive approaches have to be adopted. We shall describe some of these later on.
- The higher education participation rate of about 18 percent is large by sub-Saharan African standards, but it is a small base for a country that wishes to take the high-knowledge route. And this is exacerbated by its inefficiency and ineffectiveness in terms of throughput rates.
- Higher education faces a challenge of legitimacy in a social and political environment that demands alignment/realignment with the political goals. New political goals are being defined by the important emergence of a pan-African intellectual discourse captured powerfully for instance by the notion of a prophetic *African Renaissance* and the development of knowledge frameworks that address multiple complexes of systems, of which the *scientific method* is one. The University of KwaZulu-Natal has adopted a vision that defines it as the *premier institution for African scholarship.* This brings enormous stresses to bear on a higher education system that is so set in a particular paradigm, though there are increasingly interesting approaches emerging to address this issue.
- The aging professoriate has to be a powerful consideration in the shaping of new approaches, especially if it is not fully clear that that professoriate may be able, capable or willing to play the role of pur-

posefully and dedicatedly addressing this issue of substantial capacity development.

- The failure of the National System of Innovation to build a coherent platform for the development of high-level human resources is also an important consideration in the context that the overall science system is so small.
- South Africa has an ambiguous approach to inviting either the emigration of scientists from other countries into the system or the utilization of them.
- The universities face enormous pressure to widen access to higher education. In some senses this presents a tension since the Department of Education has capped growth in the sector on an institution-by-institution basis. Universities must then turn to a review of the shape of the institutions to assess how to manage both challenges.

This is a sample of the kinds of philosophical, policy, and implementation challenges that face the sector.

The fact that the PhD is seen as a vehicle to address this multifaceted challenge has to do with the fact that the higher education and science systems continue to see themselves as part of the global system. There is full recognition that the production of PhDs depends fundamentally on the capacity of the system to perform research, on a suitable research infrastructure and on the existence of a suitable (if not vibrant) research and academic ethos.

The throughput of PhDs is derisively small. For the last ten years only 10 percent of registered PhD students have graduated. In real numbers the system has about 8,000 students and about 800 graduate. But more importantly for every 500 first entry students, only one PhD is generated. In comparison say with India, where one PhD is produced for every 0.01 percent of the population, South Africa's output is about a tenth, one PhD for every 0.001 percent. Hence the need for a major overhaul of PhD programs and the need for a national approach rather than an institutional approach to the challenge.

INNOVATIONS

If the number of PhDs in the national system is to be the measure of the capacity of the system to be sustainable as well as enabled to meet the challenges of a nation at its current stage of development, then there are just four ways of addressing this matter. None of these methods is exclusive of the others though one or the other may be more high risk than others in terms of the importance of this issue to national development. What are these?

The first is to find ways of encouraging universities to significantly improve the throughput of PhD students, which currently rests at about 10 percent. This will entail taking a hard look at why students are not graduating and what kinds of capacity are required to achieve this.

The second is to develop the capacity and the will of universities to significantly scale up their graduate programs but with the view to understanding how to shift students through masters programs to PhDs. This may require new funding approaches from agencies such as the National Research Foundation (NRF). One immediate way of doing this would be to *require* all academic staff at universities to register for and progress towards PhDs and for universities to use push and pull strategies to achieve this. One example of this is the equity strategies that have been adopted by some of the larger historically white institutions, such as UKZN's LEAP (Leadership and Equity Advancement Programme). (For more details look at http://www.ukzn.ac.za//department/default.asp?dept=leapund).

The third is to develop special strategies to attract researchers from other parts of the world either for short- to medium-term periods on a long-term basis.

The fourth is to do what many other developing nations do, which is to send young South Africans to other systems of higher education to progress through PhD programs and to do this in a strategic way.

As was mentioned at the beginning, this is a paper about a national approach to a national challenge. Recent discussions are focusing on the following.

- Encouraging universities to address this matter in more assertive and proactive ways.
- Building a National System of Innovation approach to the problem and in particular to understand how to optimise the deployment of the national capacity in the supervision of students and in increasing the sites/contexts of study.
- Pooling higher education supervisory and coursework resources together to build graduate programs across two or more institutions.
- Reviewing the strategic thinking of the research funding agencies as a means to develop a more coherent approach to understanding the relationship between the funding of research and the production of high-level human resources. It may be necessary to consider a reversion to the definition of the role of the Foundation for Research Devel-

opment (the forerunner of the NRF) defined in the FRD Act that was *the creation of high level human resources through the funding of high quality research.* The NRF Act defines the role of the NRF as knowledge production rather than the production of human resources.

Some important and interesting steps have already been taken.

THE HIGHER EDUCATION FUNDING FORMULA

The Department of Education has reshaped the higher education subsidy system to allow the universities to play the push-pull game in terms of graduate studies. There is a full understanding that this strategy is fundamentally built on the capacity of universities to perform research. The funding formula takes this into account as well. However, this does not mean that the universities are responding positively to these subsidy pressures. In fact there is sufficient evidence to indicate that these institutions are not deploying these "directed" resources in a directed fashion. The subsidy resources generated through PhD studies are largely directed into general university funding pools.

RESHAPING THE RELATIONSHIPS OF INSTITUTIONS WITHIN THE NATIONAL SYSTEM OF INNOVATION

In the post-1994 period, in response to the issue of fragmentation, the National System of Innovation was conceived as a way to permit the relevant institutions to work coherently within a common framework. But it would appear that one of the outcomes of the process was the development of an ethos of non-differentiation, an ethos that all institutions should be "relevant" to the needs of development, meaning that they should all be involved in activities that appear to be directly relevant to the needs of the macro-economic strategy. The funding frameworks drove the system in a particular direction too, towards income generation, vicious cuts in spending, etc. This lack of differentiation produced a lack of specialized focus and a disastrous competitive edge within the system. It left the NRF performing the driving of "relevance" within the higher education system instead of focusing on its core function, the development of the research capacity of universities and their researchers. It must therefore be necessary to reshape the relationship between the institutions within the National System of Innovation—perhaps utilizing a *differentiated but articulated* approach.

One of the expectations of the national Science and Technology Green Paper was that graduate studies should be performed and supervised wherever public resources were invested in research and development activities. This policy has never been implemented and perhaps this could become a mechanism to initiate a discussion for the development of a new relationship between the science councils, private sector laboratories, universities and research funding agencies.

BUILDING NATIONAL AND INTERNATIONAL PARTNERSHIPS

In areas in which national capacity may be limited there are already excellent examples of partnerships between institutions in the building of graduate programs. These institutions need not necessarily be only universities. One of the characteristics of the unfolding knowledge era is the diffusion of knowledge production into the private and public sectors, and with this change comes a shift of capacity. The scale of the South African system is such that this diffusion has potentially serious implications for the capacity of higher education institutions to offer high-level supervision. But such partnerships also contribute to the assembling of the National System of Innovation.

These partnerships could be based on joint research activities that could facilitate not only the joint offering of courses but joint supervision as well. The establishment of such partnerships might lead to the development of networks, which in turn might provide graduate students with opportunities for diverse and complex learning/investigative spaces.

BIBLIOGRAPHY

Bawa, A., and J. Mouton. 2002. "Research." In *Transformation in Higher Education: Global Pressures and Local Realities in South Africa*, edited by N. Cloete, R. Fehnel, P. Maassen, T. Moja, H. Perold, and T. Gibbon. Juta and Co: Cape Town.

Bunting, I. 2002. "The Higher Education Landscape Under Apartheid." In *Transformation in Higher Education: Global Pressures and Local Realities in South Africa*, edited by N. Cloete, R. Fehnel, P. Maassen, T. Moja, H. Perold, and T. Gibbon. Juta and Co: Cape Town.

Cloete, N. 2002. "Policy Expectations." In *Transformation in Higher Education: Global Pressures and Local Realities in South Africa*, edited by N. Cloete, R. Fehnel, P. Maassen, T. Moja, H. Perold, and T. Gibbon. Juta and Co: Cape Town.

HSRC. 2005. Centre for Science, Technology and Innovation Indicators & Human Sciences Research Council (2005) National Survey of Research & Development 2003–2004: Provisional Report on the Sectors.

National Advisory Council on Innovation. 2003. *South African Innovation: Key Facts and Figures 2004*.

National Commission on Higher Education. 1996. *Discussion Document: A Framework for Transformation*.

7 • BRAZIL

RENATO JANINE RIBEIRO

It was in the nineteen seventies that doctoral degree programs got systematically underway in Brazil. Before that, many doctoral dissertations had been defended; but there was no nationwide policy giving priority to doctoral programs or defining their characteristics and requirements. Nevertheless, ever since the creation in 1951 of the Campaign for the Improvement of Higher Education Personnel (CAPES), a branch of the Ministry of Education, the continuing education of university professors has come to be seen as an important issue in Brazilian education and research. During the last presidency of Getulio Vargas (1951–54), which was strongly nationalistic and development-oriented, the National Research Council (CNPq) was also created. Both bodies have kept their original acronyms, although CAPES is now entitled the Coordination for the Improvement of Higher Education Personnel, while CNPq is the National Council on Scientific and Technological Development.

In the seventies, CAPES began a systematic process of evaluation of graduate programs. Even though it was a military dictatorship that was behind this initiative of the Brazilian government, the initiative was fully supported by the scientific and academic community, even including opposition groups; thus, right from the start, the Brazilian system of graduate studies has owed its success to the intensive participation of professors and scientists in the definition of evaluation criteria, decisions to grant fellowships and other financial aid, and the administration of the funding involved.

The programs have shown significant progress. The National Plan for Post-Graduate Studies 2005–2010, which is available on the CAPES homepage (http://www2.capes.gov.br/capes/portal/conteudo/10/PNPG.htm), presents a brief history of graduate studies in Brazil. In 1976, when the evaluation process got underway, we had 490 master's degree programs and 183 doctorates. By 1990, these figures had grown to 975 and 510, respectively. Expansion has been even swifter since 1996, when the figures were 1,083 and 541; by 2004, they had reached 1,959 and 1,034. This rapid rate of expansion was 6.5 percent per year in the twenty-eight years from 1976 to 2004, and 9.1 percent from 1996 to 2004. In May 2004, 568 of the doctoral programs belonged to federal institutions of higher education, while state universities accounted for 370 (of which 323 were in the three universities that belong to the state of São Paulo[1]); 96 were private.

As for the number of entering graduate students, it went from 9,440 in 1986 to 35,305 in 2003—an expansion of 374 percent. Those entering doctoral degree programs were 1,786 in 1986 and 11,343 in 2003—a 635 percent rise.

The number of master's degrees awarded was 3,647 in 1986 and 27,630 in 2003, for a growth of 757 percent in seventeen years. The success of the public policy on graduate studies is evidenced by a comparison of these figures with the number of entering graduate students. While the input rose 374 percent, the output rose 757 percent—twice as much. The number of new doctors rose from 868 in 1986 to 8,094 in 2003—an expansion of 932 percent (which is greater than the increase in the number of master's degrees awarded).

There is still much to be done. Considering that in 2003 the faculty in Brazilian higher education numbered 254,153, of whom 54,487 (21 percent) held doctorates, an important goal is to raise the number of higher education teaching personnel with doctorates to 200,000. The CAPES proposal for the draft university reform bill being discussed in the Ministry of Education, before being sent to the National Congress, is that within ten years the universities are to have 40 percent of their faculty with doctoral degrees; as for the university centers (*centros universitários*), which are more oriented toward undergraduate education, they are to have 66 percent of their faculty with master's degrees and 22 percent with doctorates by that same year; colleges should have 50 percent of their faculty holding either master's degrees or doctorates in ten years.

Furthermore, the draft legislation provides that for an institution to retain the name "university," with the autonomy guaranteed the latter by the Federal Constitution, it must have three recognized masters' degree programs and one recognized doctoral program. It is important to note that today, due to the different ways the Brazilian universities have been established (including some by state, or even municipal, laws), before there was stricter legislation, only 69 of the 168 currently in existence would meet the minimum requirement of three masters' degree programs and one doctorate.

The National Plan for Post-Graduate Studies (PNPG) 2005–2010 provides for increasing the number of doctorates granted in areas like engineering that are of relevance to economic development. The amount of money needed to maintain the current rate of expansion in the number of master's and doctoral degrees awarded (which is over 10 percent) has been calculated: it will total 1,600,000,000 *reals* in new money (660,000,000 dollars), to be invested by the various institutions, federal, state, and even private, that finance graduate studies.

WHAT HAVE BEEN THE OFFICIAL PURPOSE AND GOALS OF THE DOCTORAL DEGREE?

The goals set for scientific research have been associated with the strategic plans of the Brazilian government, especially during the presidential administration of Ernesto Geisel (1974–79), when investments were made in development with a view to self-sufficiency in the principal sectors of the economy. However, because such projects were not directed mainly at the universities, CAPES and university graduate studies were not at the core of those plans. Whether in spite of or because of this (and in contrast to other, more military-oriented projects), graduate studies had important civilian support. With the democratization of Brazil in 1985, the first civilian administration created the Ministry of Science and Technology, with the goal of sending ten thousand fellows abroad. Although over the years it has proven impossible to sustain that thrust (which, in fact, was criticized by the academic community, which gave greater priority to creating a sufficiently strong foundation for producing master's degree holders and PhDs in practically all areas of knowledge in Brazil), at least it was a results-oriented strategy. In recent years, one of the greatest challenges we have met has been to increase the linkages between academic research and the world of production. In this regard, Brazil still lacks a consistent habit of investing in R&D. If today the academic world is less reticent vis-à-vis the productive sector, the latter is still afraid to invest with no guarantee of return on its investment. The productive sector often prefers to acquire ready-made technology, even though it may not always be the most adequate to the climate and social conditions in Brazil.

WHAT WERE THE STRENGTHS AND WEAKNESS OF THE PROGRAM (PRIOR TO CHANGES)?

From what has been said, it may be deduced that the Brazilian system of graduate education is characterized by continuity, grounded in three elements: (1) evaluation by CAPES; (2) funding by CAPES, CNPq, and state foundations for supporting research, the most important of which is the Foundation for Support of Research of the State of São Paulo (FAPESP); and (3) the active participation of the academic community, through a kind of worker-management control (*cogestion*), together with governmental institutions. Even the opposition to the military regime participated in the evaluations; the opposition to this past administration largely supported the measures adopted by CAPES after 1995; and the current opposition has praised the policies of the agency.

THE MAIN ALTERATIONS HAVE OCCURRED SINCE THE MID-NINETIES. THEY ARE AS FOLLOWS:

Previously, evaluation was done by area, each of which received a grade from A to E; degree programs receiving D or E were closed down. Now, the classification ranges from 1 to 7, amplifying the scale of comparison. Classifications 1 and 2 close the degree program, while 3 means fair, 4 means good, and 5 means very good. Classifications 6 and 7 are given only to degree programs which function at an international level and/or meet international standards of excellence. The result of these changes is that the areas now face greater challenges. Before, practically all tended to have one-third A-level degree programs, one-third B, and one-third C. Today, the system as a whole has 30.1 percent of the degree programs at level 3 and 32.5 percent at level 4. The former grade A breaks down into classification 5 (24 percent), classification 6 (8 percent), and classification 7 (3.4 percent).[2] However, these figures are different in the various areas of knowledge. The excess of degree programs at the top of the hierarchy has been reduced from one third to 3 or 4 percent—which is more proper and better highlights quality. Only in the areas of the best performance do the degree programs receive classifications of 6 or 7. Thus, the evaluation has become more exemplary, forcing those areas with less scientific production to raise it; the degree to which this has occurred has exceeded expectations. Recall that scientific production, together with the awarding of master's and doctoral degrees, is the principal parameter for the CAPES evaluation.

With this, the standards for scientific production and awarding of master's and doctoral degrees have become stricter. The years of the administration of the PSDB political party, from 1995 to 2002, were very hard on the federal universities; they lost many faculty members, who were not replaced when they retired.[3] However, even without new faculty being hired, those who did remain at the universities greatly increased their production. The awarding of doctoral degrees was also accelerated. Table 6 of the National Plan for Post-Graduate Studies (PNPG) shows that while the number of master's degrees awarded in 1995 (9,265) was slightly less than the number of entering candidates in 1987 (9,440), the number awarded in 2003 (27,630) was superior to the number of entering master's degree candidates in 2000 (26,586). Whereas output used to take eight years to catch up with input, it now does so in three. Nevertheless, the problem is that we are reaching the limit of what it is possible to accomplish without new funding and without replacing professors who retire from the federal universities. This is one of the reasons why the Ministry of Education is allowing them to hire around 5,000 new faculty members in the next months.

FORCES OF CHANGE

The change process has been unleashed by the same agents who have played key roles in Brazilian graduate education over the past decades. The participation of the government is still of crucial importance, because it remains the source of the lion's share of the funding. Furthermore, although only 34.9 percent of the faculty teach at public institutions of higher education (vs. 65.1 percent in private schools), only 17.7 percent of the master's degree programs and 9.3 percent of the doctorates belong to the private sector, while the public institutions are responsible for 82.3 percent of the masters programs and 90.7 percent of the doctorates. The contrast is striking. This implies a serious problem: while most of the undergraduate programs are in the private sector, their quality is inferior to that of the public degree programs. This may be seen in the examinations of courses of study conducted by the Anísio Teixeira National Institute of Educational Studies and Research (INEP), as disseminated by the website www.inep.gov.br. The cause of this difference is that private undergraduate education is less tied to research, which is the core of graduate studies. One problem is that the private sector is still without legal regulation; the university reform currently under discussion at the Ministry of Education seeks to remedy this deficiency (with the strong opposition of the private sector, among others). Obviously, this does not imply that the public university courses of study are always the best. Because evaluation of undergraduate courses of study has only been underway for a few years, it has yet to produce results comparable to those CAPES has obtained with graduate programs; i.e., it has not yet led to the closing of any poor quality degree programs.

WHICH INTERNATIONAL AND NATIONAL FORCES BROUGHT ABOUT THESE CHANGES? HOW DID THE INTERNATIONAL AND NATIONAL FORCES INTERACT?

One noteworthy observation is that the transformation of Brazilian doctoral education has basically been decided and carried out by Brazilians. A major change has occurred over the past fifteen years: the number of full fellowships for doctoral study abroad has been gradually reduced. At the same time, a six month or one year "sandwich" period abroad has been encouraged. Thus, almost all doctoral candidates who want to study abroad for one or two semesters will have funding available to do so.[4] Furthermore, the requirement that in order to attain a higher classification, a graduate degree program must function at an international level and/or meet international standards of excellence has helped increase interaction with international centers of reference.

However, the key to the success of our model lies in the control of the entire process by the partnership between the State and the academic world. To that end, we have been very rigorous with regard to offshore masters and doctoral programs, which are illegal in Brazil if not approved by CAPES on the basis of their merit. The existence of such courses of study in the late nineties was a problem that has finally been resolved. Note that of the first one thousand students who received irregularly bestowed degrees from foreign institutions[5] and who applied for revalidation in Brazil, only one was successful (0.1 percent)—which just goes to show the poor quality of those products and how right we were not to accept education as merchandise. Indeed, the Ministry of Education has already announced that in negotiation of the General Agreement on Trade in Services (GATS), it will not agree to education being considered a service that is not subject to quality control by the Brazilian government. To be sure, none of this means the door is being closed to international cooperation, which actually has been growing. It should be recalled that since 1998, only graduate degree programs that function at an international level and/or meet international standards of excellence can attain the highest evaluations of 6 or 7.

WHAT WERE THE GOALS FOR CHANGE? WHAT WAS THE PROCESS? WHO WERE THE CHANGE AGENTS? WHICH CHANGES HAVE ALREADY BEEN IMPLEMENTED? WERE INDICATORS OF "SUCCESS" IDENTIFIED? ARE THESE OUTCOMES ALREADY VISIBLE? AND IF SO WHAT ARE THESE?

It may be seen that the principal results of the changes and the evaluation have been a continual increase in degrees granted and expanding scientific production. Now we are facing a two-fold challenge. On the one hand, there is a need for more masters and doctoral degrees among faculty members in higher education. Undergraduate education has been greatly expanded in Brazil. In the nineties, this was mostly due to private initiative. In the past two years, as a response to social movements, governments have also played an important role, e.g., through creation of the Federal University of the ABC, in the working class suburbs of the city of São Paulo,[6] as well as the campus of the University of São Paulo in the impoverished eastern zone of the capital city of the State of São Paulo. For undergraduate education to improve, it will be necessary to produce high quality faculty members.

Furthermore, it is of fundamental importance to produce high quality professionals for the productive sector, in order to increase the competitiveness of our companies in the global marketplace. We are trying to do this through the professional master's degree, which, at present, accounts for only 6 or 7 percent of all graduate courses of study. Perhaps a professional doctorate may be created in the future. We have been insisting on one innovation: that the professional master's degree can and should form competent professionals for the social areas public administration. Education, health, culture, and sports, where the social deficit is concentrated in Brazil, have serious administrative problems. Just one example: at the present time, independent production of Brazilian popular music CDs meets 40 percent of the demand. The only reason this share doesn't increase is that there are no more people trained in the economy of culture.[7] We would also like to produce more masters and doctoral degrees for the nongovernmental organizations. Considering that the country has 5,560 municipalities and twenty-seven states, the training of one professional (instead of academic) master for each would give rise to significant productivity gains in the social area.

CURRENT DOCTORAL EDUCATION

Any institution of higher education or research institute can, through the Application for Proposing New Courses of Study (APCN), send a proposal to CAPES for creation of a master's or doctoral degree program. No postgraduate academic program may have professors without a doctorate. Each area sets a minimum number of faculty members to be dedicated full-time to teaching and research, as well as other criteria. The fundamental requirement concerns the quality of faculty research, as evaluated by their publications. Depending on the area, it is necessary to have good laboratories and/or libraries. The CAPES website on periodical publications (http://www.periodicos.capes.gov.br/), currently with 9,095 periodicals, mostly international, is an instrument of decisive importance to the quality of the programs.

HOW IS DOCTORAL EDUCATION CONNECTED TO THE UNIVERSITY RESEARCH STRUCTURE?

Most doctoral programs are in public institutions. In some cases, graduate teaching is separate from undergraduate education; however, experience has shown that it is better for both to interact, so that the graduate school can help improve undergraduate education. Because evaluation of Brazilian research came into existence in graduate education, it is never just the research groups or scientific production *per se* that are evaluated, but also how the students are integrated into research; one important criterion is the education of masters and doctoral degree candidates. Although other countries may adopt other criteria, examining, for example, only the research group, we take into consideration that a research group that doesn't continually renew itself through admission of the members of the younger generation runs the risk of aging and failing to meet all sorts of demands from the outside world.

DESCRIPTION OF DOCTORAL EDUCATION

When Brazilian statistics on graduate education are discussed, the main issue is regional inequality. The country is divided into five geographical regions. The Southeast, which includes São Paulo, Rio de Janeiro, and Minas Gerais (which are the most highly developed states), is the richest region, and therefore the one with the most programs, doctoral candidates and fellows. Next comes the South, which encompasses Rio Grande do Sul, which is the fourth most highly developed state, as well as Paraná and Santa Catarina. The North, or Amazon Region, has the greatest area and a wealth of biodiversity. It is also the most sparsely populated and has the smallest number of courses of study and students; in this regard, it is comparable to the Center-West, if we exclude from this region the federal capital, Brasilia. Finally, the Northeast, which has the greatest number of states (due to the fact that it was the rich core of the colony from the sixteenth to the eighteenth centuries), has figures well below the national mean. Today, the greatest challenge for Brazil in terms of science, technology and graduate education is to reduce regional inequalities, as may be seen in table 7.1.

Even if we adjust these data to population, as in table 7.2, the inequality among the regions remains.

TABLE 7.1. Doctoral students in Brazil, according to regions

Southeast	31.274
South	6.068
Northeast	3.336
Center-West	1.058
North	.228
Brazil	41.964

Due to its bio-diversity, as well as the presence of a large number of indigenous ethnic groups, the Amazon is a top priority region for scientific research. After the failure of several attempts to induce PhD holders from other regions to move there, our administration is initiating a project called "Accelerate Amazônia," with the aim of winning over to the cause of science the inhabitants of the region, beginning in adolescence, and thus forming Amazonian scientists from among the very population of the region.

Breaking down doctoral education into eight major areas of knowledge, as we have in table 7.3, shows the modest numbers of engineering students, whom we consider of fundamental importance for increasing the productivity of our economy. The demand for new degree programs in the areas of Law, Administration, and Education is worrisome. Whatever their scientific merit may be, this phenomenon is largely due to the fact that it is cheap to install such courses of study, since they do not require laboratories. The Brazilian system includes doctoral programs in Law (243 degrees awarded in 2003) and Medicine (831 in 2003).

As for gender, table 7.4 shows our system includes 8,750 women and 7,836 men.

Thus women outnumber men in all age groups, except among those under twenty-five and over sixty-years-old, which are however negligible compared to the other age groups. With regard to nationality, even though we do not have precise data about it among doctoral students, CNPq data about the nationality of researchers holding doctorates show 14.2 percent come from Argentina, 8.7 percent from Peru, 7.7 percent from Germany, 6.2 percent from France, and 5.5 percent from the United States. Brazil grants fellowships to many foreigners. There is no discrimination, in the granting of federal and state fellowships, between Brazilians and foreigners. Furthermore, Brazilian international cooperation grants fellowships to countries with which we have special ties, such as the member countries of Mercosul (Argentineans, 26.4 percent of recipients of our

TABLE 7.2. Brazilian population and doctoral students, according to regions

Region	*Population (Millions)*	*% of global population (A)*	*Doctoral students (thousands)*	*% of students (B)*	*Inequality index (B)/(A)*
Southeast	72.4	42.65	31.20	74.53	1.75
South	25.1	14.78	6.06	14.46	0.98
Northeast	47.4	28.11	3.33	7.94	0.28
Center-West	11.6	6.86	1.05	2.52	0.37
North	12.9	7.60	0.22	0.54	0.07
Brazil	169.8	100.00	41.96	100.00	1.00

SOURCE: Instituto Brasileiro de Geografia e Estatística, http://www.ibge.gov.br/home/estatistica/populacao/censo2000/tabelagrandes_regioes211.shtm.

TABLE 7.3. Doctoral students according to the areas of knowledge, 2005

Human sciences	7,931
Health sciences	5,886
Biological sciences	5,874
Engineering & computer science	5,635
Agrarian sciences	4,843
Exact and earth sciences	4,415
Applied social sciences	3,435
Linguistics, literature & arts	3,011
Multidisciplinary studies, etc.	934
Total	41,964

fellowships in 2004) and other Latin American countries (Cuba, 13.2 percent) and, more and more under the present administration, to Africans (20 percent) and Portuguese-speaking peoples (25.2 percent), such as Capeverdians (6.4 percent), Mozambicans (5.6 percent), Angolans (1.2 percent), and East Timorese (2.4 percent).

The system of fellowships is quite comprehensive. It encourages relatively young students to get their doctorates. Of the 41,964 students enrolled in doctoral programs in 2005, 19,810, or 47 percent, were receiving fellowships. CAPES funds 49 percent of these fellowships and CNPq, 33 percent. The Foundations for the Support of Research (FAPs)[9] fund 13 percent. Of these, the most important is the Foundation for Support of Research of the State of São Paulo (FAPESP), which funds 2,132 fellows, or 5 percent of the total, and 10 percent of the 21,161 doctoral candidates residing in the state of São Paulo. Our data show that of 112,000 graduate school students, 44,112 are receiving fellowships. More than half of the remainder is not eligible, because they are employed or are enrolled in professional master's degree programs.

It should be observed that the Brazilian system of graduate education includes both masters and doctoral programs. The territorial dimensions of the country make it impossible to reduce graduate studies to the doctorate, because many of the institutions that may have masters programs would not yet be capable of administering a doctoral program. Two initiatives, the university reform bill to be proposed to Congress and a new funding program being jointly proposed by CAPES and the National Funding Agency for Studies and Research (FINEP), intend to raise the number of institutions of higher education with graduate degree programs

TABLE 7.4. Doctoral students belonging to research groups in CNPq registers, according to age and gender [8]

	Number		*%*	
Age Group	*Male*	*Female*	*Male*	*Female*
< 24	316	263	4.03	3.01
25–29	2.822	2.960	36.01	33.83
30–34	2.156	2.376	27.51	27.15
35–39	1.155	1.279	14.74	14.62
40–44	706	915	9.01	10.46
45–49	381	547	4.86	6.25
50–54	194	279	2.48	3.19
55–59	73	108	0.93	1.23
> 60	33	22	0.42	0.25
NA	—	1	—	0.01
Total	7.836	8.750	100	100

from circa 200 to 300, giving special emphasis to those situated in the Amazon, Northeast, and Center-West regions. Recently, under the leadership of a scientist who was exiled by the dictatorship and made his career in the Institut Pasteur in Paris, Luiz Hildebrando, was opened the most westerly doctoral program in the country, in Porto Velho; it is in the field of tropical diseases. We have also authorized the first doctorate on Afro-descendents, in Salvador. We are encouraging the creation of the first doctorate in ethnology in the Amazon region. In addition, we have already mentioned the professional master's degree programs.

The system of advisors assumes that there will be one advisor for each student. With the exception of areas of study in which laboratories are not needed, more than six advisees per advisor is rarely permitted. Normally, it should not take more than four years to write a doctoral thesis. While masters candidates, who are supposed to defend their dissertations within two years, generally have to take more courses, in doctoral programs the emphasis is on research, which is always oriented by a PhD professor. In some cases there is more than one advisor per candidate; this is being encouraged by CAPES. We are initiating co-tutoring and double diplomas with foreign countries, such as France and Germany. To enroll or continue one's graduate studies, it is necessary to demonstrate proficiency in one or two foreign languages, especially English. A qualification exam is required before the defense of the dissertation. Conclusion of the doctorate is attested through a public dissertation defense before a five-member examining board, a majority of which must be external to the graduate degree program and, sometimes, to the institution itself in which the program is located.

Admission criteria are left to the discretion of the program, but a competitive examination open to all interested parties who meet the minimum requirements is always required. In some cases applicants are required to have a bachelor's degree in the same area, but in most cases candidates with undergraduate degrees in other areas can be accepted, provided they undergo a period of adaptation. If a degree program selects poor students, it will be penalized in the evaluation. CAPES is not a court of last resort for particular cases, this being the responsibility of the institution of higher education itself; nevertheless, in evaluating a program's production, it winds up examining its general guidelines.

Peers do the evaluation. CAPES has a board of directors appointed by the President of the Republic, but the relationship with each area is the responsibility of forty-five area representatives chosen by the president of CAPES from lists drawn up by the graduate programs themselves for terms of three years. They put together evaluation commissions consisting of respected scientists. Evaluation focuses, in the first place, on the program's scientific production, in accordance with accepted criteria (especially the quality of the publications in which the articles are published), as well as the education of masters and doctoral candidates. A few years ago a system was created, called "Qualis," through which Brazilian academic community incorporates the criterion of citations; it also permits classification of periodicals in areas in which citations don't work (especially in the humanities). In some areas (e.g., computer science), there is a Qualis of events; in arts and music, there is a Qualis of artistic production. A Qualis of books is currently being developed. The fact that books have yet to be satisfactorily evaluated is a cause of concern considering the fact that from 2001 to 2003, a total of 8,532 books were published by authors linked to graduate programs; of these, 5,961 were in the eighteen areas corresponding to the humanities.

Finally, with regard to the destination of former students, the most accurate data we have are from the 1990s. While only one-third of the recipients of masters degrees pursue a teaching career, this has been the destiny of two-thirds of the PhDs. Today the issue of unemployment of PhDs in Brazil is controversial. CAPES believes that it is not high. Practically all the PhDs are employed—not always in the jobs they might desire, but generally in fields, such as teaching, that benefit from their experience.

SUMMARY AND CONCLUSIONS

At the present time higher education is being intensively discussed, due in large part to the fact that, for the first time in our history, we have a federal administration with its roots in the political left. To be sure, the area in which there is greatest consensus between the two poles of thought represented by the Workers' Party, which has been governing Brazil since 2003, and the Party of Brazilian Social Democracy, which governed the country from 1995 to 2002, is that of graduate education. They would rather disagree about undergraduate than about graduate education. Furthermore, there is a growing belief that evaluation of graduate programs constitutes a model for the rest of the educational system. Another belief has to do with the expansion of the system in terms of numbers of programs and of degrees awarded. There remain important tasks to be undertaken. Internationalization is attractive, but is also dangerous, because while it does make possible exchange of knowledge, it also may open the door to an invasion of poor quality courses of study. Evaluation of degree programs in the area of humanities is still insufficient, because they publish many books and it is difficult to systematically evaluate them. The destiny of former graduate students is an ever more pressing issue: on the one hand, there remain a large number of faculty members who need graduate degrees; on the other, it has been seen that most of the masters degree holders and a significant percentage of the PhDs do not go into higher education. Furthermore, precisely as a consequence of the success obtained in expansion and of the commitment of the academic community to continue expansion, the funding of research and students demands more and more financial resources, which are hard to come by. Finally, it is not easy to persuade private enterprise to place its bets on research and on graduate education itself. All are important challenges, often difficult, but they are being faced. Their very existence makes us believe we will embark, in the coming years, on a new stage in Brazilian graduate education.

NOTES

I thank Dr. Simon Schwartzmann for his comments on an almost final version of this paper, although I bear full responsibility for all opinions inside it.

1. University of São Paulo (Usp), University of Campinas (Unicamp), and Paulista State University (Unesp).

2. For the results of the 2004 three-year evaluation, covering the period from 2001 to 2003, see http://www.capes.gov.br/capes/portal/conteudo/10Resultado_AvaliacaoTrienal.htm.

3. Because of their autonomy, the universities belonging to the state of São Paulo were spared the effects of these lean years. In that same period, private institutions flourished.

4. CAPES data show that between 60 and 90 percent of the doctoral students that apply for a *sandwich* period abroad get what they wish.

5. Mostly South American, Caribbean, Portuguese, and Spanish.

6. Santo André, São Bernardo do Campo, and São Caetano, which explains the acronym ABC. They are close to Diadema, which means sometimes the acronym can be ABCD.

7. Data from Brazilian Ministry of Culture.

8. Sources: Diretório dos Grupos de Pesquisa 2004, CNPq (http://dgp.cnpq.br/censo2004/) and Instituto Brasileiro de Geografia e Estatística (http://www.ibge.gov.br/home/estatistica/populacao/censo2000/tabelagrandes_regioes211.shtm).

9. Several of the States that constitute the Federate Republic of Brazil have their FAPs.

BIBLIOGRAPHY

CAPES web site: www.capes.gov.br/capes/portal/conteudo/10/PNPG.htm.

Diretório dos Grupos de Pesquisa 2004, CNPq web site: www.dgp.cnpq.br/censo2004/.

Instituto Brasileiro de Geografia e Estatística web site: www.ibge.gov.br/home/estatistica/populacao/censo2000/tabelagrandes_regioes211.shtm.

8 • MEXICO

ARMANDO ALCANTARA, SALVADOR MALO,
AND MAURICIO FORTES

INTRODUCTION

Doctoral programs began in Mexico around the middle of the twentieth century. These programs evolved as an outgrowth of the existing scholar tradition within the humanities (philosophy) and through the initiatives of research-oriented faculty who had obtained their training mostly in Europe and in the United States. The generation of Spanish scholars that came to Mexico fleeing from Spain's Civil War enhanced this tradition. Therefore, the beginning of doctoral programs in the country may be better understood as the result of international forces rather than the normal development of its higher education (HE) system.

The exogenous nature of the origins of doctoral programs in Mexico explains some of their present characteristics. The introduction of doctoral programs created a tension between the professional and academic views of HE, as well as between the science and humanities communities regarding their positions about "truth" and their different attitudes towards research and scholarship. These differences had important effects also beyond doctoral programs, extending to other facets of university life and even further.

Before the creation of doctoral programs, universities in Mexico had very limited academic personnel in the modern sense. Professors were mostly learned professionals who taught at the various professional schools around which the universities were organized. In addition to teaching, the professors' main commitment was to satisfy their everyday practice obligations. There was little expectation of research or scholarship. However, some faculty members did in fact produce scholarly books, mainly used as textbooks. Society recognized them as distinguished professionals who spent a significant part of their time outside the universities' walls. A notable exception to this state of affairs was to be found among the professors in the relatively small schools of philosophy, literature, arts and, later, science. These, however, were then few in number and had no real influence in the running of the universities.

Even after universities evolved and full-time academic staff became the leading voice in university affairs, the professions continued to dominate the undergraduate curricula up to the current state of affairs. Thus, undergraduate education is profession-oriented and generally known as *licenciatura,* a term that indicates that graduates are *licensed* to practice their professions. The same term is applied even to graduates in academic or disciplinary fields such as philosophy, arts, humanities, and science. This means that the undergraduate syllabus is specialized, rigid and takes between 9 to 12 semesters to be completed. In contrast with bachelor's degree programs in the United States, Mexican *licenciaturas* provide less general education and more field or area content (King 1971; Osborn II 1987).

ORIGIN AND EVOLUTION

The origins of doctoral programs in Mexico can be traced back to the early 1940s when Mexico had only about a dozen public and five private universities (Rangel Guerra 1979). As with many other aspects of higher education in the country, these doctoral programs were initiated at the *Universidad Nacional Autónoma de México* (UNAM). They began in its School of Philosophy and Literature, from which the School of Sciences soon emerged as a separate entity. Doctoral programs spread out to other schools from these two and, later on, to other universities.

Three distinct periods can be appreciated in the evolution of doctoral studies in Mexico when we consider the number of programs offered and degrees awarded. These periods also constitute stages during which diverse forces can be identified as acting on the HE system. These forces resulted in different general concerns and attitudes towards doctoral programs.

The Beginnings: 1940–1970

During almost thirty years, doctoral programs remained an academic oddity. Only two or three degrees were awarded annually (Malo 1981). It was only after 1960 when other universities (including some private ones), the *Instituto Politécnico Nacional* and the *Colegio de México,* began to offer a significant number of graduate programs, although they did not award doc-

TABLE 8.1. Evolution of enrollment in the educational system

Year	*Primary School*	*Secondary School*	*Middle School*	*Higher Education*
1950	2,997,054	69,547	37,329	29,892
1960	5,342,092	234,980	106,200	76,269
1970	9,146,460	1,082,377	335,438	271,275
1980	14,666,257	3,033,856	1,265,741	935,789
1990	14,401,588	4,190,190	2,100,529	1,252,027
2000	14,792,500	5,349,700	2,955,700	1,718,000

SOURCE: 1950–1990 figures from OCDE (1997); 2000 figures from SEP (2004)

toral degrees on a regular basis. It was not until late in the sixties, once the *Centro de Investigación y Estudios Avanzados* (CINVESTAV) was fully established, that Mexico began to have constant sources of newly trained PhDs.

During this period, most Mexican PhD graduates were individuals who studied abroad either by their private means or through loans or scholarships. The *Banco de México* ran a loan program used mainly by those wishing to pursue graduate studies in economics and related fields. In addition, the *Instituto Nacional de Investigación Científica* as well as some of the recently created national research facilities (the Nuclear Energy Research and the Petroleum Institutes are two good examples) awarded graduate scholarships to students interested in pursuing research careers.

Although limited, these financial aid programs accounted for a steady increase in the enrollment of new Mexican PhD students from their inception to well into the seventies, mostly in overseas programs. Most of these doctorates received their degrees in the USA, the UK, or France. By 1976, Mexican institutions had awarded 447 doctoral degrees out of an estimated total number of 1,480 PhDs in the country. At that time, Mexico had seventy-three doctoral programs, with sixty-eight of them offered by universities situated in Mexico City (CONACYT 1976a).

During this early period, *licenciatura* enrollment increased many times over, starting from 29,892 students in 1950 to 271,275 in 1970 (table 8.1). Most of this expansion was absorbed by UNAM and a few other state universities, thus making them large universities at this early stage in their development.

Three kinds of graduate programs existed in Mexico. Specialization programs, that had the largest enrollment and also had the greatest variance in time to degree, with three-year duration for the medical profession and one- or two-year duration for other professions. Masters degree programs, usually with duration of two years, tended to have an academic or professional orientation. Finally, the doctoral degree programs, with four-year duration, were devoted to research and scholarship. In general, doctoral programs were similar to the USA model.

Differentiation and Planning: 1970–1990

During the same period, the growth of the HE system started to generate an increasing demand for graduate studies. Government officials became aware of the urgent need to produce a more highly trained labor force and of the importance of creating capacity in science and technology.

In 1970, the Mexican Government created the National Council for Science and Technology (CONACYT) with human resources development for R&D as part of its mandate. By then, the emerging community of scientists consolidated into the Mexican Academy of Sciences, founded in 1959 by less than a dozen pioneer researchers. During the seventies, the rapid growth of HE led to the creation of a new secretariat at Mexico's Ministry of Education dedicated to promoting graduate studies and scientific research at Mexican universities.

These three organizations engaged in many different activities and programs to promote and plan graduate programs throughout the country to satisfy the increasing demand for quality in HE, research and development (AIC 1973; CONACYT 1976b; SEP 1982). In 1976, CONACYT produced the first long-term plan for Mexico's scientific and technological development (CONACYT 1976c), and established the first major program for human resources development that soon was receiving international financial support.

These organizations focused on the policies needed to increase the number of doctoral graduates in the country and their influence on Mexico's development. Centralization, low productivity and imprecise rules for the conduct of graduate programs were among the more frequently mentioned obstacles for the first goal, while lack of fiscal incentives, policies and goals were often mentioned in regards to the second goal.

During the 1980s, however, masters and doctoral programs both at UNAM and elsewhere multiplied at a fast pace. Thus while in 1967 the country had only around two hundred graduate programs, twelve years later there were over seven hundred (Malo 1983). This gave a further impetus to doctoral programs, which began to multiply nationwide, and by 1980 there were fifteen universities that offered fifty-two doctoral programs (Ruiz Herrera 1986) and awarded some two hundred degrees per year.

Existing universities grew in size while new ones were created in different parts of the country, all of them requiring academic staff in large numbers. This demand raised concerns about the quality of HE and an increased interest and demand for doctoral and masters graduates. Although growth took place everywhere, it was particularly noticeable in Mexico City: UNAM expanded from about 60,000 students in 1970 to 140,000 by 1980 (Blanco 2001); it created five new campuses in the larger Metropolitan Area of Mexico City; it increased the number and nature of its research centers and institutes, and improved its academic personnel. During this decade, CINVESTAV also consolidated its departments and began to create campuses in different regions of the country. Finally, the *Universidad Autónoma Metropolitana* (UAM), established in 1974, was soon operating three campuses in Mexico City and rapidly became one of the leading institutions in Mexico, particularly in the areas of research and new doctoral programs. In 2006, a fourth campus was integrated to the UAM system.

Since conditions for pursuing a career in research at the above-mentioned three institutions were much better than in others, many of the PhDs graduating in Mexican universities (most noticeably at UNAM) were absorbed by the institutions that trained them. Thus, an informal differentiation between "research-oriented, PhD-granting" institutions and "teaching-only" institutions began to appear by the end of the seventies. This enhanced the resolve of CONACYT, the Ministry of Education (SEP) and the *Asociación Nacional de Universidades e Instituciones de Educación Superior* (ANUIES) to have state universities increase their number of graduate programs and research activities. However, no national planning policy was produced that would establish some kind of balance between the number of research oriented universities and the society's need for sufficient and good quality technical and professional institutions. By the end of the seventies a differentiation of graduate programs had also occurred. Doctorates in the medical and health fields were practice oriented whereas doctoral degrees were all research oriented.

The economic crisis that took place in 1982 changed the country's views and attitudes regarding science and HE. The fear of losing many of its best scientists to other countries or to better paid jobs led to the creation of the *Sistema Nacional de Investigadores* (SNI), a nation-wide program by which scientists' individual productivity over a period of years is assessed. Those that receive a positive evaluation obtain a regular, tax-exempt financial stipend in addition to their salary. The SNI bylaws favor individuals holding a doctoral degree.

Expansion, Privatization and Diversification: 1990 to Date

For several years—what some analysts call the *lost decade* due to the nil economic growth through the period—public HE reduced its rate of growth and the progress of public research institutions and laboratories virtually stopped, while private HE increased its size and its role. Paradoxically, during the same period graduate programs, doctoral graduates and the number of research papers produced by public universities multiplied.

The private sector expansion in the last fifteen years is the most significant phenomenon affecting the Mexican HE system. The increasing enrollments in private establishments of HE were observed for many years, and Daniel Levy (Levy 1986) anticipated the challenge this expansion posed to public dominance. The rate at which this has been taking place in the last years is remarkable. As Rollin Kent indicates, the number of private institutions grew from 358 in 1990 to 735 in 1999 out of 1,250 HE establishments (Kent 2004). Nevertheless, the enrollment in public HE establishments is still larger than in private ones. Public institutions also include the non-*licenciatura* establishments (two-year colleges) created during the last fifteen years.

Private graduate education has followed the developments at the *licenciatura* level. Since the early forties, the *Universidad Iberoamericana* (UIA) and the *Instituto Tecnológico de Estudios Superiores de Monterrey* (ITESM) offered graduate programs. During the eighties, many additional private institutions entered the provision of graduate education, most of them by way of *diplomados* (short graduate courses) and masters programs, but only UIA and ITESM and a few others had institutional doctoral programs that also comprised research activities by full-time faculty.

Over the last fifteen years the two federal government agencies directly related to HE and scientific research, the *Subsecretaría de Educación Superior* (SES) and CONACYT, have promoted different initiatives, many of which relate to doctoral studies. The former operates several programs that provide universities with grants to increase the number of their academic staff with PhD degrees or to support institutional development. In addition, SES has been instrumental in the establishment, operation and improvement of several non-government quality assurance, testing, accreditation, and certification agencies.

CONACYT on the other hand, operates the *Sistema Nacional de Investigadores*, manages the *Padrón Nacional de Posgrado* (Graduate Program Registry)—an assessment instrument that recognizes the best masters and doctoral programs in the country, the largest scholarship program for students that wish to pursue graduate studies in research related areas, and several R&D funding mechanisms.

GOALS, STRENGTHS, AND WEAKNESSES OF DOCTORAL PROGRAMS

Quality assurance mechanisms established by the above-mentioned federal agencies led to the consolidation of several doctoral programs at public universities. Moreover, students enrolled in these programs are expected to complete their degree through a PhD thesis that produces at least one publication in reputed international research journals. These programs share similar operation procedures among themselves and with the doctoral programs of US universities, such as assigning a mentor to each student admitted into the program whose main responsibility is to plan, along with the student, academic activities and supervision of the student's dissertation project. In addition, the large research institutions rely on the assessment of specific tutorial committees assigned to each student. These committees supervise student progress, assign basic course schedules during the first four or five semesters and approve the dissertation projects and the individualized students' academic plan. The tutorial system at UNAM has been remarkably successful in programs related to the natural sciences, and less so in the humanities and in the social sciences since full-time students are more numerous in the former (UNAM 2001). In spite of the increase in the number of full-time students in the humanities and social sciences, a significant number of them are still part-time.

By the end of the 1980s, UNAM, CINVESTAV and UAM together with three or four of the other larger public universities were producing a steady supply of new doctoral graduates in the country. A distinct characteristic of these graduates was that almost all of them came from public institutions and received their PhD degree mostly on basic research areas in natural sciences, life sciences and humanities. Faculty personnel at large public institutions had already reached a critical mass to compete successfully for government and institutional grants to set up laboratories and infrastructure facilities. Private universities, in contrast, had very limited experimental infrastructure and therefore focused most of their doctoral programs on areas of knowledge that did not rely on expensive investments in the operation of modern laboratories, libraries, and information facilities.

During the last two decades Mexican scientists have participated in ambitious research projects that involve graduate students and considerable subsidies through international collaboration agreements and networks to use specialized resources abroad such as particle accelerators, telescopes, or historical archives, to name but a few examples. This practice enhances graduate student and academic international mobility but it sharply contrasts with the feeble exchanges of students in different programs *within* the country, except for the intense flow of graduate students towards the leading institutions in the Mexico City Metropolitan Area. Once the student obtains his doctoral degree, it is a favored practice to apply for a faculty position at these large universities rather than return to his home institution unless he is a candidate of one of the federal, faculty-development programs mentioned elsewhere in this chapter.

International collaboration by graduate programs and research departments is exhibited by the number of publications they produce that include authors from institutions in different countries. Graduate students are encouraged to be continually aware of new developments in their fields of specialty regardless of where they originate. In fact, to avoid endogamous faculty growth, most graduate programs refrain from hiring their own students in tenure-track positions, or at least, invest considerable effort to persuade them to do postgraduate work at other institutions overseas for a minimum of one year before their job applications are considered. At UNAM, this practice has become mandatory in the exact and natural sciences areas, although it is less frequent in the social sciences and humanities programs.

Doctoral programs recognized by CONACYT as being of high quality are generally equivalent to those found in the best universities in the US or Europe, and therefore one may conclude that individuals that receive their training in these programs have the skills to make an independent contribution to the advancement of knowledge through original scholarly research. However, it is a fact that most PhD graduates involved in high-level research work in academic centers, with a negligible fraction of them stationed at the very few industries that have advanced research facilities. Thus, the increase in doctoral graduates has had a negligible influence in the country's overall growth in productivity.

One of the main weaknesses of doctoral programs in Mexico is *system inbreeding*, that is, a system devoted to the advancement of knowledge that is self-referenced. This system has doctoral programs of good—even high—quality, with ample international recognition and first-class training for graduate students, but it has not yet developed a relationship with the country's non-academic sectors and, in some cases, not even with the undergraduate programs offered by the same institutions. One may argue that one of the main objectives of a doctoral program is to produce individuals with particular skills for original research, but the job perspectives should go beyond the work at academic institutions. Additional effective mechanisms still need to be implemented to create a more innovative and synergistic relationship between industry and doctoral programs. Naturally, there are some individual exceptions, but it is a fact that many doctoral programs do not consider a wider horizon beyond the academic environment itself.

According to the Institute for Scientific Information, in 2003 Mexico produced 5,783 papers representing about 0.72 percent of the world publications, ranking twenty-first in total number of papers published of the OCDE countries and second in the Latin American region, after Brazil. About a fifth of these publications were in Physics, followed by Health Sciences (12.5 percent), Plants and Animals (12 percent) and Chemistry (11.5 percent). Each of the other disciplines represents less than 8 percent of the country's scientific contribution. The *impact factor* provides a more detailed indicator of the publication data. It is proportional to the number of citations a particular paper receives in the five-year period after its publication. This indicator shows that the disciplines that represent the largest fraction of the country's publications and also those that receive more citations—Physics, Chemistry and Plants and Animals—have an overall impact factor *below* worldwide average whereas those having the largest impact factor are, in decreasing order: Astrophysics (6.6), Immunology (5.6), Molecular Biology (5.4), Neurosciences (4.4), and Microbiology (4.3) (CONACYT 2004).

During the five-year period 1999–2003, UNAM published 12,667 articles in international journals with an impact factor of 3.1, the largest in the country. CINVESTAV follows, with 5,029 articles with impact factor of 2.8. The UAM is the third research institution, with 1,922 articles with an impact factor of 2.4.

Senior staff at research universities in Mexico still enjoy enviable intellectual freedom: professors are at liberty to choose to work on any disciplinary subject that inspires their intellect with few external pressures to modify their research agenda or adapt the methodology according to departmental or institutional planning guidelines. During the differentiation and planning period (1970–1990) mentioned above, it was assumed that in order to build critical masses of reputed researchers, it would be sufficient to require high quality in the research products instead of pressing young PhDs to contribute to the institutionally established research goals. This might be quite satisfactory to a true or potential scholar but, paradoxically, the number of respected and recognized scholars (in the universal sense) has decreased.

The *scientometric* data suggests that Mexican doctoral candidates are exposed to a very competent academic base, at least for those who pursue their degree at the main research universities. Graduate students receive good training in their specialized fields of knowledge but they do not benefit from *scholarship* in the traditional sense, as the relative number of true, multidimensional scholars in the country has diminished below what one could consider as the minimum critical mass.

There is an additional effect arising from the distinction between full-time professors devoted mostly to research activities and those that are concerned with teaching. The large public research universities in Mexico are organized in professional schools, where most of the teaching activities are carried out, together with institutes and centers, where research activities occur. The separation between the main objectives of schools and those of institutes has created an effective two-class system, where different assessment and reward programs coexist in the same institution to address the needs of "teaching" professors and those of the "research" professors. An additional inconvenience of the separation between schools and institutes is the lack of everyday contact between undergraduates and the research faculty at the institutes. The loss of the direct transmission of the research experience—the sense of discovery—to undergraduate students cancels some of the most gratifying aspects of the research university environment.

The other face of the coin is related to the question, what measures has the productive sector adapted to attract young high-level researchers? Small and medium enterprises comprise the core of Mexican industry, and they seldom invest in R&D activities to increase productivity. Large enterprises that do have a potential to benefit from innovation derived from in-house research groups prefer to rely on technological transfer and acquisition activities rather than invest in the former. The net result is a growing divide between doctoral programs and the demand for high-level researchers from the productive sectors. Recently, CONACYT launched a strategy aimed at linking researchers and business firms. The strategy includes thirty consortium projects, each with seventy researchers. Most projects consist of partnerships between enterprises and research centers sharing efforts to improve competitiveness in Mexican industry. To support this initiative, on May 2005, a World Bank 250 million USD loan was secured to fund the long-term project (2006–2015) "Innovation for Competitiveness."

FORCES OF CHANGE

The rapid expansion of the educational enrollment shown in table 8.1 reveals the strong pressures acting on the system. During the period between 1950 and 2000, the population of Mexico quadrupled from 25.8 million, with a national average age of 23.3 years, to 100.6 million at the end of the period with a national average age of 26.1 years. The education system was able to respond to the rapidly growing number of children demanding basic education services to the extent that the Ministry of Education built a large number of schools and sufficient teachers graduated to satisfy this demand.

In 2000, 34 percent of the population was under fifteen years of age and 61 percent was the economically active population (ages between fifteen and sixty-four). During the next fifteen years, the demographic distribution will demand additional HE services at an increasing rate that is stressing public finances. The nation was able to provide basic education to a population that had a considerable higher rate of growth fifty years ago, but today, when the rate of growth has diminished, the main challenge for the system is to provide more expensive HE facilities to more students while it will be closing down less expensive basic education schools. This trend explains, in part, the rapid expansion of the HE system and the proliferation of private institutions.

Although many of the new graduate programs at public and private institutions created during the last twenty years followed the pattern set by UNAM, it was soon perceived that there were marked differences in the institutions' faculty and research staff abilities. Such a state of affairs stimulated the Federal Government to develop external assessment procedures for programs, faculty and institutions. This led to the creation of peer-review evaluation organizations since the early nineties, and to the improvement and strengthening of the graduate program registry administered by CONACYT. More recently, formal program accreditation organizations have begun to operate in collaboration with the existing professional colleges and certifying bodies. Although program accreditation procedures are not yet mandatory, society perceives this distinction as a mark of good quality.

In addition to the above-mentioned changes that deal with increased interest in external and objective assessment of HE, there has been a renewed interest in increasing assessment of doctoral education. For example, the Mexican Academy of Sciences initiated an examination of doctoral programs at UNAM in collaboration with the US National Academy of Sciences, also assisted by the Mexican academies of engineering and medicine in a combined effort to identify the best Mexican programs in these areas and to promote new networks, mostly within the Latin American context.

Perhaps the most important force of change is the rapid and multifaceted internationalization of HE. Several factors intervene in this phenomenon caused by the expansion of a global economy. In addition, the negotiation of trade agreements within large geographical regions; the availability of scholarships and financial aid programs to attract graduate students to North American and European universities, and the trends to increase the mobility of students and academic staff such as the Erasmus and Socrates programs of the European Union (EU) have also contributed. Internationalization of HE, in its many forms, is an interesting development and in fact, science has evolved as an essentially international endeavor. However, it may also represent a risk to national educational systems, particularly in the area of doctoral education. Students are lured by extremely attractive programs offered in several countries. For example, the creation of a European Research Area (with an extraordinary funding as a fraction of the European Union GNP) will attract many of the most brilliant minds involved in R&D activities in Mexico and other countries in Latin America. Furthermore, European universities are also providing generous financial aid to bring foreign graduate students to their institutions, and many may not return to their home countries after obtaining their degrees. According to current European projections, "In order to have the same proportion of researchers in the labor force as the high performing US, the EU needs an additional 550,000 researchers by 2010. This is equivalent to roughly 50,000 extra researchers per year with the proviso that the US does not increase its proportion of researchers in the short to medium term" (European Commission 2003).

A historical perspective of the paradigmatic transformation in the economies of several countries demonstrates the enormous importance of long-term planning for R&D as an essential condition for advancement and progress. The examples are plentiful, of which we only mention the following: the drastic reforms introduced by emperor Meiji, in Japan at the end of the nineteenth century that brought Western science and culture into that country; the large investment in scientific research promoted by Vannevar Bush's report to the US president in 1945 that laid the blueprint for the impressive growth in American science and technology during the next fifty years, and the well known economic growth of South Korea, Taiwan, Singapore, India, Ireland and Israel based on knowledge. In contrast, it is unfortunate that such long-term national policy plans have not yet been developed in Mexico. Current federal legislation mandates each new federal administration to produce a state plan for education and, specifically, for the much-needed influence of doctoral training in research and technological development activities. But these plans almost never survive beyond the next administration.

THE CURRENT STATUS OF DOCTORAL EDUCATION

Academic personnel in science and technology in Mexico is limited. It represents only 0.7 people devoted to research and development (R&D) per 1,500 persons of the economically active population, with a total annual graduation of doctors of about 1,000 individuals. Only ninety institutions of HE in Mexico offer doctoral programs and most of these are concentrated in a handful of universities: thirty-seven of them have just one program, and three quarters of the total offer less than five programs. Institutions with more than ten doctoral programs account for 10 percent. Table 8.2 shows those with the highest number of programs.

It is worth noting that only two of these institutions are private: the UIA and ITESM. The others are concentrated in five states in the country (out of thirty-two). According to ANUIES, in 2004 universities and other institutions of HE offered 3,628 graduate programs, of which 897 were at the specialization level, 2,223 were at the master's degree level and 508 were at the doctoral level (ANUIES 2004)

Total enrollments in Mexico's Educational System for the 2001–2002 academic year accounted for almost thirty million students (29,023,459), of which 81.9 percent attended elementary school; 10.81 percent secondary education; 6.9 percent HE; and only 0.4 percent graduate studies. More than two million students (2,147,075) enrolled in HE. The number of graduate students was 132,473 (6.1 percent of the total), distributed in professional schools (22.4 percent); masters (70.3 percent) and only 7.3 percent at the doctorate level (SEP 2002).

A historical review of enrollment patterns in HE shows that in 1970 the number of students was 252,236. This number grew to 853,239 in 1980 and increased to 1,252,027 in 1990; figures for 2002 accounted for an enrollment of 2,236,811 students. However, at the graduate level, the increase in enrollment has been rather moderate: it has grown only 23 percent from 1998 (107,149) to 2002 (132,473). Table 8.3 shows the number of graduate students since the mid-1980s.

In the school year 2005, 70.5 percent (105,594) of graduate students attended masters programs, and 20.9 percent pursued a professional program, while only 8.5 percent enrolled in a doctoral program. Moreover, the enrollment in graduate programs was highly concentrated in a few states. In the year 2000, of the total enrollment (118,099), 38 percent of

TABLE 8.2. Institutions with the highest number of doctoral programs in Mexico

Institution of Higher Education	*Programs*
Universidad Nacional Autónoma de México	32
Universidad Autónoma de Nuevo León	23
Centro de Investigación y de Estudios Avanzados	22
Universidad de Guadalajara	20
Colegio de Graduados. Universidad Autónoma de Chapingo	19
Instituto Politécnico Nacional	18
Universidad Autónoma Metropolitana	15
Instituto Tecnológico de Estudios Superiores de Monterrey	13
Universidad Autónoma del Estado de México	11
Universidad Autónoma de Puebla	11
Universidad Iberomericana	10

SOURCE: COMEPO, *Plan de Desarrollo del Posgrado Nacional* (National Graduate Studies Development Plan), p. 15.

students were located in Mexico City; 8 percent attended graduate studies in Nuevo León; 7.9 percent in Jalisco; 7 percent in Puebla; and 6.7 percent in the State of Mexico. At the doctoral level, near half of the total enrollment is located in the country's capital. As expected, the number of doctoral graduates per million inhabitants has remained rather low, despite its increase during the last decade: it went from 2.5 in 1990 to 8.7 in 1998 and to 10.9 in the year 2000 (CONACYT 2000). Table 8.4 shows the slow evolution of doctoral enrollment in Mexico during the 1990s and the beginning of the twenty-first century.

As the leading institution for teaching and research in Mexico, it is worth noting that UNAM employs the largest number of research personnel in the country (more than 4,000 researchers). It also has the highest number of SNI members of any institution of HE (2,733). UNAM allocates 25 percent of its total budget to research activities. Scientific research is conducted at its eighteen institutes and ten centers. Research in the humanities and the social sciences is carried out in nine institutes and seven centers. (UNAM 2003; UNAM 2004). In addition, it has a considerable number of major research facilities (including two ships to conduct oceanographic studies) scattered throughout the Mexican republic.

CINVESTAV, created in 1961, is the second most important research institution. Today, it employs more than five hundred researchers (almost

TABLE 8.3. Enrollment in graduate education by levels of study, 1985–2002

Year	Total	Doctorate %	Masters %	Professional
1985	37,040	3.5	63.2	33.1
1990	43,965	3.0	61.2	35.6
1995	65,615	6.8	64.5	28.5
2000	118,099	7.1	69.6	23.2
2005	149,676	8.5	70.5	20.9

SOURCE: ANUIES 2002, *Anuario Estadístico* (Statistical Yearbook), México, 2002

TABLE 8.4. Evolution in the number of doctoral students in Mexico (1990–2006)

Year	Students
1990	1319
1991	1438
1992	1617
1993	2133
1994	3075
1995	4462
1996	5127
1997	6139
1998	7501
1999	7899
2000	8385
2001	9413
2002	9670
2003	10,415
2004	11,711
2006	12768

SOURCE: COMEPO *Plan de Desarrollo del Posgrado Nacional* (National Graduate Studies Development Plan), p. 16; ANUIES 2006.

all of them are SNI members) that work in its eight departments located in Mexico City, and in the cities of Guadalajara, Irapuato, Mérida, Querétaro and Saltillo. During the 2003 academic year, CINVESTAV granted 151 doctoral degrees in natural and exact sciences; biological and health disciplines; technology and engineering, and social sciences and humanities (CINVESTAV, web page). Among the public universities, UAM, *Universidad de Guadalajara* and *Universidad Autónoma de Nuevo León* also have significant numbers of researchers with a large fraction of which are SNI members: 629, at UAM, 201, at UdG and 183, at UANL (quoted from the institution's web pages).

Research constitutes a substantial activity only in a handful of the numerous private universities in Mexico. ITESM, the *Universidad de las Américas* (UDLAP), and UIA are good examples. In ITESM—one of the best well-known private institutions—research is focused on innovation, technological development and competitiveness; planning for sustainable development; protection of the environment; and the improvement of education. UDLAP's main areas of interest are anthropology, political science, economics, history, international relations, sociology, computing and communications. Research at UIA is organized in different departments where scientific and humanistic disciplines are strong. Although the number of researchers at these three universities that are SNI members was until recently low (less than 100), their number is growing. Recent figures show ITESM and UIA graduating each some twenty-five PhDs per year and ITESM as having 194 members in their staff belonging to SNI (UIA 2005; ITESM 2005)

In order to strengthen the quality of masters and doctoral programs offered by the Mexican system of HE, in 1991 CONACYT began to operate the *Padrón Nacional de Posgrados* (PNP), a registry of good quality graduate programs. It classifies masters and doctoral programs in two categories: a) Competitive at an international level, *i.e.*, excellent, and b) High-level. This is the most important instrument of the Federal Government to assure the quality of graduate education and in fact, it is the most widely accepted form of accreditation within the Mexican academic community (Alcantara and Canales 2004; Rodriguez 2004). During the 1999–2000 academic year, only 406 (13.9 percent) programs were incorporated into the PNP out of 2,908 graduate programs (masters and doctoral).

This instrument, along with the *Programa Integral para el Fomento del Posgrado* (PIFOP) is part of the *Programa para el Fortalecimiento del Posgrado Nacional* (PFPN), launched by the federal government at the beginning of the 2000–2006 Federal administration. The PFPN's main objective is to improve and assure the quality of graduate programs offered by the country's institutions of HE. Another goal of this national program is to expand opportunities for training scientists, humanists and technologists through good quality graduate education.

It is worth acknowledging that during the last decades, the growth of graduate education in Mexico has been an uneven process, both in terms of program quality and in the scope of different fields of knowledge. In some cases, there exists a weak relationship between doctoral education and the needs of the social and productive sectors. The strong concentration of enrollment in a few fields of knowledge has also restricted the creation of a diversified scientific and technological basis in order to overcome the challenges facing the nation. The Mexican scientific community is small and it is strongly concentrated at the public institutions of HE. This is in part due to the low levels of investment in research and development made by the productive sector. Therefore, the flux of technological transfer from universities to industry is very weak.

According to CONACYT's 2001–2003 report, of the total number of doctoral students enrolled in the year 2000 (8,385), only 1,220 completed their degrees (CONACYT 2004). Distribution of enrollment by field in doctoral studies shows that the highest concentration is in the natural and exact sciences (29.7 percent), and the social sciences and administration (20.7 percent), followed by engineering and technology (16.5 percent); education and humanities (16.2 percent); health sciences (11.3 percent); and agriculture (5.6 percent). Table 8.5 shows the evolution of new doctors by field from 1986 to 1998.

According to the COMEPO development plan, it is likely that the number of doctoral programs and doctoral students in Mexico will continue to increase in the near future due to the current policies being implemented through several programs, such as the Program for the Improvement of the Professoriate (PROMEP), launched in 1996 by the Ministry of Education. During the last three years, this program has granted 2,461 scholarships to pursue graduate studies in Mexico and abroad. Another important instrument is the National Program for the Improvement of Academic Personnel (SUPERA), established by ANUIES. In addition, CONACYT's Integral Program for the Consolidation of Graduate Studies (PIFOP) provided support to 372 graduate programs in 2002 (COMEPO 2004)

As most public universities in Mexico have an autonomous status, they have the prerogative of establishing their own admission policies. Usually, applicants for graduate studies must meet some requirements, including an interview with one or several professors, a review of previous studies,

TABLE 8.5. Evolution of new doctorates by field (1986–1998)

Fields	*1986*	*1988*	*1990*	*1992*	*1994*	*1996*	*1998*	*Total 1986–1998*
Natural and Exact Sciences	53	54	66	85	98	143	185	1249
Agriculture	5	4	3	12	22	44	61	242
Health Sciences	8	21	36	39	44	71	87	594
Engineering and Technology	7	13	9	27	44	52	91	456
Humanities and Education	13	26	32	21	33	75	144	538
Social Sciences	46	63	55	81	83	125	166	1175
Total								4254

SOURCE: COMEPO, *Plan de Desarrollo del Posgrado Nacional* (National Graduate Studies Development Plan), p. 17.

a presentation of a research project, proficiency in a foreign language, and professional and research experience in order to be admitted into a doctoral program.

Although tuition and fees at most public institutions in Mexico are negligible, there are agencies that provide scholarships and financial aid for doctoral studies, either in Mexico or abroad. Since its creation in 1970, CONACYT has offered students and academic personnel a large number of scholarships and research grants. Scholarships for doctoral studies in Mexico help students to dedicate full time to their academic programs. In 2003, Mexico's federal agencies awarded 23,804 students with scholarships to pursue graduate studies (CONACYT 2004).

A COMPARATIVE EXPERIENCE IN DOCTORAL EDUCATION

A recent study conducted by Clements and Alcantara (2005) attempted to investigate primary stakeholder perspectives of doctoral education at three research-intensive institutions in Mexico and the United States. By exploring the insights of doctoral students, faculty and administrators using surveys, taped and transcribed interviews and content analysis of documents, this study triangulated observations of doctoral programs at three locations. The purpose of this array of methodological approaches was to analyze in depth the varied viewpoints of students, faculty and administrators on their experiences of, satisfaction with, and importance of, mentor-protégé relationships with regard to student degree completion in the two countries.

The authors observed that mentoring at the doctoral level is comprised of a number of both perceptible and barely visible activities, behaviors, experiences and interactions between professors and doctoral students. For this critical relationship to rely so heavily on the goodwill and conscientiousness of a single mentor may indicate one of the haunting problems of doctoral degree programs.

In this study professors and academic coordinators identified the factors that, in their view, favor or make difficult the mentoring association. The positive aspects include: personal trust (empathy), students' involvement in research projects preferably lead by mentor, full-time faculty and students, clear lines of research, strong commitment of the professor in the students' academic progress, and so on. On the other hand, a failed mentoring relationship could be due to the lack of the "pedagogical authority." This situation may happen when the student does not recognize that his/ her mentor is an expert in a specific field and that he/she is able to support and conduct the entire academic process that would eventually lead to the completion of the student's dissertation. Lack of authority may be attributed to little experience in the field and insecurity, as happens with young professors.

Student autonomy is also required to find and process data; autonomy also implies initiative and the search for new ideas and methodologies. A mentoring relationship could also fail when there is not enough empathy between the two partners, or when either the professor or the student is not able to dedicate enough time to the program. It is frequent, particularly in the Mexican case, that students have to work twenty to thirty hours per week outside the university. Problems exist also when the professor does not have tenure and has to comply with heavy teaching loads. Good academic facilities are a necessary condition for a program to be successful. These are taken for granted in the prestigious institutions, but, for example, at some of UNAM schools not all full-time professors have office space and a computer.

CONCLUSION

Although graduate education has long been present in Mexico, its development has been slow and its productivity is still low. It is only in the last score of years that it has become widespread, rather than being limited to a handful of universities in two or three cities; when the total number of graduates each year have consistently reached more than a thousand; and when program diversification has allowed many fields of study to be covered instead of just a few.

Doctoral programs have followed the above trends, but at a smaller scale and lower pace of development. The annual number of PhD graduates is small when compared to Mexico's total population, and the numbers of students enrolled in programs leading to a doctoral degree remain less than 1 percent of total enrollments in HE. In addition, the numbers of institutions offering doctoral programs are still limited, mostly public, and concentrated in few geographical locations.

It is worth noting both that public policies keep supporting programs that assist universities to administer good doctoral programs as well as to have more PhDs in their staff. And there is a growing interest shown by private institutions in recruiting doctoral graduates and offering doctoral programs. In addition, while it is true that yearly PhDs output is low, most doctoral programs have good quality.

However, the demand for PhD graduates from business, industry and even government continues to be small, and the non-university positions open for them every year are quite limited. Furthermore, the slow pace of the Mexican economy, the absence of clearly stated and well known national development policies, and the country's narrow interest in innovation, science and technological development indicate that the demand for PhDs will remain restricted to that exerted by the HE sector.

GLOSSARY

AIC	Mexican Academy of Sciences
ANUIES	National Association of Universities and Higher Education Institutions
CENEVAL	National Assessment Center for Higher Education
CIEES	Peer Review Committees for Higher Education
CINVESTAV	Center for Research and Advanced Studies
COMEPO	Mexican Council for Graduate Studies
CONACYT	National Council for Science and Technology
COPAES	Accreditation Council for Higher Education
FOMES	Improvement Fund for Higher Education
ITESM	Monterrey Technological Institute for Higher Education

OCDE	Organization for Economic Co-operation and Development
PFPN	National Program to Consolidate Graduate Studies
PNP	National Registry of Graduate Programs
PROMEP	Program for the Improvement of the Professoriate
SEP	Ministry of Education
SES	Under Secretariat for Higher Education
SNI	National Researchers System
SUPERA	National Program for Academic Improvement
UAM	Metropolitan Autonomous University
UDLAP	Las Americas University, Puebla
UIA	Iberoamerican University
UNAM	National Autonomous University of Mexico

BIBLIOGRAPHY

AIC, Academia de la Investigación Científica (Mexican Academy of Sciences). 1973. *Coloquios sobre políticas nacionales en Ciencia y Tecnología*, (*National public policies on science and technology colloquia*), México.

Alcántara, Armando, and Alejandro Canales. 2004. "Tendencias y Disyuntivas en la Evaluación del Posgrado" ("Trends and conflicts in graduate studies assessment"). In *La Academia en Jaque. Perspectivas Políticas sobre la Evaluación de la Educación Superior en México* (*Academia at risk, political perspectives on higher education assessment in Mexico*), edited by Imanol Ordorika, 113–30. México: UNAM-Miguel Ángel Porrúa.

ANUIES, Asociación Nacional de Universidades e Instituciones de Educación Superior (National Association of Universities and Higher Education Institutions). 2002. *Anuario Estadístico* (*Statistical yearbook*) México: ANUIES.

Blanco, José. 2001. *La UNAM: su estructura, sus aportes, su crisis, su futuro (The National Autonomous University of Mexico: its structure, its contributions, its crisis, its future).* Mexico: CONACULTA-CONACYT-FCE, Fondo de Cultura Económica, 45.

Clements, Margaret, and Armando Alcántara. 2005. "Mentoring Practices in Doctoral Programs in Mexico and the United States: Growing Wiser Together." Paper Prepared for the 49th Annual Meeting of the Comparative and International Education Society, 22–26 March. Palo Alto, CA: Stanford University

COMEPO, Consejo Mexicano de Estudios de Posgrado, A. C. (Mexican Council of Graduate Studies, A.C.). *Estrategia Nacional de Autoevaluación de Programas de Posgrado (National strategy for graduate programs self assessment).* http://www.comepo.org.mx.

SEP, Coordinación Nacional para la Planeación de la Educación Superior (National Coordination for Higher Education Planning). 1982. *El desarrollo del posgrado en la educación superior* (*The development of graduate studies in higher education*). México: SEP-ANUIES.

———. 2004. *Plan de Desarrollo del Posgrado Nacional (National Graduate Studies Development Plan)*. http://www.comepo.org.mx.

CONACYT, Consejo Nacional de Ciencia y Tecnología (National Council for Science and Technology). 1976a. *Plan Nacional Indicativo de Ciencia y Tecnología (National Plan for Science and Technology)*. México.

———. 1976b. *Programa Nacional Controlado de Becas* (*National Plan for Controlled Scholarships)*. México.

———. 2000. *Indicadores de Actividades Científicas y Tecnológicas (Science and Technology Indicators)*. México.

———. 2001. *Programa de Fomento al Posgrado Nacional* (*National program for the advancement of graduate studies)*. http://www.conacyt.mx.

———. 2004. *Informe 2001–2003 y Perspectivas para el 2004. (2001–2003 Report and perspectives for 2004)*. http://www.conacyt.mx.

European Commission. 2003. Directorate-General for Research Information and Communication Unit, http://europa.eu.int/comm/research/rtdinfo_en.html.

ITESM. 2005. "La investigación y el Posgrado 2003–2004" ("Research and Graduate Studies") Mexico: Tecnológico de Monterrey (Monterrey Institute for Technology and Hogher Studies), 22, 34–37.

Kent, Rollin. 2004. "Private Sector Expansion and Emerging Policy Responses in Mexican Higher Education", AIHEPS, 17th Annual Conference of the Consortium of Higher Education Researchers, The Netherlands.

King, Richard G. 1971. *The Provincial Universities of Mexico*. New York: Praeger Publishers.

Levy, Daniel. 1986. *Private Higher Education in Latin America: Private Challenges to Public Dominance.* Chicago: University of Chicago Press.

Malo, Salvador, Jonathan Garst, and Graciela Garza. 1981. *El egresado de posgrado de la UNAM* (*The degree recipients of UNAM graduate programs)*. México: UNAM.

Malo, Salvador, and Isabel Menocal. 1983. La Academia y los estudios de posgrado (*Academia and graduate studies). Ciencia* 34: 77–89.

OECD. 1997. *Reviews of National Policies for Education: Mexico, Higher Education.* Paris: OECD.

Osborn II, N. Thomas. 1987. *La educación superior en México* (*Higher education in Mexico)*. México: Fondo de Cultura Económica.

Rangel Guerra, Alfonso. 1979. *La educación superior en México* (*Higher education in Mexico)*. México: El Colegio de México.

Rodríguez, Roberto. 2004. "Acreditación, ¿Ave Fénix de la Educación Superior?" ("Accreditation: The phoenix of higher education?"). In *La Academia en Jaque. Perspectivas Políticas sobre la Evaluación de la Educación Superior en México (Academia at risk, political perspectives on higher education assessment in Mexico)*, edited by Imanol Ordorika, 175–222. México: UNAM-Miguel Ángel Porrúa.

Ruiz Herrerá, José. 1983. "Desarrollo del Posgrado" Foro de Consulta Popular: el Sistema Universitario ("Graduate studies development", Community Survey Forum: The university system). México: SEP-ANUIES.

Secretaría de Educación Pública. 2002., *Estadísticas de la Matrícula de Educación Superior (Statistics on higher education enrollment).* http://www.sep.gob.mx.

Poder Ejecutivo Federal (Federal Executive Branch). 2001. *Programa Especial de Ciencia y Tecnología 2001–2006. (2001–2006 Special program on science and technology).* México: PEF.

UIA. 2005. Primer Informe del Rector 2004–2005, Universidad Iberoamericana (2004–2005 Rector's Report). México, 203.

Universidad Nacional Autónoma de México. 2001. *Reglamento General de Estudios de Posgrado (Graduate studies bylaws of the National Autonomous University of Mexico).* México: Dirección de General de Estudios de Legislación Universitaria (General Office for University Legislation).

· III ·

DOCTORAL EDUCATION IN AUSTRALASIA

9 • AUSTRALIA

TERRY EVANS, BARBARA EVANS, AND HELENE MARSH

Australia is a large country geographically, but with a small population of about twenty million people. It has the eighteenth largest economy in the world. It is significant geo-politically partly due to it its historical and linguistic connections and its treaty arrangements with the UK and USA, and partly due to its location in the Asia-Pacific region. Australia has thirty-nine universities, the largest of which has around 40,000 students and the smallest less than 5,000 students. The oldest universities were established in the 1850s and the newest established in the past decade. Two universities are small private universities (one Catholic, one secular), and there is a large publicly funded Catholic university. All universities offer doctoral degrees, although the new small universities have tiny enrollments of less than one hundred doctoral students, whereas the larger universities have enrollments of well over one thousand. Australia has a federal system of government with six states and two territories. Most universities are established under state acts of parliament and formally report to their state's parliament. However, the bulk of government funding to universities comes from the Australian Government, and higher education policy is deliberated and enacted principally at that level of government. In recent years, the proportions of funding those universities have derived from Australian Government sources have decreased markedly, with about 40 percent of all funding now coming directly from this source. Increasing proportions of funding have come from students' fees and from non-government sources.

Most domestic undergraduate students' tuition in Australian universities is subsidized by the Australian government, whereas most post-graduate coursework students (or their employers) pay for their own tuition. However, PhDs are classified as research, as distinct from coursework, degrees and the tuition costs are met by the Australian Government. Changes in this funding formula are a focus of this paper. Masters and doctoral degrees are classified as research degrees if at least two-thirds of the program consists of the design, development, implementation, and reporting of research or scholarship leading to the production of new knowledge or creative works.

Research is seen as fundamental to the PhD in Australia (see Council of Deans & Directors of Graduate Studies Guidelines, http://www.ddogs.edu/au/cgi-bin/papers.pl). The PhD commenced in Australia in 1946 with the first three awards being made at the University of Melbourne in 1948, although higher doctorates (for example, DSc, DLitt) were awarded in the nineteenth century (Pearson 2005). The form of PhD education adopted in Australia derived principally from the United Kingdom in the early twentieth century. Research on early Australian PhD theses by Evans and Tregenza (2004) shows that it was common for the first PhD candidates (typically in the sciences) to spend time at a UK university and/or for a UK academic to be involved in their supervision or mentoring. Early Australian doctoral pedagogy emulated the UK personal tutor relationships in undergraduate education within a disciplinary departmental system (Simpson 1983; Pearson and Ford 1997; Becher, Henkel, and Kogan 1994). Individual students were closely associated with individual professors or other academic staff who "supervised" the research and otherwise generally supported it with material, social, and intellectual resources. This approach has been described by Clark as an "extension of the BAHons with some research" (Clark 1995, 79).

The numbers of PhD students in Australia grew rapidly through the early twenty-first century. Most recently the increase in domestic numbers has slowed somewhat, whereas the numbers of international students have increased sharply in the past decade. A particularly strong growth occurred in the 1990s following the expansion of the university system to incorporate the former Colleges of Advanced Education (Holbrook and Johnston 1999; Pearson and Ford 1997). In addition, doctoral study has further diversified in terms of the range of fields of study being pursued (ARC/NBEET 1996; Evans, Macauley, Pearson, and Tregenza 2003a, 2003b). With this growth arose concerns about the nature, purpose and quality of doctorates, or more broadly "research training" as research masters and research doctorates are known (AVVC 1987; Dawkins 1988; Kemp 1999). Concerns continued to be raised about completion times and rates (DEET 1988; Martin, Maclachlan, and Karmel 2001), "wastage" of resources (Kemp

1999; Martin, Maclachlan, and Karmel 2001), the relevance of the award (Sekhon 1989; Mullins and Kiley 1998) and calls for new approaches and programs (Clarke 1996). Increasingly, PhD graduates have varying employment outcomes and circumstances, so that the PhD is no longer seen only as principally an apprenticeship for being a university academic or a research scientist (Thomson and others 2001).

One response to changing expectations of doctoral study was the development of professional doctorates (Evans 1997; Trigwell and others 1997; McWilliam and others 2002). McWilliam and others (2002) reported that a total of 131 professional doctorate programs were offered by thirty-five Australian universities, especially in the fields of education, health, psychology, and business. Another response has been a liberalization of PhD rules to accommodate new specialties and ways in which research can be carried out and theses presented (Pearson and Ford 1997, 23–24; Evans, Macauley, Pearson, and Tregenza 2003a). What seems evident is that the PhD in these professional fields is proving more attractive than professional doctorates. McWilliam and others (2002, 55) stated that in 2001 thirteen professional doctorate programs were either "suspended or not commenced." Evans, Macauley, Pearson & Tregenza (2004), based on substantial bibliometric study of all Australian PhD thesis titles, (Macauley, Evans, Pearson, and Tregenza 2004) concluded that the PhDs awarded in professional fields were increasingly outnumbering the professional doctorates in those same fields to the extent that in most cases the professional doctorate programs appeared unviable.

Australian scholars have shown a growing interest in research and scholarship in doctoral education, especially since the early 1990s. There have been government-funded reports on doctoral education (Cullen, Pearson, Saha, and Spear 1994; Parry and Hayden 1994; Pearson and Ford 1997; Trigwell and others 1997; McWilliam and others 2002; Neumann 2003); government policy reviews that included aspects of doctoral education (Kemp 1999; West 1998); conferences on doctoral education (for example, the Quality in Postgraduate Research conferences, the Professional Doctorate conferences, and more specific conferences such as the Research on Doctoral Education conferences and the Australian Association for Research in Education mini-conference on Defining the Doctorate in 2003); a new journal *Studies In Research: Training, Evaluation and Impact* was launched in 2005; special issues of journals (for example, the *Australian Universities' Review* [38: 2 & 43: 2] in 1995 and 2000 respectively, *Higher Education Research and Development* [21: 2] in 2002 and [24: 2] in 2005,

Australian Educational Researcher [29: 3] in 2002); books (for example, Green, Maxwell, and Shanahan 2002; Bartlett and Mercer 2001; and Holbrook and Johnston 1999), as well as many articles, papers and chapters in various locations. Within this important work there has been considerable focus on the theory and practice of doctoral education, especially concerning contemporary circumstances and conditions, or particular elements of policy and practice (for example, Brennan 1998; Evans 1995, 2000, 2001, 2002; Evans and Pearson 1999; Holbrook, Bourke, Farley, and Carmichael 2001; Johnson, Lee, and Green 2000; Kiley and Mullins 2002; Lee, Green, and Brennan 2000; McWilliam and Taylor 2001; Pearson 1996, 1999; Pearson and Brew 2002; Seddon 2001). However, published work that takes a broader social and historical view of the PhD is much less evident and more limited in scope (see Coaldrake and Stedman 1998, 115, 214; Pearson 2005).

DOCTORAL PROGRAMS IN AUSTRALIA—DESCRIPTION AND DATA

The PhD has continued to evolve over recent decades. It has become increasingly flexible, accommodating new areas of human endeavor such as the creative and performing arts as appropriate "disciplines" for research. It has also accommodated an increased demand from governments and the community for relevance and applied value of the work undertaken. As noted above, PhDs in professional fields have increased strongly since the late 1980s.

As described earlier, doctoral programs in Australia include PhDs (by far the most common) and other doctorates. Many of the "other doctorates" are self-described as "professional doctorates"; other programs, such as Doctor of Psychology, Doctor of Creative Arts, or Doctor of Divinity, preceded the "professional doctorate" nomenclature and may or may not be described as such today. However, the more fundamental distinction (because it affects funding and status) is between doctorates by research and doctorates by coursework. Tables 9.1 and 9.2 show, respectively, the numbers of all doctoral students and then numbers of research doctoral students in 2003 by institution, and mode and type of attendance (the most recent year for which data are available).

The numerical differences between the enrollment figures in the tables show that there are very few (about 1,700) coursework doctorate students in Australia. The balance between male and female total enrollments is very close, with 51 percent male and 49 percent female enrollments. "Internal enrollments" are those who enrolled to attend on-campus; external being those who are enrolled off-campus; that is, studying by distance education.

TABLE 9.1. All doctoral students by institution, and mode and type of enrollment, and gender, 2003

	Internal			*External*			*Multi-modal*			*Gender*		*Persons*
Institution	*Full-time*	*Part-time*	*Sub-total*	*Full-time*	*Part-time*	*Sub-total*	*Full-time*	*Part-time*	*Sub-total*	*Males*	*Females*	
Adelaide University	898	439	1,337	18	34	52	3	0	3	738	654	1,392
Australian Catholic University	80	195	275	2	2	4	0	0	0	141	138	279
Australian Defence Force Academy	58	59	117	3	1	4	0	0	0	104	17	121
Australian Maritime College	12	0	12	1	1	2	2	1	3	14	3	17
Australian National University	1,270	317	1,587	0	0	0	0	0	0	886	701	1,587
Bond University	54	28	82	0	0	0	0	1	1	50	33	83
Central Queensland University	94	55	149	17	68	85	2	0	2	130	106	236
Charles Darwin University	69	51	120	2	12	14	26	23	49	95	88	183

TABLE 9.1. *(continued)*

	Internal			*External*			*Multi-modal*			*Gender*		*Persons*
Institution	*Full-time*	*Part-time*	*Sub-total*	*Full-time*	*Part-time*	*Sub-total*	*Full-time*	*Part-time*	*Sub-total*	*Males*	*Females*	
Charles Sturt University	84	29	113	39	234	273	3	1	4	198	192	390
Curtin University of Technology	480	422	902	33	393	426	20	42	62	777	613	1,390
Deakin University	350	113	463	85	285	370	4	3	7	404	436	840
Edith Cowan University	258	163	421	39	72	111	14	9	23	269	286	555
Flinders Univ of South Australia	388	319	707	10	42	52	0	5	5	352	412	764
Griffith University	587	445	1,032	16	48	64	8	20	28	541	583	1,124
James Cook University	340	198	538	13	28	41	1	0	1	276	304	580
La Trobe University	510	519	1,029	5	0	5	0	0	0	396	638	1,034
Macquarie University	437	409	846	12	54	66	5	11	16	478	450	928

Melbourne College of Divinity	19	10	29	4	12	16	2	6	8	35	18	53
Monash University	1,303	842	2,145	19	113	132	4	13	17	1,092	1,202	2,294
Murdoch University	437	198	635	13	24	37	4	3	7	308	371	679
Queensland Univ of Technology	557	279	836	16	80	96	15	19	34	508	458	966
Royal Melbourne Inst of Technology	523	519	1,042	20	24	44	0	0	0	653	433	1,086
Southern Cross University	157	106	263	46	108	154	2	3	5	256	166	422
Swinburne University of Technology	260	187	447	0	0	0	0	0	0	267	180	447
Tabor College	4	0	4	1	0	1	0	0	0	4	1	5
University of Ballarat	84	58	142	0	0	0	0	0	0	70	72	142
University of Canberra	106	98	204	0	0	0	0	0	0	115	89	204

TABLE 9.1. *(continued)*

	Internal			*External*			*Multi-modal*			*Gender*		*Persons*
Institution	*Full-time*	*Part-time*	*Sub-total*	*Full-time*	*Part-time*	*Sub-total*	*Full-time*	*Part-time*	*Sub-total*	*Males*	*Females*	
University of Melbourne	2,223	860	3,083	4	10	14	2	0	2	1,362	1,737	3,099
University of New England	211	52	263	79	214	293	2	2	4	287	273	560
University of New South Wales	1,615	535	2,150	43	33	76	2	0	2	1,251	977	2,228
University of Newcastle	394	398	792	38	51	89	9	4	13	486	408	894
University of Notre Dame	20	16	36	0	0	0	0	0	0	19	17	36
University of Queensland	2,042	1,013	3,055	0	3	3	3	4	7	1,609	1,456	3,065
University of South Australia	929	476	1,405	11	81	92	10	2	12	932	577	1,509
University of Southern Queensland	74	18	92	34	105	139	1	0	1	138	94	232

University of Sydney	1,853	854	2,707	13	49	62	5	2	7	1,300	1,476	2,776
University of Tasmania	449	365	814	1	4	5	2	8	10	430	399	829
University of Technology, Sydney	449	345	794	3	4	7	2	2	4	417	388	805
University of the Sunshine Coast	20	23	43	0	9	9	0	1	1	36	17	53
University of Western Australia	1,088	368	1,456	0	0	0	0	0	0	745	711	1,456
University of Western Sydney	371	340	711	0	1	1	0	1	1	348	365	713
University of Wollongong	628	280	908	2	9	11	2	0	2	490	431	921
Victoria University	254	280	534	0	0	0	0	0	0	287	247	534
Total	22,039	12,281	34,320	642	2,208	2,850	155	186	341	19,294	18,217	37,511

SOURCE: DEST

TABLE 9.2. Research doctoral students by institution, and mode and type of enrollment, and gender 2003

	Internal			External			Multi-modal			Gender		Persons
Institution	*Full-time*	*Part-time*	*Sub-total*	*Full-time*	*Part-time*	*Sub-total*	*Full-time*	*Part-time*	*Sub-total*	*Males*	*Females*	
Adelaide University	869	435	1,304	18	33	51	3	0	3	717	641	1,358
Australian National University	1,266	317	1,583	0	0	0	0	0	0	886	697	1,583
Australian Catholic University	69	192	261	2	2	4	0	0	0	138	127	265
Australian Defence Force	56	49	105	3	1	4	0	0	0	92	17	109
Australian Maritime College	12	0	12	1	1	2	2	1	3	14	3	17
Bond University	35	10	45	0	0	0	0	0	0	32	13	45
Central Queensland University	79	42	121	7	59	66	2	0	2	96	93	189
Charles Darwin University	68	43	111	0	0	0	26	23	49	85	75	160

Charles Stuart University	78	27	105	36	180	216	3	1	4	158	167	325
Curtin University of Technology	480	422	902	33	393	426	20	42	62	777	613	1,390
Deakin University	350	113	463	85	285	370	4	3	7	404	436	840
Edith Cowan University	205	123	328	8	69	77	10	8	18	209	214	423
Flinders Univ of South Australia	384	280	664	8	25	33	0	4	4	331	370	701
Griffith University	577	432	1,009	16	48	64	8	20	28	536	565	1,101
James Cook University	340	194	534	0	1	1	1	0	1	272	264	536
La Trobe University	501	497	998	5	0	5	0	0	0	393	610	1,003
Macquarie University	437	409	846	12	54	66	5	11	16	478	450	928
Melbourne College of Divinity	19	7	26	4	0	4	2	2	4	23	11	34
Monash University	1,303	842	2,145	19	113	132	4	13	17	1,092	1,202	2,294

TABLE 9.2. *(continued)*

	Internal			*External*			*Multi-modal*			*Gender*		*Persons*
Institution	*Full-time*	*Part-time*	*Sub-total*	*Full-time*	*Part-time*	*Sub-total*	*Full-time*	*Part-time*	*Sub-total*	*Males*	*Females*	
Murdoch University	429	180	609	13	24	37	4	3	7	299	354	653
Queensland Univ of Technology	553	279	832	16	80	96	15	19	34	505	457	962
Royal Melbourne Inst of Tech	517	499	1,016	20	24	44	0	0	0	635	425	1,060
Southern Cross University	157	106	263	46	108	154	2	3	5	256	166	422
Swinburne Univ of Technology	260	187	447	0	0	0	0	0	0	267	180	447
University of Ballarat	84	58	142	0	0	0	0	0	0	70	72	142
University of Canberra	104	96	200	0	0	0	0	0	0	111	89	200
University of Melbourne	2,140	818	2,958	4	10	14	1	0	1	1,340	1,633	2,973

University of New England	204	51	255	70	200	270	2	2	4	277	252	529
University of New South Wales	1,615	535	2,150	43	33	76	2	0	2	1,251	977	2,228
University of Newcastle	394	324	718	38	51	89	9	3	12	420	399	819
University of Notre Dame	20	16	36	0	0	0	0	0	0	19	17	36
University of Queensland	2,013	988	3,001	0	0	0	0	0	0	1,595	1,406	3,001
University of South Australia	400	448	848	11	81	92	7	2	9	521	428	949
Univ of Southern Queensland	62	9	71	32	43	75	1	0	1	78	69	147
University of Sydney	1,834	849	2,683	13	49	62	5	2	7	1,298	1,454	2,752
University of Tasmania	449	362	811	1	2	3	2	8	10	428	396	824

TABLE 9.2. *(continued)*

	Internal			*External*			*Multi-modal*			*Gender*		*Persons*
Institution	*Full-time*	*Part-time*	*Sub-total*	*Full-time*	*Part-time*	*Sub-total*	*Full-time*	*Part-time*	*Sub-total*	*Males*	*Females*	
Univ of Technology, Sydney	449	345	794	3	4	7	2	2	4	417	388	805
University of the Sunshine Coast	20	23	43	0	9	9	0	1	1	36	17	53
University of Western Australia	1,088	368	1,456	0	0	0	0	0	0	745	711	1,456
University of Western Sydney	371	336	707	0	0	0	0	0	0	343	364	707
University of Wollongong	619	271	890	2	9	11	2	0	2	487	416	903
Victoria University	245	261	506	0	0	0	0	0	0	284	222	506
Total	21,155	11,843	32,998	569	1,991	2,560	144	173	317	18,415	17,460	35,875

SOURCE: DES

TABLE 9.3. Australian Indigenous research doctoral students by broad field of study, 2003

Field of study	*Doctorates*
Natural & Physical Sciences	14
IT	2
Engineering & Related Technology	5
Architecture & Building	1
Agriculture, Environment and Related Studies	3
Health	21
Education	37
Management & Commerce	11
Society & Culture	71
Creative & Performing Arts	10
Food, Hospitality & Personal Services	0
Total	175

SOURCE: DEST

However, in practice there can be a considerable overlap between these two enrollment modes across institutions, with some on-campus students working for most or a substantial part of their candidature away from the campus (even overseas), and some university staff enrolled off-campus as part-time doctoral students of their own university where they work and attend each day. "Multi-modal candidature" is a strange category for doctoral study. It is really an enrollment category used by the Government (in effect, the Department of Education, Science & Technology (DEST)) to indicate undergraduate and postgraduate students who are enrolled on-campus for one or more units (courses) and off-campus for the balance. Individual institutions provide the data to DEST categorized in the appropriate enrollment categories; however, for doctoral students it is unclear what this data really means. The best estimate is that it means that multi-modal enrollments are those where the doctoral students have a mix of both on-campus and off-campus doctoral experience. However, to some degree, this probably applies to many other doctoral students in Australia!

Table 9.3 shows the numbers of Aboriginal and Torres Strait Islander (Indigenous) students enrolled by their Broad Field of Study (the classification system of subjects and disciplines used by government). Only those fields in which Indigenous students are enrolled are represented in the table.

The proportion of Indigenous doctoral students is low but increasing

TABLE 9.4. Growth in Australian PhD completions

Year	*No. of completions*
1950	8
1960	97
1970	584
1980	836
1990	1367
2000	3247

SOURCE: DEST

FIGURE 9.1. National completions data—doctorates by research

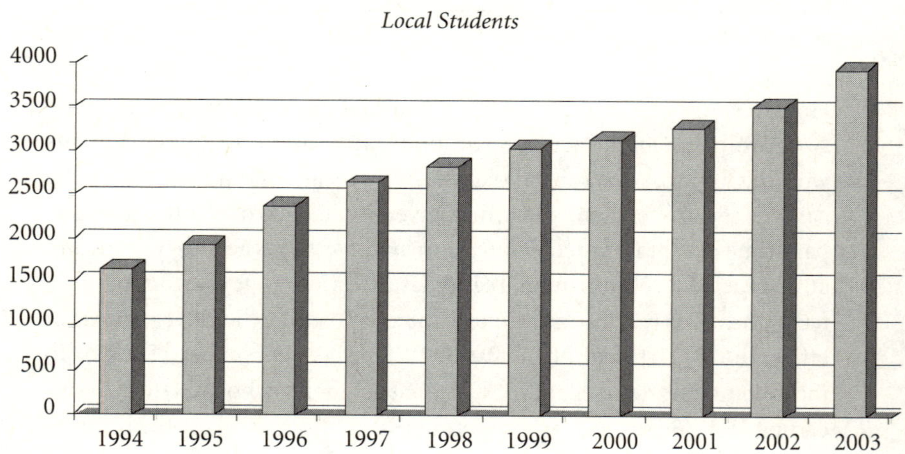

SOURCE: DEST

slowly; it remains much less (0.5 percent) than the proportion of Aboriginal and Torres Strait Islander peoples in the Australian population (about 2 percent). However, the number and proportion of doctoral students may be a slight underestimate because data collectors rely on voluntary declaration by students at enrollment. Table 9.3 shows a high proportion of these students in the Education and Health Fields, which are areas of major concern and emphasis within and for Indigenous communities.

FIGURE 9.2. National completions data—doctorates by research

International Students

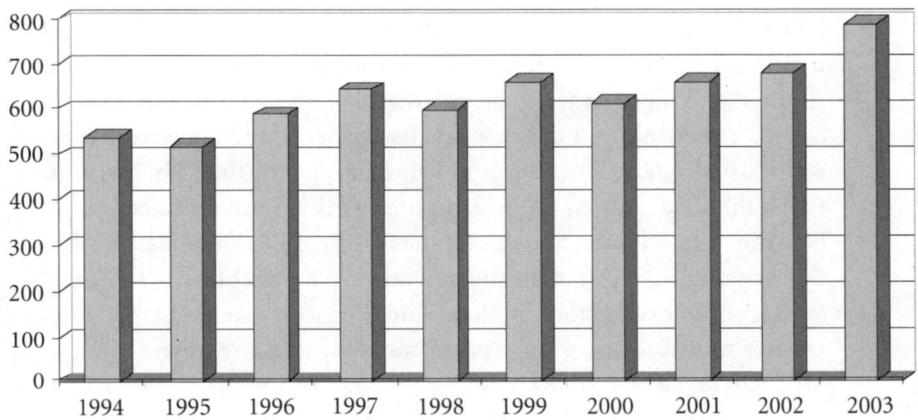

SOURCE: DEST

Table 9.1 lists all thirty-nine universities, plus four other institutions that have a profile in doctoral education (table 9.2 has one institution less, Tabor College—"a multi-denominational charismatic Christian college"—did not offer research doctorates). All Australian universities are entitled to award doctoral degrees. The age and size of the universities involved, and their research profiles vary markedly, and concerns have been raised about the capacity of the newest and smallest universities to provide good quality doctoral programs, given their limited research capacity and experience. These, and other concerns, have led the Council of Australian Deans & Directors of Graduate Studies (DDOGS) to discuss quality, quality assurance and best practices in Australian doctoral education (the authors are members if the Council and have been actively involved in this work). The Council has developed national guidelines on best practices regarding the structure, content and examination of doctoral programs (see http://www.ddogs.edu.au/cgi-bin/papers.pl).

Nationally, PhD completions have increased continuously since 1950 (table 9.4), particularly in recent years. National completions data for doctorates by research over the years 1994–2003 show continuing growth for local students (figure 9.1) and a somewhat flatter, but increasing, growth for international students (figure 9.2). It is noteworthy that international students have a lower attrition rate than local students.

ENTRY PROFILES AND PATTERNS OF DOCTORAL CANDIDATURE

As noted above, there are approximately 36,000 students enrolled in Australian doctoral programs by research in 2005 (with approximately a further 1,700 in doctorates by coursework). There are roughly equal numbers of male and female students, with slightly more female local students and slightly more male international students. Approximately 6,000 are international students and 14,000 students are enrolled part-time, which usually means that the candidate is also in full-time employment. Part-time candidature in Australian universities is usually calculated as half-time candidature. Sometimes the acronym EFT (Equivalent Full-Time) is used in government and other data to represent doctoral "load" (that is volume of doctoral students, funding, workload etc). Therefore, 500 full-time students and 500 part-time students are represented as 750 EFT load for these purposes.

With regard to the age of entry to PhD study, two general patterns are seen. Many students (often full-time and on a scholarship) enter immediately after completing their undergraduate study at between twenty-three and twenty-six-years of age, and another group (mostly part-time and employed full-time) enters in their thirties or later. The average age of Australian PhD students is thirty-seven years.

THE PHD

In Australian universities the PhD is awarded by "the university" itself, as opposed to the faculty. Typically, undergraduate and postgraduate coursework degrees are awarded by the particular faculties on behalf of the university. Universities adopt one of these approaches for other coursework and professional doctorates, and also for research masters degrees. Although Australian PhD work is located within particular department(s), school(s), or faculty(ies), once it comes to the examination (see sub-heading "Examination" below), the university manages the processes centrally and offers the award itself. The fact that in some universities some doctoral candidates are not examined and awarded by the university but rather by the faculty, leads to greater uncertainty and variability in the quality and standards of these degrees.

In Australia the PhD program is typically a three to four year full-time program of supervised research and scholarship culminating in the preparation of a thesis (as it is called in Australia, rather than dissertation as in the USA) of 80,000 to 100,000 words that is judged by external examiners to make a significant contribution to knowledge and scholarship in the discipline.

ENTRY

Students typically enter the PhD after having completed at least a four year honors program (or its equivalent) with Honors First Class (H1) or Honors Upper Second Class (H2A) grades (equivalent to a Grade Point Average of about 3.3 to 3.5). Honors programs include a significant research component in their final year. There has been a recent trend for higher-achieving students to complete two undergraduate degrees "combined" before entering an honors year in one of their disciplines. Entry to the PhD after completion of a research master's degree has been declining over recent years, although entry with a coursework master's degree with similar research components and grades to honors degrees has increased, especially for part-time students entering mid- or late-career in professional areas.

PROGRAM STRUCTURE AND CONTENT

Usual elements of Australian PhD programs include the major research project, research skills preparation, preparing relevant ethics and grant applications, attending and presenting seminars, defined writing requirements at each stage of candidature, developing generic skills, oral presentations, and overseas research visits. Publication during candidature is encouraged, particularly in the sciences. Discipline-based research is conducted in academic departments. Graduate Schools exist in many, but not all, Australian universities and these provide additional support, academic activities and generic skills programs, leadership programs, and career planning. They usually have overall authority for candidature, supervision, internal policy and quality assurance.

For students enrolled "full-time" (sometimes only if they are also holding a scholarship), "allowable" outside work commitments are to be no more than six to eight hours per week. Whilst developing teaching experience is encouraged, it is expected to be within the allowable six to eight hours. Students who are not on a scholarship may not have such limitations placed upon them; however, normal progress for a full-time student is expected and monitored.

There is considerable variation in the amount of "coursework" required in different PhD programs. However, most programs include some components that could be broadly described as coursework. Government regulation precludes more than 33.3 percent coursework in a research doctorate. In the sciences, often no formal discipline-based coursework is required. Other disciplines have variable amounts of supporting "hurdle coursework" that must be completed at an appropriate standard before the student may continue to the research project. Where formal discipline-based coursework is required, this is often in the newer PhD fields or where the undergraduate qualification is more professionally oriented (for example, Economics and Commerce). Most universities have a rigorous hurdle confirmation of candidature at about twelve months. This normally includes the acquisition of necessary technical and methodological skills, completion of any required coursework subjects, completion of an adequate amount of research, submission of a significant piece of writing, a public presentation on their project, and an interview by a "confirmation committee."

Developing an international perspective is becoming increasingly important in the training of PhD students. The international mobility of PhD students during their candidature is increasing and joint doctoral programs, such as the French "cotutelle," are becoming more popular. But does the academic community see the PhD as an international degree? And if we do, are there consequent issues regarding common doctoral standards that should be adopted? Perhaps we see the beginning of this in the European Bologna Process, which aims to bring consistency and harmony to university education across Europe.

EXAMINATION

Successful completion of an Australian PhD is based on the assessment of the research thesis by two or more independent examiners who are external to the candidate's university. International examiners are encouraged. These arrangements provide an external quality assurance of PhD standards and outcomes. Internal examiners (all staff of the home university, including supervisors) are NOT permitted in Australian universities that require two examiners, although some that require three examiners may permit one examiner to be from within the university, providing the examiner is independent of the candidate and the doctoral work. However, supervisors may provide advice and context information to the examining panel through the Chair of Examiners. In effect, the examiners provide advice and recommendation to the university over the award of the degree. Their advice is highly influential and normally followed, except where there are disagreements or irregularities. Typically, the department or faculty in which the student is enrolled nominates examiners to the university, and usually an appropriate senior person reviews the examiners' reports before the responsible university committee deliberates on the outcome. In these ways, the faculty does have important roles to play in the examination process.

An oral defense of a candidate's thesis is rarely required of candidates in Australia (which is a significant departure from the UK heritage). However, a public presentation of their work before academic colleagues from within and often beyond their department is becoming increasingly expected or required. This would normally occur prior to final submission, thus providing an opportunity for collegial commentary and critique, and for verification of the student's "ownership" of the work.

FUNDING FOR HIGHER DEGREE RESEARCH STUDENTS

In 2005, the Australian Government provided over AUS $550 million to universities to support research training through the Research Training Scheme (RTS). This RTS funding is distributed to universities based on their research performance compared with all other universities. The components of this formula are 50 percent higher degree by research (HDR) completions, 40 percent research income, and 10 percent publications. (These are weighted for "high-cost (science)" or "low cost (humanities)" disciplines at 2.35 to 1.00, and at 2:1 for doctorates: masters programs.) This effectively provides "fee-free" places for domestic research students for up to two years for masters and four years for doctoral programs. Some universities enroll more HDR students than they have RTS places; however, universities rarely charge fees for these places. Therefore, almost all domestic HDR students do not pay tuition fees, which is a marked contrast to undergraduate and postgraduate coursework programs.

Most full-time students also receive a scholarship of approximately AUS $19,000 a year for up to three-and-a-half-years to cover living expenses. These scholarships are funded from a number of sources, including the Federal Government (1,550 scholarships), universities, research funding bodies such as the Australian Research Council or National Health and Medical Research Council, or through other research projects, organizations, and foundations. Part-time students normally fund their living costs from their employment income and are, therefore, less expensive on the public purse.

The Federal Government also provides 330 tuition scholarships to international students who then normally receive a scholarship for living expenses from the university at which they are enrolled. Through its foreign aid programs, the Federal Government also provides other scholarships to international students from particular developing countries, for both tuition and living expenses. There are also other scholarships for international students that are available from trusts and other agencies. However, many international students are funded from within their own countries by their governments or employers, or they pay themselves, sometimes with the help of family members.

POSSIBLE DIFFERENCES TO NORTH AMERICAN DOCTORAL PROGRAMS

Unlike American universities, all universities in Australia offer doctorates. There is also some evidence that doctoral education is more discipline focused in Australia than the US, with Canada somewhere in between. If one includes the coursework component, the expected (and actual) duration of candidature for full-time enrolled Australian doctoral students is shorter, at between three to four years.

There is less (if any) formal discipline-based coursework required of most Australian students, although there is an increasing amount of "generic" and "research training" "non-credit" coursework being expected in Australia. Unlike the US, and to a lesser extent Canada, the Australian examination system is dependent almost entirely on examiners external to the conferring university. The costs of doctoral study (by research) appear less for Australian students than in the US. Therefore, diversity, affirmative action, and minority issues are less evident in Australian doctoral policy and programs, although there are some specific sources of support to encourage Indigenous students to undertake doctorates. Postgraduate student associations play a significant role in providing support for doctoral students in most Australian universities.

SOME DOCTORAL PROGRAM ISSUES BY STAGE OF CANDIDATURE

Selection and Entry: Some Questions

How do we understand and accommodate the diverse purposes of doctoral study in contemporary Australia? What are the interests of students, universities, communities, government, business, industry, and research? In these contexts, do we have appropriate procedures to select the "right" students? Who are the "right" students? Should selection criteria be designed to choose those with the greatest "likelihood of success"? (A powerful incentive under the RTS.) If so, how do we balance providing opportunity for qualified students against certainty of outcome? How do we balance minimizing risks of non-completion against the potential of "risky" innovative research? How do these choices rest with requirements over anti-discrimination and other legislation? Do we focus sufficiently on the entire program—that is, getting the right student with the right supervisors in the right project at the right time?

Induction

Effective "transition" programs assist students to "hit the ground running." Early in candidature we need to establish clear responsibilities and agreed expectations of all those involved, and to identify the particular needs of individual students.

During Candidature

Procedures should be available to monitor student progress, maintain both structured and informal communication, and ensure collegiality and inclusion of students into the academic community. There should also be ways of identifying and supporting students "at risk" of non-completion.

Completion Issues

Exit surveys can provide valuable information, which if used effectively can significantly improve programs. Career planning should be considered throughout the program, not just at completion so that students are prepared and eager to move on.

Completion Rates (Attrition) and Times (Time to Degree, TTD)

It is very important to understand that international comparisons of these measures are extraordinarily difficult because the measures available in different countries are not comparable. This makes useful benchmarking of practices and outcomes equally difficult. Nevertheless there are some patterns that can be seen in these parameters across national boundaries. For example, there are clear discipline differences in attrition rates that are consistent internationally. In Australia, there was a dramatic increase in the importance of completions following the implementation of the RTS in late 2001 for the 2002 academic year (see section entitled Funding for Higher Degree Research Students above).

Fundamental questions that arise from considering these parameters are:

- Is attrition a problem, an indicator of a problem or both?
- Is there "good" attrition and "bad" attrition?
- Should we measure attrition after confirmation or qualifying exams?
- When does attrition become "wastage"?

Only one Australian study has been conducted: the National Study on Postgraduate Completion Rates DETYA 2001 (Martin, Maclachlin, and Karmel 2001). It examined the 1992 entering cohort of 5,550 local HDR students (2,650 doctorates) and evaluated outcomes in 1999 after seven to eight years. The findings showed that the actual doctoral completion rate in 1999 was 53 percent and the predicted overall doctoral completion rate was 65 percent. The average doctoral completion time was 3.7 years. There was no correlation with the research intensiveness of the university or the average commencing academic ability of postgraduates. Calculated "wastage" (i.e., candidature achieved but did not complete) was 23 percent.

Variability in completions rates was found to be due to:

- gender—female completion rates higher;
- study mode—full-time students much more likely to complete (~ 60 percent cf. ~ 40 percent);
- age—actual completion rates in 1999 decreased with increasing age;

<24	66 percent
25–29	52 percent
30–39	50 percent
40–49	40 percent
> 50	37 percent

- field of study—completion rates were higher for health sciences, sciences, engineering and lower for social sciences and humanities;

Ranked from highest to lowest	*Estimated completion rate percent*
Health	67
Veterinary science	65
Science	59
Engineering	55
Agriculture	55
Business	48
Education	46
Arts, humanities, social science	41
Law	38
Architecture	31

CHANGES AND INNOVATIONS

Prior to 2001, Australian universities were funded for domestic research masters and PhD students on the basis of an agreed load negotiated between the relevant federal department and individual institutions. All institutions charged fees for international research students; some institutions also charged fees for research training of domestic students above the agreed load target. This situation changed with the introduction of the RTS from late 2001. The RTS is part of a package of reforms initiated by the Australian federal government in 1999 with knowledge and innovation: a policy statement of research and research training released by the then Minister for Education Dr. David Kemp (Kemp 1999). The goal of the RTS was to improve the quality of postgraduate research education in response to a number of criticisms:

- There is too little concentration by institutions on areas of relative strength.
- Research degree graduates are often inadequately prepared for employment.
- There is unacceptable wastage of private and public resources associated with long completion times and low completion rates for research degree students (Kemp 1999).

Since 2002, the RTS has drastically changed the way postgraduate research student places are funded in Australia. The RTS formula's (see sub-heading "Funding for HDR students" above) values for each institution are averaged over a two-year period to moderate the impact of variability between years. The RTS also reduced the duration of maximum funding from five to four years for a research doctoral candidate and from three to two years for a research master's candidate. The introduction of the RTS also effectively reduced the number of research places funded by the federal government by more than 13 percent from 24,980 EFTSU to 21,644 FTE. These reductions affected the universities disproportionately. The largest "research-intensive" universities lost a low proportion of research student places, while some newer minimal research universities lost almost half of their places.

Because the RTS was expected to adversely affect regional universities located outside the major state capital cities, two mechanisms were introduced to reduce this impact: (1) "Regional Protection": a scheme designed to ensure no regional institution suffers a deterioration in its research funding from its starting position; and (2) "A Cap on Winners," a rule whereby no institution was able to gain more than a 5 percent increase in funding in comparison with its allocation in the previous year in each of the transition years (2002–2004). Increases over 5 percent were redistributed to other institutions with priority being given to those with the most significant decline in funding. Much of the controversy surrounding the early years of the scheme centered on the mechanism to implement its phased introduction. Not all funding was allocated according to the above formula, which was applied only to the funding generated by the "separations pool"—the funding support for completing students and those students who "separated" before completing their degree by withdrawing or temporarily suspending their candidature. Unlike the RTS formula, which is averaged over two years to moderate the impact of variability between years, the separations pool was calculated each semester, which had adverse impacts and unintended consequences in respect to institutional behavior.

In response to strident criticisms about the RTS, including a court challenge (later withdrawn) from a leading research university, the Federal Government reviewed the scheme in 2003 and modified the operational details from 2004. The separations pool was abolished. Seventy-five percent of each institution's funding for any given year is now based on its previous year's allocation; the remainder is funded on the basis of the allocative formula. The overall effect of this change is that universities receive about 80 percent of the payment for training most domestic research students only after the student graduates (20 percent is still funded on the basis of load through a research block funding scheme). The first installment of this payment is not received until two years after the student graduates, and the payment is phased in over many years (about 95 percent is received in the twelve years after a student graduates).

Further changes to the RTS may be introduced in response to the forthcoming Research Quality Framework (RQF), an initiative the federal government designed to "develop a more consistent and comprehensive approach to assessing the quality and impact of publicly funded research" in Australia (DEST 2005). This initiative is envisaged as an adaptation of the research assessment exercises conducted in several other countries, especially the United Kingdom and New Zealand. The format of this initiative is still being negotiated, but it is almost certain to lead to changes in the allocative formula of the RTS to incorporate measures of research quality and impact. Whether these measures will be applied to the outcomes of research training is the subject of robust discussion.

IMPACT OF CHANGE AND INNOVATION

The RTS significantly increased the profile of graduate research education in Australia. For the first time, there was an explicit line in the federal funding to universities for research training. This change catalyzed universities to nominate their areas of research strength, concentrate research training places in these areas, develop the generic skills of their research students, and improve their completion times and completion rates. The resultant changes are summarized in table 9.5, which presents the results of an informal survey of the thirty-seven Australian universities we conducted for this paper. Twenty-eight universities responded (76 percent), including five of the Group of Eight, large research-intensive universities which collectively win some 60 percent of the performance-based RTS funding. Our survey shows that most universities have increased emphasis on research training in the last five years, particularly with respect to generic skills training, measures to improve timely completions including a formal conformation of candidature process, increase stipend scholarship support and quality assurance. Our survey showed that most of these changes are central university level initiatives (rather than Faculty or School/Departmental initiatives). A significant proportion of institutions attributed at least some their changes to the introduction of the RTS scheme. The compulsory audits carried out by the Australian University Quality Agency (AUQA) seem to have been a less powerful driver of change, except with respect to quality assurance processes such as student surveys.

There was considerable concern that the RTS would have unintended consequences, but the supporting evidence for these is largely anecdotal. For example, it was claimed that if demand for HDR places exceeds supply, universities will be reluctant to enroll students whom they regard as having a higher than average risk of failing to complete, e.g., part-time students and students with significant family responsibilities. CAPA (2002) presented evidence from several universities' Research and Research Training Management Reports to the government to make the case that several universities were discouraging part-time enrollment.

One of the concerns raised in the "Knowledge and Innovation: A policy statement of research and research training report" (Kemp 1999) was that "research degree graduates are often inadequately prepared for employment." Ironically one of the results of the RTS is to provide a strong disincentive for universities to encourage students to spend time gaining work experience in industry placements because of the increased emphasis

TABLE 9.5. Numbers of universities making changes, and reasons for changes, to research training at twenty-eight Australian universities between 2000 and 2005

	Present in 2000[1]	*Introduced/ upgraded since 2000*[1]	*Planned introduction*	*RTS reason/ influence for change*	*AUQA reason/ influence for change*
Graduate School or equivalent	9	2	3	2	
Dean of Graduate Studies or equivalent	16	9		4	
Generic skills program	10	14		8	2
Measures to improve timely completions	7	22	1	23	
Increase in number university-funded stipend scholarships	8	21		12	
Increase in value of university-funded stipend scholarships	4	12	2	2	
Formal compulsory confirmation of candidature process	16	11	4	7	1
Surveys of student satisfaction during candidature	10	14	3		5
Surveys of student satisfaction on exit	12	8	4	2	2

SOURCE: DDOGS Survey 2006

[1] Some universities subsequently upgraded initiatives that were in place in 2000.

on timely completion, which is clearly the most unambiguous response to the RTS reforms (table 9.1).

LOOKING TO THE FUTURE

The future for doctoral studies in Australia is being shaped by various forces, not only the RTS and RQF and their developing interconnections, but also the Australian Government's requirements for compliance on a range of quality, financial and industrial (labor relations) matters. There is no certainty or stability ahead; however, this should not be taken to imply that doctoral education is in turmoil. Indeed, we would argue that the highly fluid and interconnected forces that bear upon Australian doctoral education are no more than a local version of global forces that bear upon most developed nations. (Developing nations share some of these forces, but those nations also have other forces with which to contend). In one sense, if new "creative" economies (as Florida 2003, 2005) require the talent of a sustainable "creative class," then one important element is the production of new researchers and new research. This should mean that doctoral education, assuming it adapts to the emerging needs and conditions, should have a strong future. However, the New Right/Neo-Conservative ideologies that dominate much of contemporary Western policy seem to induce features in government and business that eschew the creation of new ideas, theories and knowledge, unless they have a commercial potential or are at least congruent with these prevailing ideologies.

A challenge, therefore, is to ensure that universities are allowed to flourish within contemporary societies in ways that do not stultify the creation of new, and sometimes challenging or provocative, ideas both from the academic staff and the doctoral students. The consequences of the application of the RTS, RQF, and other measures in Australian universities may change the policies and practices in ways which detrimentally affect at least some universities, and may lead universities to become risk averse to the extent that some new research and some potential research students never come into being. It will be difficult to assess what the effect of such omissions will be: how do you miss what you never had? However, one can imagine it will affect the long-term vitality of societies and economies.

Alongside these developments, two more positive trends can be identified. One is that the Council of Australian Deans and Directors of Graduate Studies is becoming ever more effective and influential as an organization. It actively engages in debate about matters pertaining to doctoral study, engages in its own small pieces of data gathering and analysis, and lobbies government and other agencies, often with the Council of Australian Postgraduate Associations, on matters of doctoral policy and their impact on universities and candidates. The other positive trend is the increasing amount of research and publication on doctoral study in Australia. This is also helping to provide research-led debates and discussions on various aspects of doctoral study and its social and economic impacts.

SUMMARY AND CONCLUSION

PhDs have been offered in Australia for about sixty years. The programs are seen as an important marker of what it means to be a university, and being a PhD graduate is an important marker of being an academic staff member in an Australian university. However, in recent years the increase in doctoral students and the diversity of their needs, interests, and national contexts indicates that doctorates are being pursued for a variety of purposes and reasons, not connected to becoming a university teacher. This demand presents universities and others with some challenges as to how to provide a high quality doctoral experience that meets both the personal needs and circumstances of the students, as well as the broader institutional and national needs. The growth in numbers and the diversity of doctoral students, especially in numbers of mid-career professionally oriented students and their topics, suggest a growing vibrancy, at least on the "demand side" of the "doctoral business."

The RTS and RQF have many performance-related aspects that are driving a reshaping of doctoral practices in universities, and may well reshape the doctoral profile in Australia, perhaps in risk-averse and less diverse ways. The growth in activity in the professional and scholarly activity surrounding Australian doctoral studies is an encouraging sign that within the university sector there is an increasing motivation to shape debates, policies and practices in doctoral study.

BIBLIOGRAPHY

ARC/NBEET. 1996. "Patterns of research activity in Australian universities: Phase one: Final report." Canberra: Australian Government Publishing Service.

AVCC. 1987. "Report of AVCC Sub-committee on Academic Standards to the AVCC." Canberra: AVCC.

Bartlett, A. and G. Mercer, eds. 2001. *Postgraduate Research Supervision: Transforming (R)elations*. New York: Peter Lang.

Becher, T., M. Henkel, and M. Kogan. 1994. *Graduate Education in Britain*. London: Jessica Kingsley Publishers.

Brennan, M. 1998. "Struggles Over the Definition and Practice of the Educational Doctorate in Australia." *Australian Educational Researcher* 25(1): 71–90.

Clark, B. R. 1995. *Places of Inquiry: Research and Advanced Education in Modern Universities*. Berkeley, University of California Press.

*Clarke, J. A. 1996. "Why EdD and not PhD? Some student perceptions." In Proceedings of the Which way for Professional Doctorates? Conference, Faculty of Education, Health and Professional Studies, University of New England, edited by T. W. Maxwell and P. J. Shanahan, 71–78.

Coaldrake, P. and L. Stedman. 1998. *On the Brink: Australia's Universities Confronting their Future*. Brisbane: University of Queensland Press.

Council of Deans and Directors of Graduate Studies Guidelines http://www.ddogs.edu.au/cgi-bin/papers.pl.

Council of Australian Postgraduate Associations (CAPA). 2002. "Implementing the Research Training Scheme: The Consequences for Postgraduate Research Students." Council of Australian Postgraduate Associations, Research Paper, November.

Cullen, D. J., M. Pearson, L. J. Saha, and R. H. Spear. 1994. "Establishing Effective PhD Supervision." Canberra: Australian Government Publishing Service.

Dawkins, J. S. 1988. "Higher Education: A Policy Statement." Canberra: Australian Government Publishing Service.

DEET. 1988. "Report on Progress of Postgraduate Research Award Holders: 1979 Cohort." Canberra: AGPS.

Department of Education, Science, and Technology (DEST). 2005. "Research Quality Framework: Assessing the Quality and Impact of Research in Australia: Issues paper." Canberra: DEST.

Evans, T. D. 1995. "Postgraduate Research Supervision in the Emerging "Open" Universities." *Australian Universities Review* 38(2): 23–27.

Evans, T. D. 1997. "Flexible Doctoral Research: Emerging Issues in Professional Doctorate Programs." *Studies in Continuing Education* 19(2): 174–82.

Evans, T. D. 2000. "Meeting What Ends?: Challenges to Doctoral Education in Australia." Proceedings of the Quality in Postgraduate Research National Conference, Adelaide.

Evans, T. D. 2001. "Tensions and Pretensions in Doctoral Education." In *Doctoral Education and Professional Practice: The Next Generation?*, edited by B. Green, T. W. Maxwell, and P. Shanahan, 275–302. Armidale, NSW: Kardoorair Press.

Evans, T. D. 2002. "Part-time Research Students: Are They Producing Knowledge Where it Counts?" *Higher Education and Research and Development* 21(2): 155–165.

Evans, T. D., P. Macauley, M. Pearson, and K. Tregenza. 2003a. "A Brief Review of PhDs in Creative and Performing Arts in Australia." Proceedings of the Defining the Doctorate: Doctoral Study in the Creative and Performing Arts Conference, Australian Association for Research in Education, Newcastle. http://www.aare.edu.au/conf03nc/ev03007z.pdf.

Evans, T. D., P. Macauley, M. Pearson, and K. Tregenza. 2003b. "A Decadic Review of PhDs in Australia." Proceedings of the Joint Australian Association for Research in Education/New Zealand Association for Research in Education Conference, Auckland. http://www.aare.edu.au/03pap/eva03090.pdf.

Evans, T. D., and M. Pearson. 1999. "Off-campus Doctoral Research in Australia:

Emerging Issues and Practices." In *Supervision of Postgraduate Research in Education,* edited by A. Holbrook and S. Johnston, 185–206. Coldstream, Victoria: Australian Association for Research in Education.

Evans, T. D., and K. Tregenza 2004 "Some Characteristics of Early Australian PhD Theses." Proceedings of the Australian Association for Research in Education Conference, University of Melbourne, November.

Florida, R. 2003. *The Rise of the Creative Class.* Melbourne: Pluto Press.

Florida, R. 2005. *The Flight of the Creative Class: The New Global Competition for Talent.* New York: Harper Business.

Green, B., T. W. Maxwell, and P. Shanahan, eds. 2001. *Doctoral Education and Professional Practice: The Next Generation?* Armidale, NSW: Kardoorair Press.

Holbrook, A., and S. Johnston, eds. 1999. *Supervision of Postgraduate Research in Education.* Coldstream, Victoria: Australian Association for Research in Education.

Holbrook, A., S. Bourke, P. Farley, and K. Carmichael. 2001. "Analysing PhD Examination Reports and the Links between PhD Candidate History and Examination Outcomes: A Methodology." *Research and Development in Higher Education* 24: 51–61.

Johnson, L., A. Lee, and B. Green. 2000. "The PhD and the Autonomous Self: Gender, Rationality and Postgraduate Pedagogy." *Studies in Higher Education* 25(2): 135–47.

Kemp, D.A. 1999 "Knowledge and Innovation: A Policy Statement on Research and Research Training." Canberra: Department of Education, Training, and Youth Affairs.

Kiley, M. and G. Mullins. 2002. "It's a PhD, not a Nobel Prize": How Experienced Examiners Assess Research Theses." *Studies in Higher Education* 27(4): 369–86.

Lee, A., B. Green, and M. Brennan. 2000. "Organisational Knowledge, Professional Practice and the Professional Doctorate at Work." In *Research and Knowledge at Work: Perspectives, Case Studies and Innovative Strategies,* edited by J. Garrick and C. Rhodes, 117–36. London: Routledge.

Macauley, P., T. D. Evans, M. Pearson, and K. Tregenza. 2004. "Using Digital Data and Bibliometrics for Researching Doctoral Education." *Higher Education Research & Development* 24(2): 189–99.

Martin, Y. M., M. Machlachlan, and T. Karmel. 2001. *Postgraduate Completion Rates.* Canberra: DETYA.

McWilliam, E., and P. Taylor. 2001. "Rigorous Rapid and Relevant: Doctoral Training in New Times." In *Doctoral Education and Professional Practice: The Next Generation?,* edited by B. Green, T. W. Maxwell, and P. Shanahan, 229–46. Armidale, NSW: Kardoorair Press.

McWilliam, E., P. G. Taylor, P. Thomson, B. Green, T. Maxwell, H. Wildy, and D. Simons. 2002. "Research Training in Doctoral Programs: What Can Be Learned from Professional Doctorates?" Department of Education, Science and Technology.

Mullins, G., and M. Kiley. 1998. "Quality in Postgraduate Research: The Changing Agenda." In *Quality in Postgraduate Research: Managing the New Agenda,* edited by M. Kiley and G. Mullins, 1–13. Adelaide: The Advisory Centre for University Education, The University of Adelaide.

Neumann, R. 2003. "The Doctoral Education Experience." Evaluation and Investigation Programme, Department of Education, Science and Training, Commonwealth of Australia.

Parry, S. and M. Hayden. 1994. *Supervising Higher Degree Research Students*. Canberra: Australian Government Publishing Service.

Pearson, M. 1996. "Professionalising PhD Education to Enhance the Quality of the Student Experience." *Higher Education* 32: 303–20.

Pearson, M. 1999. "The Changing Environment for Doctoral Education in Australia: Implications for Quality Management, Improvement and Innovation." *Higher Education Research and Development* 18(3): 269–88.

Pearson, M. 2005. "Framing Research on Doctoral Education in Australia in a Global Context." *Higher Education Research & Development* 24(2): 119–34.

Pearson, M. and A. Brew. 2002. "Research Training and Supervision Development." *Studies in Higher Education* 27(2): 235–50.

Pearson, M. and L. Ford. 1997. *Open and Flexible PhD Study and Research*. Canberra: Department of Employment, Education, Training, and Youth Affairs, Evaluation and Investigations Program.

Seddon, T. 2001. "What Is Doctoral in Doctoral Education?" In *Doctoral Education and Professorial Practice: The Next Generation?*, edited by B. Green, T. W. Maxwell, and P. Shanahan, 303–36. Armidale, NSW: Kardoorair Press.

Sekhon, J. G. 1989. "PhD Education and Australia's Industrial Future: Time to Think Again." *Higher Education Research and Development* 8(2): 191–215.

Simpson, R. 1983. *How the PhD Came to Britain: A Century of Struggle for Postgraduate Education*. Gildford, Surrey: Society for Research into Higher Education.

Thomson, J., M. Pearson, G. Akerlind, J. Hooper, and N. Mazur. 2001. "Postdoctoral Training and Employment Outcomes." Canberra: Department of Education, Training, and Youth Affairs, EIP Report.

Trigwell, K., T. Shannon, and R. Maurizi. 1997. "Research-Coursework Doctoral Programs in Australian Universities." Canberra: Department of Employment, Education, Training, and Youth Affairs.

West, R. 1998. *Learning for Life: Final Report: Review of Higher Education Financing and Policy*. Canberra: Australian Government Publishing Service.

10 • JAPAN

SHINICHI YAMAMOTO

INTRODUCTION

In June 2005, the National Council on Education (well-known as "Chukyo-shin" in Japanese), which is an advisory body to the Minister of Education, published an interim report on graduate education policy titled "Graduate Education in a New Age: Toward the Formation of an Internationally Attractive System" to enrich graduate programs in Japan. The council listed four major functions of graduate education in Japan and suggested an approach to reform. These four functions are to train 1) researchers for R&D who are rich in creativity and imagination, 2) professionals with highly sophisticated skills, 3) academics with good teaching and research skills, and 4) highly talented people who play an active role in the developing knowledge-based society. Doctoral programs are understood to focus on training researchers and academics, while master's degrees focus on producing professionals and highly talented people (MEXT 2005).

After World War II, Japan introduced an American-style graduate education system that had two-year masters programs followed by three-year doctoral programs. However, it was difficult for academics in Japan to change from the traditional apprenticeship mode to the newly introduced coursework mode. Before World War II, under the German-style higher education system, graduate schools had been regarded as a place for future academics to be trained individually by their mentors. The system of graduate schools itself began with the Imperial University system in 1886.

There had been no category of professional schools that were different from graduate schools until 2004, when the government created a new type of school called "professional school" or "senmon-shoku-daigakuin" in Japanese. Thus, graduate schools in Japan had included all the functions of postgraduate education, i.e., research training, professional education, and other functions until 2004.

Until the late 1980s, the mainstream for the reform of graduate education had been to secure professional education in the masters programs rather than to enrich research training in the doctoral programs. That was partly explained by the fact that masters programs had tended to be regarded as preparatory to doctoral programs and thus, in spite of a growing demand for professionals, the main aim of the masters programs also tended to be academic research training. Another explanation was that most of the faculties had been trained at graduate schools and directly got jobs at universities. Thus faculty members did not know much about training people who would work for industry and in other non-academic settings. They therefore were not interested in teaching practical and professional matters.

To improve this situation, the government occasionally revised "The Standard for the Establishment of Graduate Programs," which is the order of the Minister of Education that each university must follow when they plan to establish or expand graduate programs. By the terms of the revised standard, graduate schools today can open their programs in the evening, can enroll part-time students, can set their goal as professional education rather than research training, and can employ faculty who have special and practical knowledge and skills and who come from non-academic sectors such as industry.

In the 1990s, the national push for advances in science and technology again pushed doctoral programs to emphasize research training. Research training in the 1990s, however, could not be in the same mode as in the 1950s and '60s. A new government initiative set research priorities, with selective allocation of resources, encouragement for university-industry collaboration and a goal of globally competitive research outputs. One of the most epoch-making facts that should be mentioned is the Science and Technology Basic Plan, which started in 1996. In that plan, universities are regarded as important players for the promotion of science and technology. Today, doctoral education is regarded as an engine for the promotion of science and technology by training students to be future researchers and by performing research in various fields, including the most advanced scientific research.

EXPANSION OF GRADUATE PROGRAMS IN JAPAN

According to the survey by the MEXT (Ministry of Education, Culture, Sports, Science, and Technology) in 2004 there were 162,712 masters students and 73,446 doctoral students. Although these numbers are still small

CHART 10.1. Expansion of Japanese higher education (enrollment)

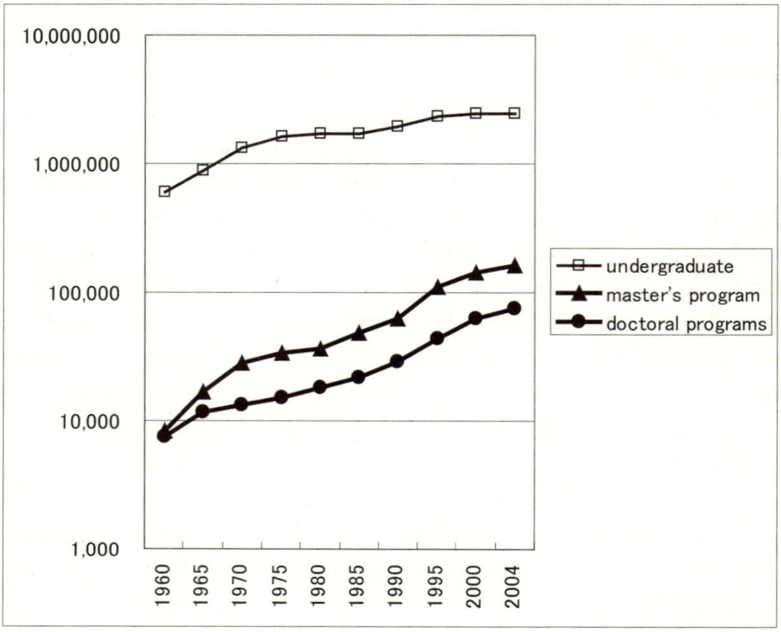

SOURCE: MEXT Survey

if we compare them with undergraduate enrollments, enrollment in graduate programs almost doubled from the early 1990s. It should be noted that the expansion of graduate education has been much faster than that of undergraduate education (see chart 10.1). The largest proportion of masters students study engineering; in doctoral programs most enrollment is health related, while social sciences play a large part in undergraduate programs (table 10.1). Judging from the figures in 2004, it is estimated that about 32 percent of the young generation is studying in undergraduate programs, about 3 percent masters programs and about 1 percent in doctoral programs (MEXT 2005).

The expansion of masters programs is explained by the fact that in the 1960s and early '70s the demand for well-trained engineers grew due to rapid economic growth. Moreover several economic plans by the government pushed universities to expand their masters programs in engineering. In the 1990s, on the contrary, expansion of masters programs was mostly due to the emerging popularity of the humanities and social sciences. Due to government encouragement of lifelong learning and adult education, a growing number of adult students enrolled in masters programs in the

TABLE 10.1. Enrollment of Higher Education by Programs and Field of Study

	Humanities	*Social Science*	*Science*	*Engineering*	*Health*	*Others*	*Total*
Undergraduate							
1960	77,888	257,979	16,206	92,572	23,026	133,793	601,464
1965	113,723	386,178	27,220	174,655	27,557	166,132	895,465
1970	170,907	562,162	42,071	283,674	37,994	247,550	1,344,358
1975	215,933	688,667	50,225	333,959	57,515	305,704	1,652,003
1980	239,990	704,737	54,579	337,767	71,413	333,018	1,741,504
1985	246,850	671,001	59,678	343,590	74,750	338,523	1,734,392
1990	302,594	787,325	66,778	390,646	69,883	371,346	1,988,572
1995	374,964	933,624	82,764	456,707	65,667	417,105	2,330,831
2000	410,979	985,617	87,901	467,162	64,309	455,787	2,471,755
2004	408,186	961,762	87,398	439,107	63,501	545,969	2,505,923
Master's							
1960	2,870	2,370	987	1,223	140	715	8,305
1965	3,104	3,355	2,198	5,657	512	1,945	16,771
1970	5,157	4,607	2,983	10,251	909	3,807	27,714
1975	5,975	4,596	3,226	13,514	1,018	5,231	33,560
1980	5,469	4,050	3,741	14,864	1,497	6,160	35,781
1985	5,645	4,373	4,598	20,668	2,053	10,810	48,147
1990	6,009	6,366	6,484	28,399	2,710	11,916	61,884
1995	9,707	13,161	11,153	48,256	4,241	23,131	109,649
2000	12,234	21,457	12,785	59,076	6,492	30,786	142,830
2004	13,182	21,536	13,954	65,235	10,531	38,274	162,712
Doctoral							
1960	1,016	894	900	391	3,709	519	7,429
1965	1,281	1,086	1,245	1,282	6,101	688	11,683
1970	1,876	1,727	2,263	2,356	3,769	1,252	13,243
1975	2,465	2,198	2,355	2,522	3,795	1,569	14,904
1980	2,860	2,430	2,589	2,358	6,191	1,783	18,211
1985	3,227	2,437	2,472	2,403	9,062	1,940	21,541
1990	3,594	2,654	3,067	4,315	11,794	2,930	28,354
1995	4,675	3,727	5,033	9,030	15,311	5,998	43,774
2000	6,871	6,195	6,410	11,818	20,051	11,136	62,481
2004	7,600	7,478	6,344	13,584	23,491	14,949	73,446

SOURCE: MEXT Survey

humanities and social sciences, including programs in such fields as business management and teachers' training. The expansion of doctoral programs during the 1990s was due to the fact that the government stimulated leading universities to expand doctoral programs to promote science and technology. "The Graduate Program Intensive," was a program to put a priority on graduate programs more than on undergraduate programs. This program is known as "Jutenka" in Japanese (Yamamoto 1999).

The decline of an eighteen-year-old population makes higher education institutions difficult to run because they have relied heavily on young undergraduate students. In 2004, about 30 percent of private four-year institutions and 40 percent of two-year institutions had difficulty recruiting enough students. The population of eighteen-year-olds will continue to decline, reaching 1,200,000 in 2009 and 820,000 in 2050. Institutions have already sought other types of students such as adult students and foreign students. Masters programs and professional schools are expected to make up the shortage of undergraduate students. From an international viewpoint, the government has encouraged universities and colleges to accept more foreign students under the initiative called "100,000 students from overseas." We have already had more than that. In 2004, the MEXT survey shows that there are 101,601 foreign students in Japanese universities, of which about 30,000 are enrolled in graduate programs. Most of the foreign graduate students come from Asian countries, chiefly China, Korea, and Taiwan.

GRADUATE PROGRAM INTENSIVE UNIVERSITIES—RESEARCH UNIVERSITIES IN THE JAPANESE MODE

We have observed the large expansion of graduate education in Japan. The reason for the expansion, however, is explained differently by experts in different circles. According to the academics, the expansion was desirable to raise the status of their institutions in an increasingly competitive academic community. For the individual professor who teaches and does research at a graduate school, increasing the number of graduate students means enlarging the power of those who do research. For the staff at the Ministry, stepping into graduate school policy is desirable because there is a great possibility to increase their budgets and to promote science and technology.

Jutenka, or The Graduate Programs Intensive, made every national university think seriously about expanding graduate programs. The policy gave national universities additional resources when they quickly added or enlarged doctoral programs. For the expansion of doctoral programs, how-

TABLE 10.2. Research vs. Teaching

	Primarily in Teaching (%)	*Leaning to Teaching*	*Leaning to Research*	*Primarily in Research*
Australia	13	35	43	9
Brazil	20	42	36	3
Chile	18	49	28	5
Germany	8	27	47	19
Hong Kong	11	35	46	8
Israel	11	27	48	14
Japan	**4**	**24**	**55**	**17**
Korea	5	40	50	6
Mexico	22	43	31	4
Netherlands	7	18	46	30
Russia	18	50	29	3
Sweden	12	21	44	23
United Kingdom	12	32	40	15
United States	27	36	30	7

SOURCE: Boyer 1994

ever, they needed to be authorized both by the Ministry of Education and by the Ministry of Finance, according to the rules of budget procedure. During this period most national universities shifted their priority of management from undergraduate programs toward graduate programs. They submitted budget requests to the Ministry of Education every year for creating new programs and/or for expanding existing programs. They said their graduate programs would be useful for training experts who would work not only for academia but also for industry and regional society.

Professors at universities that followed the mandates of Jutenka were in some cases granted the title of graduate professors rather than just professors. Being a graduate professor became a symbol of high status among academics. In addition to the symbolic merit, these faculty enjoyed higher salaries and more resources. Moreover, in science and engineering areas, professors needed manpower to assist them in their research activities. The more effectively they recruited large numbers of graduate students, the more desirable their laboratories would be for their research activities. According to my survey, academics in science and engineering prefer to be granted additional research associates and research assistants rather than

TABLE 10.3. Preference of resource

	Humanities	*Social Sciences*	*Science*	*Engineering*	*Agriculture*	*Health*	*Others*	*Total*
Time	42.2	39.3	30.5	26.7	26.2	16.8	35.7	30.8
Money (non-competitive)	13.0	14.3	12.1	13.2	16.7	20.4	14.0	13.8
Money (competitive)	3.5	3.5	4.0	4.5	6.0	8.4	4.1	4.5
Domestic travel	5.8	6.4	1.8	2.1	2.0	0.4	7.0	3.0
Overseas travel	8.8	11.8	3.8	2.9	2.1	0.4	9.4	4.8
Space	4.3	2.7	5.2	5.0	4.5	4.0	5.8	4.6
Facilities	0.8	0.6	7.3	9.6	9.7	4.0	6.4	6.6
Books and journals	10.6	9.3	2.7	0.8	0.9	1.3	2.9	3.6
Research associates and assistants	7.7	9.1	21.2	23.5	21.4	27.0	11.1	18.8
Technicians	1.1	0.6	7.0	6.2	5.9	10.2	1.2	5.1
Clerical staff	2.2	2.3	4.4	5.5	4.5	7.1	2.3	4.3
Total	100.0	100.0	100.0	100.0	100.0	100.0	100.0	100.0

SOURCE: Yamamoto, 2004-1

additional funding for other purposes. Their preference is very different from those in humanities and social sciences, where professors prefer time and books to manpower (table 10.3).

Another survey indicates that most Japanese academics prefer research to teaching as their first priority, even if they work for junior colleges or technical colleges (table 10.2). Although Jutenka was implemented only at major national universities, like the University of Tokyo and the University of Kyoto, most academics were eager to expand graduate programs. By expanding, as I mentioned above, they get more resources for their research. Thus "expansion for the sake of expansion" becomes their primary attitude, which may easily cause a mismatch between the demand for and supply of graduate students.

PREDICTED DEMAND AND SUPPLY OF DOCTORAL STUDENTS

The University Council, which was one of the advisory councils to the Minister of Education during the 1990s, made various recommendations on higher education policy. Among those, in 1998, the council made a recommendation entitled "Universities in the 21st Century and their Reform." This policy statement recommends that graduate schools train people who have highly professional knowledge and skills as well as future researchers who will work in academia. It reflects a recent trend toward life-long learning in Japan, where keeping up with new professional knowledge and practical skills will be more important for the people in their jobs than ever. Thus graduate programs are expected to expand. In addition to this, as I mentioned before, the strong desire of academics and universities to participate in Jutenka also affected this recommendation. This recommendation predicted the future supply and demand for graduates of masters and doctoral programs. The result was as follows: in 2010, demand for graduates with masters degrees will exceed supply, while the supply of doctorates will exceed demand. This prediction was based on the past ten-fifteen years' data on graduate enrollments.

MEXT asked a research group composed of several scholars of higher education research and economics to study and predict future demand and supply of graduate students. I myself was a member of the group. This study was done in 1997–98 and funded by MEXT. The main issues of the study were 1) trends of enrollment in graduate programs; 2) job market trends for graduate degree holders, including universities and other academic sectors, and industry; 3) predicted enrollment of graduate programs in 2010; and 4) predicted demand for graduate students in 2010. The year of 2010 was regarded as an important year because the eighteen-year-old

TABLE 10.4. Prediction of Supply of and Demand for Students

	Supply of Students		*Demand for Students*	
	Case A	*Case B*	*Case A*	*Case B*
Master's Course	171,928	168,141	181,298	164,989
Doctoral Course	82,009	81,446	60,108	55,786
Total	253,937	249,587	241,406	220,775

SOURCE: Ushiogi, et al. 1988.
Case A is based on past 10 years' trend and Case B is based on past 15 years' trend.

population will continue to decline until that year, and therefore enrollment will also continue to decline. The decline would cause serious problems for higher education management. Thus various kinds of systemic change will have to be implemented by that year. The graduate education system is no exception to these trends.

We made several findings during our study.

1. Japan experienced a rapid expansion of graduate enrollment between 1980 and 1997. The percentage of students going to graduate programs from undergraduate education increased from 4.5 percent in 1980 to 10.9 percent in 1997. This trend was higher in science and engineering than in the social sciences and humanities. The enrollment of adult and foreign students grew faster than that of traditional young Japanese students.

2. Judging from past trends, the percentage of students going to masters programs after graduating from undergraduate programs will increase from 8.6 percent in 1997 to 12.2–12.6 percent in 2010, and the percentage admitted to doctoral programs will rise from 2.2 percent to 3.0–3.1 percent in 2010. From these calculations, we obtained the conclusion that in 2010, 87,000 students (up from 57,000 in 1997) will join masters programs and 23,000 students (15,000 in 1997) will enroll in doctoral programs.

3. Students who finished masters programs increased from 15,258 in 1980 to 50,430 in 1997. It is fortunate that in spite of this rapid growth most of the students could find jobs after graduation, mainly in industry. On the other hand, about 30 percent of students who graduated from doctoral programs could not find a job on a full-time basis. The number of students who finished doctoral programs increased from 3,600 in 1980 to 9,860 in 1997. Some students in the "30 percent" cohort could be funded as post-doctoral researchers. Jobs for those who complete masters' degrees are mostly in industry, while doctorates find their jobs both in academia and industry.

CHART 10.2. Prediction in 2010 and actual growth of enrollment in recent years

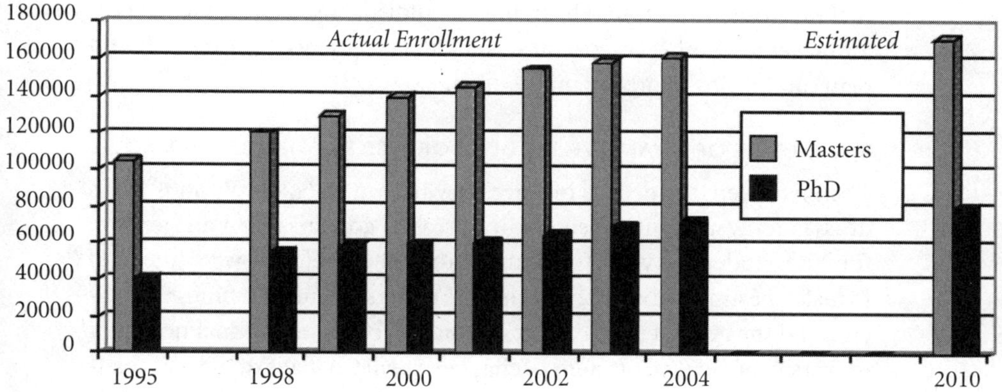

SOURCE: MEXT Survey and Yamamoto 2004–2

Then we analyzed the findings and predicted the future demand and supply of graduate students. The brief outline is as follows. First, it is not easy for students to find jobs at universities and colleges. Due to the decline of the eighteen-year-old population, the academic job market will shrink. Our prediction was that the number of academic staff (professors and others on full-time basis) would be 153,000 in 2010, while it was 158,000 in 1995. The new positions opened for new doctorates will be 2,300 to 2,500 annually. The industrial sector will therefore play a key role. According to our prediction, in the manufacturing industry, the demand for graduates with masters degrees will grow to between 25,800 and 28,400 in 2010, which is 1.5–1.7 times as many as in 1997. In service industries, the demand will be 12,500–14,800, which is 2.2–2.8 times as many as in 1997. The demand for doctorates will also grow in 2010 (1.5–2.5 times as many as in 1997). In sum, the growth in the industrial sector will determine demand. We concluded that the supply of graduate degree holders in 2010 would be 249,587–253,937, while the demand from academia and industry would be 220,775–241,406. The difference between supply and demand could be called the national "mismatch," which will be taken in consideration during the formation of future science policy.

However, we wish to point out that these predictions were mainly based on the past ten to fifteen years' trends and did not necessarily include elements such as technology innovation and the reform of graduate schools. Those are also important factors that will determine the future supply and demand of graduate students. Actually the growth of doctoral enrollment has been larger than our prediction. As shown in chart 10.2, in 2004, enrollment in doctoral programs is currently 73,446 and will be larger than 82,000 that we estimated in 2010. The trends we studied, however, signal that policy makers and other important stakeholders in science education should plan carefully to improve Japanese science.

THE FUTURE OF JAPAN: WHERE DOCTORATES PLAY IMPORTANT ROLES

The 1990s were the decade of university reform in Japan. Various kinds of changes were undertaken in such areas as governance, management, funding, student services, and curriculum. These reforms were intended to make the university more accountable to the students, the funding agencies, and the general public, in contradiction of the traditional notion of university or faculty autonomy. It has been realized that expanded, broadened higher education and the progress of scientific research have made the Japanese university system no longer appropriate to meet the needs of the people. University reform mode has continued since then and thus the early 2000s should also be called another decade of reform.

A new set of important reforms has been introduced recently. First is the introduction of the external assessment system for universities and colleges. Starting in 2004, each institution must have its quality of education and research assessed every seven years by the authorized assessment agencies. Several assessment agencies have been authorized by the Minister of Education. To some extent this new system is similar to the accreditation system in the United States. This external assessment, along with the growing need for global quality assurance, will make universities and colleges more carefully design their educational and research system.

Second is the new system of national universities. In April 2004, all existing national universities became incorporated and separated from the main body of the government. This new system is called "National University Corporations," which have independent legal status, although they are given their mission and mostly funded by the government. This corporation system was originally discussed in the 1990s as a measure of government-wide reform that would reduce the number of government employees by separating non-clerical departments from the main body of the government. MEXT decided that creating a separate National University Corporation was an effective method to achieve this goal and guarantee the autonomy of universities. Under this system, each national university will compete for effective management and better performance.

A third new reform is the introduction of various kinds of competitive funding for universities and colleges. In addition to competitive individual research grants, the government introduced institutional-based competitive funds such as the "Centers of Excellence Programs for the 21st Century (COE)" in 2002 and "Good Practice of Educational Activities (GP)" in 2003, which encouraged institutional effort toward university reform. Increasing competitive funding is the worldwide trend for improving science education, and Japan is no exception (OECD 2003). In fiscal 2004, competitive funding for universities and colleges is estimated to be about 360 billion yen.

According to the MEXT, there are three reasons for current university reform: first, to respond to progress in scientific research and changes in human resource development; second, to respond both to the rise in the percentage of students continuing to higher education and to their diversification; third, to respond to the growing need for lifelong learning and the rising expectations of society for universities. In this situation, each institution should identify its own mission, whether it is research-intensive or not.

The role of doctoral programs impinges on academia, industry, service industries and other economic sectors. Globalization and changes in industrial structure are leading to changes in the demands for professionally and academically trained workers. One national problem is that existing graduate programs do not fully respond to those needs. If there are mismatches between supply of and demand for PhD students, the gap should be filled up by improving the quality and system of graduate education as well as making people in industry be aware of recent reforms of graduate education in Japan.

In Japan, outside of academia, PhDs are still regarded as a special kind of people who are difficult to manage. Many employers believe that PhDs tend to worry about their specialty and thus are not flexible in the changing environment of business. Overcoming this belief and giving PhDs important roles, I think, are the solutions that will respond to globalization. Universities and the government have much to do to accomplish this objective.

APPENDIX: CURRENT SYSTEM OF HIGHER EDUCATION AND GRADUATE EDUCATION IN JAPAN

Higher Education in Japan was completely changed after World War II. The main components are 1) four-year undergraduate programs and 2) five-year graduate programs that are usually divided into two-year masters programs and three-year doctoral programs. Students must graduate from high schools and be more than eighteen years old to enroll in undergraduate programs, although the government recently introduced a new rule that allows admission of talented seventeen-year-old students. To enroll in graduate programs, students must finish undergraduate programs that usually take four years. Thus, almost all Japanese graduate students are more than twenty-two years old.

Graduate programs in Japan are divided into three categories: masters programs, doctoral programs, and professional schools. The last category was introduced only a few yeas ago. Masters programs aim at training various kinds of professionals who will work for industry, although some MA students prepare to enter doctoral programs. It takes two years to get most masters degrees but in some programs it takes only one year. Doctoral programs mainly aim at training future researchers who will work for academia and industry. It takes five years to get a doctoral degree if a student directly enrolls from an undergraduate program and three years after finishing a master's program. However, in some cases, it is possible to get a doctoral degree in three years at five-year programs and one year at three-year programs. The aim of professional schools is to train highly skilled professionals in specific fields. The typical ones are law schools, business schools, and schools of technology management. However in medical and dental training, we have no professional schools as in the United States. Instead, we train such people in six-year undergraduate programs that are followed by four-year doctoral programs. Doctoral programs in the medical and dental fields are a mixture of academic and professional training for those who already have medical or dental doctors' licenses. In other words, we have no distinction between PhDs and professional doctoral degrees like a doctor of education and a doctor of medicine.

One of the biggest problems in doctoral programs is the low rate of degree granting in the humanities and social sciences field. The total number of doctoral degrees granted was 16,314 in 2002. This figure was large enough if we compare this with the total number of students who finished their course work in the same year. The number was 13,462 in total. However, if we examine the numbers by field, we see a very different picture. In the humanities, for example, there were 1,174 students who finished their course work in 2002, while there were only 739 doctoral degrees granted. On the other hand, in science, there were 1,607 students who finished and there were 1,651 doctoral degrees granted. We must carefully consider that about one-third of doctoral degrees are so called "theses doctors," which are granted without coursework.

According to the estimation by the MEXT, only 27.0 percent of doc-

CHART 10.3. Graduate program system in Japan

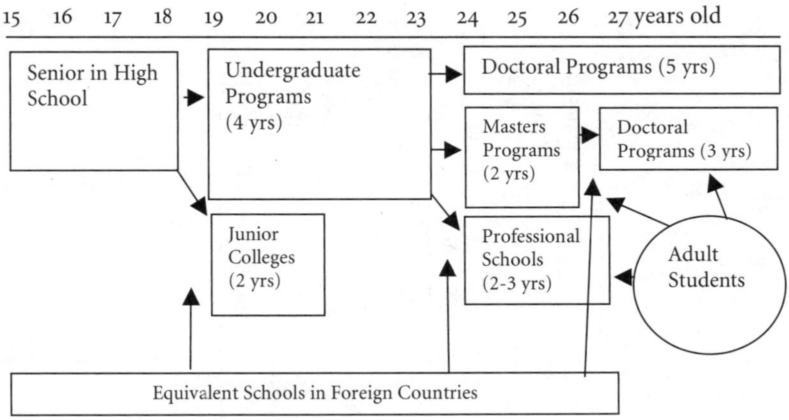

toral students were granted degrees in humanities in 2004, while 80.2 percent took degrees in science. More students are completing doctoral degrees in the humanities than in the past, however. In 1991, only 4.7 percent of doctoral degrees were granted in the humanities. Such a low rate is explained by the fact that some people still believe, especially in the humanities and social sciences, that PhDs should be given only to established scholars who have created great works and should not be given to young students even if they show by their theses enough ability to become researchers. It was fortunate that Japanese students in humanities and social sciences used to be able to get jobs in Japanese academia without PhDs. But globalization of higher education does not allow such a special situation to continue. We must grant PhDs to the students from overseas according to the global standard. And Japanese students in the humanities and social sciences must have a PhD degree when they look for appropriate posts in the international job market.

Another problem is financial support for doctoral students. Financial support is important for attracting students into graduate programs and promoting research training. There are various kinds of support implemented in Japan. For graduate students, a scholarship loan (basically with no interest) provided by the Japan Student Services Organization (called Japan Scholarship Foundation until 2004) has played the biggest role, enabling competent students who lack financial resources to attend graduate schools and maintain their daily lives. More than 40 percent of

TABLE 10.5. Financial supports for graduate students

	Fellowship by JSPS	*TA*		*RA*		*Scholarship Loan*
		National Universities	*Private Universities*	*National Universities*	*Private Universities*	
Budget (million yen)	7,559	4,414	1,400	1,843	600	104,100
Eligible doctoral students	3,220	9,281	7,271	4,267	469	27,444
Eligible master's students		4,384	1,213			61,936
	Fiscal 2004	Fiscal 2003	Fiscal 2003	Fiscal 2003	Fiscal 2003	Fiscal 2004

SOURCE: MEXT, 2005

masters program students and more than 60 percent of doctoral program students took advantage of these loans in the 1970s. Although the growth in this scholarship funding has not followed the expansion of the student population, the fund still provides basic financial support for graduate students. The amount of this scholarship is 88,000 yen monthly for masters program students and 122,000 yen (about 1,100 US dollars) for doctoral students. Additional support is available if the students pay interest. Students who after graduation serve as researchers for universities or related institutions for a certain period have not needed to repay this scholarship loan until the governmental revision in 2004 that abolished this privilege.

In 1985, MEXT established a new, more competitive fellowship program for young researchers, called "Fellowships for Young Japanese Scientists." With the aim of cultivating young researchers who will conduct innovative and trail-blazing research, this program provides a limited number of promising young researchers with fellowships and research grants so as to allow them to concentrate on their research, which they conduct in laboratories or under supervising researchers of their choice for a specified period (two to three years). This new fellowship, which is administered by the Japan Society for the Promotion of Sciences (JSPS), is provided for graduate students and post-doctoral researchers on a highly competitive basis. It has been playing an important role in supporting graduate students and post-doctorates. If funded, a PhD student is paid 200,000 yen (about 1,800 US dollars) monthly and, in the case of a post-doctorate, 364,000 to 446,000 yen monthly. In addition, they are given up to 1,500,000 yen (about 14,000 US dollars) in the form of a research grant every year.

In addition to the scholarship loan and the fellowship, research assistantship and teaching assistantship are also available. Table 10.5 is a summary for various schemes of financial support for graduate students drawn up by MEXT.

BIBLIOGRAPHY

Boyer, Ernest L. 1994. "The Academic Profession, An International Perspective." Stanford: The Carnegie Foundation.

MEXT. 2005. "Graduate Education in a New Ages toward the Formation of Internationally Attractive System." Interim Report by the Central Council on Education.

MEXT Survey. "Statistical Handbook of MEXT," published annually.

OECD/CSTP. 2003. "Governing the Science System—Challenges and Responses.

Ushiogi, Morikazu et.al. (Study Group on Graduate Education). 1998. "Report of the Study on Graduate Education from the Perspective of Quantitative Development" (Daigakuin no Ryoteki Seibi ni kannsuru Chosa Kenkyu).

Yamamoto, Shinichi. 1999. "The Growing Sophistication of Research at a Time of Broadened Participation in Higher Education." In *University-Industry Linkages in Japan and the United States*, edited by Lewis Branscomb, Fumio Kodama, and Richard Florida, 531–46. Cambridge: MIT Press.

Yamamoto, Shinichi. 2004–1. "An Analysis of Resource Allocation for Research." *The Journal of Science Policy and Research Management*, Vol.19, No.1/2: 68–69

Yamamoto, Shinichi. 2004–2. "Mismatches in Supply and Demand for S&T Graduates at PhD Level." In *Fostering the Development of Human Resources for Science and Technology*, edited by Sveva Avveduto, 153–66. Roma: Biblink editori.

11 • INDIA

NARAYANA JAYARAM

The Doctor of Philosophy (PhD) is the highest academic degree awarded by universities and university-level institutions of higher education in India. Although beginning only in the second decade of the nineteenth century, doctoral education in India expanded rapidly as a part of the general expansion of higher education, with state patronage, after independence (in 1947).[1] In 1990, with the adoption of structural adjustment reforms by the Government of India, there has been a gradual withdrawal of state patronage for higher education and a coterminous privatization of that sphere. However, under the growing impact of the globalization of the economy and the internationalization of education, and with the government dithering about the long-term policy to be adopted for higher education, higher education in India is now passing through a period of stunted growth and uncertain future (see Jayaram 2004). This has implications for doctoral education, too.

This essay discusses the development of doctoral education in India and examines its problems and prospects in the changing scenario of higher education in the country. The essay is divided into six parts: Part One outlines the historical background of doctoral education in India. Part Two discusses the major developments in doctoral education since independence. Part Three analyzes the data on enrollment in doctoral programs and the doctoral degrees awarded. Part Four discusses the structure and functioning of doctoral programs. Part Five examines the problem of quality in doctoral education. And Part Six reflects on the prospects of research-oriented education in India.

THE HISTORICAL BACKGROUND

The foundation for India's present system of higher education was laid by the British colonial regime in the mid-nineteenth century (Ashby and Anderson 1966, 54–146). The initial efforts of the Christian missionaries and the East India Company generated a protracted controversy between the "Anglicists" commending a Western course and the "Orientalists" favoring an indigenous direction. William Bentinck finally resolved this controversy in favor of the Anglicist orientation, barely a month after Thomas Babington Macaulay had penned his (in)famous *Minute* (on 2 February 1835). Charles Wood's *Dispatch* (of 19 July 1854) reaffirmed his policy. Upon the recommendation of the Committee appointed on 26 January 1855, the first three universities were established at Bombay (now Mumbai), Calcutta (now Kolkata), and Madras (now Chennai) in 1857.

Modeled after the University of London (established in 1836), these pioneer universities were largely affiliating and examining bodies with very little intellectual life of their own. All the universities that were subsequently established developed in an isomorphic fashion set on the pattern of the original universities. The British educational implantation in India was conceived to serve the economic, political and administrative interests of the British, and in particular, to consolidate and maintain their dominance in the country. It emphasized English, which not only was taught as a language, but also was made the exclusive medium of instruction in higher education. The content was biased in favor of languages and the humanities, and against science and technology.

Although the first three universities were established as early as in 1857, the first-ever doctorate awarded by any of these universities was conferred as late as in 1911,[2] and the growth in the number of such degrees was also slow. The colleges affiliated to these universities, and those that were established subsequently, only offered instruction in courses leading to the award of the first degree (namely, BA, BSc, etc.). No systematic attempt was made to establish research-oriented education in the universities or to train students in research methods. Thus the best of Indian scientists and scholars of the colonial era went abroad, many to the United Kingdom and some to the United States of America, for research-oriented or high quality higher education.[3]

It was only in 1914 that the first postgraduate departments were started in the country. The credit for this goes to Sir Asutosh Mookherjee, who founded the first postgraduate departments at the University of Calcutta and laid the foundation for postgraduate-level training and research

(UEC 1950, 144).[4] After World War I, several new universities were started, and some of these were "teaching universities" (as different from "affiliating universities") and they began offering postgraduate training and research in certain fields of study. The PhD, DLitt, and DSc degrees were instituted and awarded to students on successful completion of their research. The opening of the doctoral education program was characterized by caution, and comparisons were always made to the best institutions in England. Not surprisingly, the Indian University Education Commission (1948–49) observed that, "both in quality and quantity the level of scientific research was at its best in Indian universities between the years 1920 and 1945" (UEC 1950, 145).

In its report, The Scientific Man-Power Committee observed in August 1948, that the number of PhD and DSc degrees in six basic disciplines awarded by all the universities in India during the preceding ten years was 260, an average of twenty-six per year. Considering that in England, at Cambridge alone in 1935, 365 students (174 Cambridge graduates and 191 overseas students) were registered for the PhD degree, the Indian numbers were not at all impressive (quoted by UEC 1950, 147).

DOCTORAL EDUCATION SINCE INDEPENDENCE

The University Education Commission (popularly known as the Radhakrishnan Commission), appointed immediately after India attained independence, observed that the aim of the universities was "to undertake research in as many branches of knowledge as possible, and to produce an army of trained research workers, who, by their studies, will not only set high standards of intellectual life in scholarship and scientific research, but will also actively advance the moral and material progress of our country" (UEC 1950, 141). The Science Policy Resolution of the Government (March 1958) also stressed the importance of the acquisition and application of scientific knowledge. And the Education Commission (1964–66) (popularly known as the Kothari Commission) forwarded a well-articulated proposal for reorienting the university system toward research (ME 1971).

It is tempting to view the growth of doctoral education in India as an essential part of the phenomenal growth of higher education in the country since 1947 resulting from such policy recommendations. The growth in the number of students enrolling for research degrees (from 1,434 in 1950–51 to 13,612 in 1970–71 to 53,193 in 1995–96), however, was a direct consequence of the doctorate being made a mandatory qualification for appointments to permanent teaching positions in universities and colleges. This was part of the recommendation of the University Grants

Commission's (UGC)[5] committee for the revision of pay scales of teachers, headed by Dr. S. N. Sen in 1973. The committee was of the opinion that a research qualification would make for a better teacher. Whether this assumption is reasonable or not is a moot question. The implementation of the recommendation, however, led to a sudden demand for enrollment in doctoral education, and a concomitant growth in the number of guides to supervise the research work of the students so enrolled.

Since employment was the primary driving force behind this demand rather than pursuit of knowledge (which was until then stressed as the main objective of research-oriented higher education), there was a gradual decline in the standards of doctoral education and the quality of doctoral theses produced. There was also no visible improvement in the quality of doctorate-holding teachers entering the profession. Realizing the inadvertent deleterious consequence of the earlier policy measures, in 1983 the UGC's committee on pay revisions, headed by Professor R. C. Mehta, recommended the removal of the doctorate as an essential qualification for recruitment to the post of lecturer in universities, colleges and institutes. Irrespective of whether a candidate had a doctorate or not, passing of an eligibility test became mandatory for appointment to teaching positions from 1989.[6] However, considering the mounting pressure from the candidates who had already obtained a doctorate or had submitted their thesis for evaluation, the passing of this test was waived for such candidates initially until 31 December 1993. This waiver was later extended to 31 December 2002.

For appointment to teaching positions in universities and colleges (especially those receiving financial assistance from the central or state government), it is now mandatory to pass a test called the National Eligibility Test (NET). The NET is conducted by the National Educational Testing Bureau of the University Grants Commission at the all-India level twice a year (generally in the months of June and December). The test consists of two components: aptitude for research and proficiency in a subject chosen by the candidate. Candidates who pass this test may become eligible for both (a) a doctoral research fellowship (called Junior Research Fellowship [JRF], for the first two years, and Senior Research Fellowship [SRF], for the next three years) awarded by the UGC; and (b) appointment to entry-level teaching positions (Lecturer or Assistant Professor) in universities, colleges and institutes; or (c) for the latter only.[7] Those who qualify for JRF through the NET must enroll themselves in an Indian university, Indian Institute of Technology (IIT) or an institution of national importance within two years from the declaration of their results to be eligible to get the fellowship.

The NET is conducted in seventy-seven subjects covering the humanities (including languages), social sciences, forensic science, environmental sciences, computer science and applications, and electronic science. The Council of Scientific and Industrial Research (CSIR) conducts the UGC-CSIR NET for other science subjects jointly with the UGC, namely, the life sciences, physical sciences, chemical sciences, mathematical sciences, and earth, atmospheric, ocean, and planetary sciences. Additionally, several state governments have been authorized by the UGC to conduct their own state-level eligibility tests (SET). While candidates qualifying through the NET become eligible for appointment all over the country, since June 2002 those qualifying at the SET are eligible for appointment only in the state from which they have qualified.

Although the doctorate is no longer a requirement at the entry level now, those holding that degree at the time of their appointment are given two increments (monetary incentives) in their basic pay. Those acquiring doctoral qualification in-service (that is, after becoming a Lecturer/Assistant Professor) get this monetary incentive from the date on which they are awarded the doctorate. Furthermore, under the Career Advancement Scheme now in vogue, a Lecturer/Assistant Professor will become eligible for appointment to the next higher academic position, namely, Reader/Associate Professor, only if s/he has a doctorate. That is, while experience may bring some monetary benefits, it would not substantially improve one's status in the academic profession unless the teacher possesses a doctorate.

Furthermore, under the Pension Scheme for tenure appointments made until January 2004, those entering the profession with the doctorate would get the notional benefit of three years of service for counting of pension benefits. The logic behind this is that the teacher concerned would have worked for a minimum of three years for her/his doctorate after obtaining the basic qualification (a masters' degree) before entering the job, and would be at a disadvantage vis-à-vis those entering the profession without the doctorate.

Thus, the doctorate is now mandatory for a teacher to be appointed to the position of Reader/Associate Professor in a university or institute, and Principal of a college. However, the doctorate is not insisted on for appointment to a Professor's post, the highest teaching position to which a teacher can be appointed. A scholar of eminence (as evidenced by her/his publications) can be appointed as Professor even without the doctorate. While this was a norm until about the 1970s, it is rarely that one comes across such an appointment nowadays.

The UGC has been encouraging in-service lecturers/assistant professors to acquire higher academic qualifications like MPhil or PhD by providing them with fellowships under the Faculty Improvement Program. Most universities and institutes grant study leave to teachers to complete their doctoral work; many state governments grant such leave to teachers working in colleges assisted by them.

TRENDS IN DOCTORAL EDUCATION: ENROLLMENT AND AWARDING OF DEGREES

India has witnessed massive growth of student enrollment in higher education: from a total of 173,696 in 1950–51 to 8,399,443 in 2000–01 (see table 11.1). Early on, student enrollment in courses leading to research degrees (MPhil and PhD) was modest: 1,434 in 1950–51. Over the next two decades, the number increased steadily: to 5,083 in 1960–61 and 13,612 in 1970–71. It then galloped to 53,193 in 1995–96; and to 57,411 in 2000–01. Provisional figures for 2002–03 show an all-time high enrollment at 62,213.

While in absolute terms this growth of enrollment in research courses appears impressive, as a proportion to the growth of enrollment in higher education it has never exceeded 1 percent. It peaked in 1960–61 (0.91 percent), as part of the general expansion of higher education in the country. It peaked again in 1995–96 (0.81 percent), this time as a result of the UGC making the doctorate mandatory for appointment to entry-level teaching positions in universities and colleges. However with the UGC revising its stance on this issue, the proportion has declined and remained stable at around 0.68 percent (see table 11.1).

In 2000–01, in all 57,411 students were enrolled in research courses: 11,964 (20.84 percent) in MPhil and 45,447 (79.16 percent) in PhD. Those enrolling in PhD programs constituted only 0.54 percent of the enrollment in higher education. In 2000–01, arts (including social sciences) and science faculties accounted for nearly 75 percent of enrollment in research courses (see table 11.2). The enrollment in these faculties was more pronounced in MPhil (85.95 percent) as compared with PhD (71.56 percent) program. In doctoral programs, the percentage of students enrolling in arts (35.74 percent) and science (35.82 percent) faculties were the same, and so was the percentage of students enrolling in engineering (7.94 percent) and agriculture (7.12 percent). Enrollment in doctoral education is still biased in favor of the traditional "liberal sciences," as distinguished from the "applied sciences."

Gender-wise, women accounted for 39.36 percent of the enrollment in higher education, and their enrollment in research courses (39.20 percent)

TABLE 11.1. Trends in enrollment in higher education in India

Year	Total Enrollment	Enrollment at different levels (in percentages)			
		Graduate	Postgraduate	Research	Diploma/ Certificate
1950–51	173,696	83.70	11.51	0.83	3.96
1960–61	556,559	84.75	10.58	0.91	3.76
1970–71	2,009,134	89.43	8.13	0.68	1.76
1995–96	6,574,005	89.61	8.60	0.81	0.98
2000–01	8,399,443	89.16	9.23	0.68	0.93

SOURCE: Kaul (1974, p. 8) for 1950–51, 1960–61, and 1970–71; UGC (2002–03) for 1995–96 and 2000–01.

is commensurate with this (see table 11.3). The enrollment of women in research courses has improved since 1995–96, when it was 35.67 percent. It must be noted, however, that much of women's enrollment in research courses is at the MPhil level (44.79 percent); they constitute only 33.62 percent of the enrollment at the PhD level, and this has increased only marginally (that is, by 1.83 percentage points) since 1995–96.

At the PhD level, men outnumber women in all faculties, and their concentration in the faculties of commerce/management, engineering, medicine, agriculture, veterinary science, and law is noteworthy. Women are relatively better represented in the arts, sciences, education, and other faculties. A column-wise reading of the table confirms this: 80.67 percent of 15,277 women PhD students are in the arts and science faculties, where as only 66.95 percent of their male counterparts are in these faculties, and 19.14 percent of women are in engineering and agriculture faculties.

An analysis of the data on doctorates (PhD/DLitt/DSc) awarded is perhaps a better pointer to the trends in doctoral education. The number of doctorates awarded increased from 18,286 during 1973–78 to more than 50,000 during 1993–98 (Bandyopadhyay 2003, 2). During the past two decades, on an average, Indian universities and university-level institutions have been turning out 10,000 doctorates per year. During 1999–2000, in all 11,296 doctorates were awarded (see table 11.4): arts/social science (4,280 or 37.89 percent) and science (3,885 or 34.39 percent) faculties together accounted for over 72 percent, and the remaining 28 percent by commerce (571 or 5.05 percent), education (364 or 3.22 percent), engineering/technology (723 or 6.40 percent), medicine (228 or 2.02 percent), agriculture

TABLE 11.2. Faculty-wise and gender-wise student enrollment in MPhil and PhD programs, 2000–01

Faculty	M Phil			PhD		
	Men	*Women*	*Total*	*Men*	*Women*	*Total*
Arts, including Oriental Learning	3,873	3,200	7,073	9,973	6,268	16,241
	(54.75)	(45.25)	59.12	(61.40)	(38.60)	35.74
	58.64	59.71		33.06	41.03	
Science, including Home Science, Computer Applications,	1,717	1,493	3,210	10,224	6,056	16,280
Computer Science, etc.	(53.49)	(46.51)		(62.80)	(37.20)	35.82
	26.00	27.86	26.83	33.90	39.64	
Commerce/Management	364	227	591	1,368	419	1,787
	(61.60)	(38.40)	4.94	(76.55)	(23.45)	3.93
	5.51	4.24		4.53	2.74	
Education, including Teacher Training, Shastri	133	84	217	506	461	967
	(61.30)	(38.70)	1.81	(52.32)	(47.68)	2.13
	2.02	1.57		1.68	3.02	
Engineering/Technology, including Agricultural Engineering	98	44	142	3,015	594	3,609
and Technology, Dairy Technology and Architecture	(69.01)	(30.99)	1.19	(83.54)	(16.46)	7.94
	1.48	0.82		9.99	3.89	
Medicine, including Homeopathy, Ayurveda, Unani, Tibbia,	57	73	130	840	348	1,188
Dentistry, Physiotherapy, Naturopathy, Nursing, etc.	(43.84)	(56.16)	1.09	(70.70)	(29.30)	2.61
	0.86	1.36		2.78	2.28	

Agriculture, including Horticulture, Sericulture, and Forestry	6	4	10	2,761	473	3,234
	(60.00)	(40.00)	0.08	(85.37)	(14.63)	7.12
	0.09	0.07		9.15	3.09	
Veterinary Science, including Fisheries, Dairy Science,	0	0	0	550	93	643
Animal Science, etc.				(85.53)	(14.47)	1.41
				1.82	0.61	
Law	18	3	21	377	110	487
	(85.71)	(14.29)	0.18	(77.41)	(22.59)	1.08
	0.27	0.05		1.25	0.72	
Others (Music/Fine Arts, Drawing and Painting, Library	339	231	570	556	455	1,011
Science, Physical Education, Journalism, Social Work, etc.	(59.47)	(40.53)	4.76	(55.0)	(45.00)	2.22
	5.13	4.31		1.84	2.98	
Total	6,605	5,359	11,964	30,170	15,277	45,447
	(55.21)	(44.79)	100	(66.38)	(33.62)	100
	100	100		100	100	

SOURCE: Adapted from UGC (2002a, pp. 26, 29)

TABLE 11.3. Level-wise student enrollment, 2000–01

	Total Enrollment		*Gender Distribution*	
Level	*Number*	*%*	*Men (%)*	*Women (%)*
Graduate	7,488,736	89.16	60.69	39.31
Postgraduate	775,303	9.23	59.34	40.66
MPhil	11,964	0.14	55.21	44.79
PhD	45,447	0.54	66.39	33.62
Diploma/Certificate	77,993	0.93	65.73	34.27
Total	8,399,443	100.00	60.64	39.36

SOURCE: Adapted from UGC (2002a, p. 29)

(787 or 6.97 percent), veterinary science (146 or 1.29 percent), law (74 or 0.66 percent), and "others" (including music/fine arts, library science, physical education, journalism, and social work) (238 or 2.11 percent) (UGC 2002b, 1).[8] (See table 11.4.)

A subject analysis of these doctorates reveals that in arts/social sciences, of the 4,280 degrees awarded, languages and literature alone accounted for nearly 40 percent (1,685 or 39.37 percent), followed by economics (830 or 19.39 percent), political science (362 or 8.46 percent), sociology (257 or 6.00 percent), psychology (199 or 4.65 percent), and others (947 or 22.13 percent). Similarly, of the 3,885 degrees awarded by the science faculties, more than 76 percent (or 2,954) were in seven disciplines: chemistry (965 or 24.84 percent), physics (533 or 13.72 percent), botany (495 or 12.74 percent), zoology (438 or 11.27 percent), mathematics (265 or 6.82 percent), biochemistry (142 or 3.66 percent), and home science (116 or 2.99 percent) (UGC 2002b, 27–30, 31–33). With 621 PhD awardees, Hindi stood first in the award of the PhD degrees in the arts faculty, and with 965 awardees, chemistry alone accounted for 24.84 percent of all PhDs awarded in science faculty and recorded the highest number of awardees in any subject in any faculty.

Gender-wise, the award of doctorates is reflective of the gender distribution of enrollment in doctoral education (see table 11.4): 65 percent of all doctorate awardees are men. However, in terms of the faculty from which they have obtained their doctorates, there are interesting differences. As compared with their proportion in the total doctorate awardees (35 percent), women account for a relatively higher proportion of awardees in the arts (42.31 percent), education (49.45 percent), medicine (43.42 percent),

TABLE 11.4. Number of theses accepted (faculty-wise) for the award of doctorate degrees—1999–2000

	Number of degrees awarded		
Faculty	*Men*	*Women*	*Total*
Arts/Social Sciences	2,469	1,811	4,280
	(57.69)	(42.31)	37.89
	33.63	45.79	
Science	2,476	1,409	3,885
	(63.73)	(36.27)	34.39
	33.73	35.63	
Commerce	471	100	571
	(82.49)	(17.51)	5.05
	6.42	2.53	
Education	184	180	364
	(50.55)	(49.45)	3.22
	2.50	4.55	
Engineering/Technology	632	91	723
	(87.41)	(12.59)	6.40
	8.61	2.30	
Medicine	129	99	228
	(56.58)	(43.42)	2.02
	1.76	2.50	
Agriculture	670	117	787
	(85.13)	(14.87)	6.97
	9.13	2.96	
Veterinary Science	131	15	146
	(89.73)	(10.27)	1.29
	1.78	0.38	
Law	57	17	74
	(77.03)	(22.97)	0.66
	0.78	0.43	
Others	122	116	238
	(51.26)	(48.74)	2.11
	1.66	2.93	
Total	7,341	3,955	11,296
	(64.99)	(35.01)	100
	100	100	

NOTE: All universities combined, including institutions "deemed to be universities."
"Others" includes Music/Fine Arts, Library Science, Physical Education, Journalism, and Social Work.
Adapted from UGC (2002b, p. 1, Table 1)

and "others" (48.74 percent) faculties. A column-wise reading of the table reveals that 81.42 percent of all women doctorate awardees are from the arts and science faculties; the corresponding percentage for men is 67.36, and 24.16 of men obtained their doctorates in commerce/management, engineering/technology and agriculture. The gendered nature of doctoral education is manifest in its extreme in subjects such as music and fine arts, where 87.10 percent (54/62) and 73.68 percent (28/38) of all doctorates are women!

In brief, in spite the impressive growth in enrollment in research courses in absolute terms, as a percentage of total enrollment in higher education doctoral program enrollment has been very low, and the enrollment in doctoral programs has stabilized at less than 0.7 percent during the last decade. Much of the enrollment in doctoral education and the doctorates awarded are from the conventional liberal education faculties of the sciences and arts/social sciences. Women account for one-third of the enrollment in doctoral education; there has been a slow but steady increase in their proportion in doctoral education over the decades. But the enrollment of women in doctoral education appears to be skewed in favor of the arts, sciences, education, and other faculties; doctoral education in the faculties of commerce/management, engineering, medicine, agriculture, veterinary science, and law appears to be generally a male preserve.

THE STRUCTURE AND FUNCTIONING OF DOCTORAL EDUCATION

Under the UGC Act 1956, only universities established by an act of Parliament or State Legislative Assemblies and institutes "deemed to be universities" under Section 3 of that Act can award the doctorate.[9] The IITs, though not coming under the purview of the UGC, are overseen by the All India Council of Engineering and Technology Education (AICTE), and are authorized to award the doctorate. However, the Indian Institutes of Management (called IIMs) are not so authorized; they offer a "fellowship program" which is regarded as equivalent to the doctoral programs of the universities and the IITs. That is, the IIM Fellowship is treated as equivalent to the doctorate, but its holder is not entitled to use the title "Dr."

Candidates desirous of pursuing doctoral education register for a formal program in a university or institute where it is offered, often undergo a course of taught curriculum and prepare a thesis as part of the requirements for the award of the doctorate. However, many universities confer the doctorate *honoris causa* on individuals in recognition of their lifetime achievement in a given field or as a mark of their esteem. Obviously, by definition, those who are conferred the doctorate *honoris causa* neither undergo a course of study nor submit a thesis for evaluation. Some of them, in fact, may not have any formal education to their credit! The pressures of popular democracy and compelling group interests or the obligations to return favors often result in such degrees being awarded to "undeserving" persons and politicking about it. Considering the likely controversy about such awards, there are instances of individuals declining the award. Generally, those who are conferred the doctorate *honoris causa* do not use "Dr." as a title.

ADMISSION TO DOCTORAL PROGRAM

As early as 1948–49, the University Education Commission recommended that utmost care should be exercised in selecting students for doctoral programs: "The student should not only have attained a proper background in the fundamentals of his subject, but should have a certain innate originality of mind, apart from mere learning, that is essential for a research worker" (UEC 1950, 148). The Commission further emphasized that admission to this program "should be made entirely on merit and on an all-India basis" (UEC 1950, 149).

However, a decade and half later, the UGC's committee on standards of university education noted that

> There seems . . . to be a tendency in some universities to register candidates without due attention being paid to their research aptitudes. The usual procedure is that an application is made by a candidate to supplicate for a research degree, indicating the topic together with or without a synopsis of the work proposed to be done. This is placed before a Research Degree Committee, which quite often has to judge the fitness or otherwise of the candidates in a hurried way, as the committee has to deal with a large number of applicants.—UGC 1965, 44

This situation has hardly changed since then.

The minimum academic qualification for admission to the doctoral program in most universities/institutes is a Second Class Master's or equivalent degree in the subject of research awarded by a recognized university in India or abroad with at least an average of 55 percent of aggregate marks, or a grade point average of 3.5 under the seven-point grade system of the UGC. The IITs and some universities prescribe a higher minimum, that is, First Class (60 percent or 4.05 grade point average). For the candidates belonging to the Scheduled Castes and Scheduled Tribes,[10] however, the minimum eligibility is reduced by 5 percentage points in aggregate marks or 0.45 points in the grade point average. Additionally, the IITs prescribe a valid GATE score or an award of a CSIC/UGC/NBHM research fellowship for admission to their doctoral programs. Often, more so in IITs than in the universities, some departments/centers or schools/faculties prescribe additional eligibility requirements focused more on the subject of research.

All central universities, IITs and IIMs, and some state universities conduct an entrance test for admission to the doctoral program to ascertain the aptitude and knowledge of the applicants. Some of the universities expect letters of recommendation from teachers who are familiar with the applicants' academic careers certifying their suitability for pursuing the doctoral program. All documents relating to applicants are scrutinized by a committee, whose nature and composition varies from university to university. In some universities, an interview is also conducted.

The purpose of an elaborate selection process is "to look out for the quality of the candidate's mind" and her/his "fitness for research" rather than her/his paper qualifications (UGC 1965, 45). However, in most universities, the process is carried out perfunctorily, and the entrance test and the interview serve only as a sieve—that is to select few students from a large number of applicants—rather than as a guide to aptitude for research or as an indicator of "innate originality of mind."

PRE-DOCTORAL TRAINING

For most students enrolling in doctoral programs in India, such a program is their first encounter with research. This is because in most universities in the country there is no component of research-based dissertation, and if it exists at all, it is often optional. Some universities and institutes offer Master of Philosophy (MPhil) programs (of one- or two-year duration) as an intermediate research degree, and in these universities, an MPhil may be a requirement for enrollment in the PhD program.

The provision of an intermediate research-degree is expected to improve the quality of doctoral research. The pedagogy at the Master's level is oriented more to the transmission of knowledge, and there is little or no emphasis on its generation or refinement. Based on the recommendation of the University Education Commission (1948–49) that "students should be given training in the methods and principles of research" (UEC 1950, 148), many universities introduced a course in research methodology at the master's level (and some even at the bachelor's level), especially in social sciences (and languages). At this stage, however, very few students would have decided about enrolling in a doctoral program. Hence, neither the students nor their teachers treat the course on research methodology with the seriousness that it deserves.

That is, in most universities, for all practical purposes, the training in the theory and practice of research begins at the doctoral level. Realizing the inadequate training that the students have at the time of entering doctoral studies, several universities have introduced a component of pre-doctoral training that the students have to complete successfully before their registration for the doctoral program is confirmed. While generally such pre-doctoral training is "self-taught" (with the assistance of the guide/supervisor), in IITs and in some universities the students have to complete a minimum number of credit hours of lecture courses, laboratory sessions, seminars, etc.

DOCTORAL RESEARCH WORK

Even in universities and institutes where course work is prescribed for doctoral students, it is only a partial requirement, generally a condition for the confirmation of registration for the program. The basic requirement for the award of the doctorate is a thesis to be submitted by the student. The thesis is expected to embody the results of a piece of original research work carried by the student characterized either by the discovery of facts or by a fresh approach toward the interpretation of facts or theories.

In many arts subjects (especially philosophy, and languages and literature) and in mathematics or statistics, the research work may be exegetical in nature. However, in science subjects, the emphasis is on laboratory work; and in the social sciences, on fieldwork. Irrespective of the subject of study, the student must prove her/his capacity for critical examination and sound judgment. The thesis must also be satisfactory as regards its literary presentation. Most universities also prescribe the physical layout of the thesis, and some even expect the thesis to be cleared by the library or the publications division before it is submitted for examination.

Most universities do not allow doctoral students to publish their research work before the declaration of results. Some expect the examiners to certify whether the thesis is publishable, and the student has to obtain permission from the university to publish her/his thesis. However, a few universities have begun permitting, if not expecting, students to publish their research work prior to the submission of the thesis. For instance, Jawaharlal Nehru University (a premier central university) permits the students to submit, along with their thesis, any original papers pertaining to the area of specialization published by them during the course of their doctoral research and their MPhil dissertation (if any) as subsidiary or supporting material in favor of their candidature for the doctorate.

EXAMINATION OF DOCTORAL THESIS

The system of examination of the doctoral thesis is varied. However, all universities invariably send their thesis outside the university for evaluation, a system known in Indian parlance as "external examination." In some universities, the definition of "external examination" is so rigid that even guides are not associated with the process of examination; one of the external examiners is appointed as the Chairperson of the Board of Examiners for the thesis. However, the general practice is to appoint the guide as the Chairperson or Coordinator of the Board of Examiners, whether s/he is an examiner or not.

Until the early 1970s, universities used to send the doctoral thesis to experts from outside the country (especially the UK and USA) for examination. This was particularly the case when expertise in several subjects was not available in the country, or the pool of examiners was too small to draw upon. While some universities continue to appoint at least one examiner from outside the country (as mandatory even), most universities now appoint examiners only from within the country. Experts are now available in practically all subjects, and, in fact, in some subjects, like languages, music and fine arts, it is difficult if not impossible to find examiners from outside the country. Furthermore, in the experience of most universities, sending a thesis outside the country for examination implies inevitable delay in the announcement of results. Of course, there is also the ideological objection to appointing examiners from outside the country: that it is tantamount to voluntary submission to intellectual neo-colonialism (mostly of the English-speaking world). All the same, the system is defended on the ground that it is in the best interest of the quality of doctoral programs.

In most universities and institutes, a viva voce examination is mandatory before the thesis is finally accepted for the award of the degree. However, in very rare cases, it is held only if the external examiners recommend it. This examination has certain advantages: the examiners get an opportunity to confirm their impressions of the candidate and her/his thesis, and the student is offered an occasion to defend her/his thesis and prove her/his knowledge of the field. Conventionally, the viva voce has been held in camera, with only the Chairperson of the Board of Examiners (who is generally the guide), at least one external examiner and the candidate present. However, it is increasingly becoming a "public defense" of the thesis before a gathering of faculty members, students and others who may be interested in the subject. In either case, however, the ultimate recommendation on the award of the doctorate to the student is made by the Board of Examiners. It is extremely rare that a candidate who is asked to defend her/his thesis is failed at the viva voce examination. That is, viva voce examination is more a formality than a definitive test.

Viva voce examination is conducted only when the examiners appointed for the thesis unanimously recommend it for the award of the doctorate. If any examiner recommends revision of the thesis, the candidate is generally advised to revise the thesis and resubmit it after a stipulated period (generally not earlier than six months). The resubmitted thesis is referred to the examiner who had recommended the revision, and only after he/she approves the thesis, the viva voce examination is conducted. If an examiner recommends rejection of the thesis, it is generally referred to a third examiner, whose verdict is regarded as final.

DURATION OF DOCTORAL PROGRAM

The duration of doctoral programs varies from two to five years. The IITs and some universities prescribe a minimum period of two years before which a student cannot submit her/his thesis, though under certain conditions this prescription is waived. Similarly, the maximum period, which is five years in most universities, is relaxed in exceptional cases by six months or a year.

Generally, students registering for doctoral programs are required to engage in research *full-time*, and not to engage in any employment that would affect their research work. However, to encourage employed persons to pursue doctoral education, some universities enroll students on a *part-time* basis. Part-time students are permitted a slightly (about 40 percent) longer duration than their full-time counterparts to submit their theses. Full-time students, in most universities, are required to spend at least two years in the territorial jurisdiction of the university in which there are enrolled. However, this rule is not insisted upon, and students living outside the location of the university generally meet this rule by giving a local address.

STATUS OF DOCTORAL STUDENTS

The status of doctoral students in Indian universities and institutes is best described as marginalized. Generally, they view themselves as superior to the Master's students, and often maintain a distance from the latter; in fact, they call themselves "research scholars" or "research fellows" as different from "students." If at all, the Master's students grudgingly endorse this self-conferred status of doctoral students.

For the faculty, and more so the administration, doctoral students are "students." However, they subtly distinguish the doctoral students from the Master's students: the doctoral students are often assigned work as teaching assistants or tutors, and are asked to invigilate at the examinations, assist in the admission process, etc. This gives doctoral students greater access to the faculty and the administration.

As part of state-supported higher education, doctoral programs are highly subsidized. Nevertheless, the students have to support themselves during the program period; if they are not residents of the place where the university/institute is located, they have to meet hostel and other living expenses. This is in addition to the deferred earnings resulting from their not being gainfully employed. Some doctoral students take up employment at the cost of their research work, and this results in delay in the submission of thesis and often in the student dropping out of the program.

To arrest this tendency and to encourage bright students to pursue doctoral education, the UGC offers five-year research fellowships (Junior Research Fellowship, during the first two years; and, if the progress of the student is satisfactory, Senior Research Fellowship for the next three years). The fellowship amount is about 60–70 percent of a Lecturer's salary at the entry level. The fellowship holders are entitled to a housing allowance and contingency grant. However, to be eligible to get this fellowship a student has to pass the National Eligibility Test referred to earlier.[11] Several charities, foundations, and philanthropic organizations also award fellowships to academically proficient doctoral students who find it difficult to finance their educations. The Indian Council of Social Science Research offers short-term research grants to doctoral students in social sciences to do library work and data analysis.

SUPERVISORY SYSTEM

Research work leading to MPhil and PhD degrees is supervised by a teacher, called "guide" in the Indian parlance. Often a guide is assisted by a co-guide. The institution of co-guide is of instrumental significance: generally, a co-guide is taken if the subject of research is interdisciplinary in nature, requiring expertise in more than one field. However, a co-guide is also taken for administrative convenience—if the guide dies or leaves the university/institute when the student is about to submit the thesis—or to meet some administrative requirement—as, for example, when the expert in a field is located in an institution outside the university/institute where the student is enrolled.

As per the UGC guidelines, in most universities, professors and readers/ associate professors are automatically recognized as guides. A lecturer/ assistant professor is generally recognized as guide provided he/she has a stipulated period of experience after obtaining the doctorate and has published a specified number of articles in refereed journals. In some universities and institutes, however, the recognition of a teacher as a guide is not automatic; there is a process for recognition, which in some cases involves review by external experts of the bio-data of the teacher wanting to be recognized as a guide.

Most universities stipulate the maximum number of doctoral students that a guide can supervise at any point in time: the number is more (about six) in humanities and social sciences) and less (about four) in sciences. The overall responsibility for supervising the research work of a student rests with the guide. In some universities, the guide is assisted by a committee—called variously a doctoral advisory committee, faculty research committee, etc.—consisting of colleagues from within and outside the faculty and even experts from outside the university/institute.

A few universities have a special provision for self-guidance by a doctoral student. For instance, Goa University allows a teacher who has put in ten years of service at the undergraduate level in a college affiliated to it or five years of service at the postgraduate level, and who has done "sufficient research work" to register for the doctorate on her/his own. A self-guiding doctoral student, however, has to comply with all other requirements prescribed by the University. The Head of the Department of the subject concerned will co-ordinate the work of such candidates.

THE PROBLEM OF QUALITY

Pursuit of research as a career or for its own sake has never been an option for most students completing higher education in India. In the decades immediately following independence, the best students preferred to enter government service, as it offered better salaries and career prospects. Today, the prospects in computer science and information technology and allied applied fields attract the best of students. Excepting the central universities and top-ranking institutes of technology and management, universities invariably complain about the poor quality of students enrolling for doctoral education. The students are found not only to be inadequately prepared for doctoral education, but also to lack the aptitude for research.

No wonder the problem of quality of doctoral education is a matter of serious concern in the Indian university system. This problem has many dimensions. The most obvious is the poor quality of the theses submitted by the students. Most theses that are awarded doctorate degrees are read for the first and last time by the student, her/his guide, and the examiners before it is stacked in the library shelves or deposited in a documentation center. Very rarely are they published by reputed publishers or in scholarly journals. As such, doctoral research in India hardly makes any impact on the knowledge in any given field.

Normally, evaluation is expected to ensure quality of the thesis to be awarded the doctorate. However, it is at this stage that the system seems to have fared the worst. In the mid-1960s, the UGC's committee on the standards in higher education had observed that "it is important to ensure that theses are referred only to competent scholars in the filed. We understand that this is not always done" (UGC 1965, 45). The problem seems to have become grim with the increasing number of theses being submitted for evaluation.

Regional universities in India have always suffered from a lack of resources, and the gradual withdrawal of state patronage for higher education has aggravated their financial predicament. To minimize expenditure on examiners visiting universities to conduct viva voce examinations, most universities appoint examiners from within the state or from the neighboring universities. Compounding this is the tendency among guides to recommend the names of their friends on the panel of examiners, as *quid pro quo*, so that the theses supervised by them pass muster.

An important aspect of the colonial implantation of higher education in India was English, which was not only taught as the most important language, but was also the medium of instruction in postsecondary education. Even after half a century of independence, higher education in India has not been able to deliver itself from this colonial legacy completely; it is still the predominant medium of instruction in higher education. Excepting in the language subjects, doctoral theses are largely written in English, a language in which most students are not proficient.

In some regional universities, doctoral students now have the option of writing their theses in the regional (Indian) language, say Hindi, Kannada or Tamil. Generally, this option is exercised by students enrolled in the faculties of humanities and social sciences. Since the library language in higher education is still predominantly English and the Indian languages are not developed enough to facilitate scientific writing, such students are at a disadvantage. Moreover, since there are many Indian languages, there is also the problem of finding external examiners who can evaluate the thesis written in a given Indian language. As a consequence, the examiners are drawn from the same limited pool repeatedly, irrespective of their expertise.

Be it in English or in the Indian languages, there is hardly any emphasis on original writing in the Indian education system; for most students, the PhD thesis is their first essay at original writing. There is now growing appreciation of the need to impart training in academic writing skills. The Tata Institute of Social Sciences has introduced a "Workshop on Academic Writing Skills" (an auxiliary course) in its MPhil-PhD program. In some universities, guides persuade their doctoral students to attend similar workshops.

Given the lack of aptitude for research and the linguistic proficiency required to write a good doctoral thesis, students often look for easy alternatives. Some students use ghostwriters, usually a teacher familiar with the art of writing theses. This often passes under the name of professional consultancy! Then, there is the intractable malady of plagiarism: instances of doctoral students lifting passages from published material and of copying from dissertations already awarded degrees are gossip topics in all universities, and are even reported in newspapers. The easy accessibility to material on the Internet has evidently facilitated the "cut-and-paste" culture among students.

Plagiarism, however, is not easily detectable, especially if the thesis is written in an Indian language. Theses written in English language submitted to one university have been translated into Indian languages and submitted in another university. Some second-hand bookshops clandestinely sell MPhil dissertations and PhD theses. Since plagiarism in doctoral education tarnishes the image of the university and its faculty, universities generally brush complaints of plagiarism under the carpet, or conduct a perfunctory inquiry to bury the case.

By law, the UGC has the responsibility of regulating the quality of education in universities.[12] However, considering the inordinate number of universities it is required to oversee, and being endowed with very little power, the UGC has been incapable of enforcing its own recommendations. For instance, with research being accepted as a necessary function of the university system, the UGC has been a mute witness to inadequately staffed and ill-equipped institutions enrolling large numbers of students for doctoral programs. As a step in the direction of quality control in higher education, in 1994, the UGC set up an autonomous body called the National Assessment and Accreditation Council. However, this body has no special provision for assessment and accreditation of doctoral programs.

CONCLUSION: WHITHER DOCTORAL EDUCATION

Starting late and growing slowly during the colonial era, doctoral education is now established as an integral part of the higher education system in India. If not as a proportion to the total enrollment in higher education, in absolute terms at least, there has been a phenomenal increase in the enrollment for doctoral education over the decades. Correspondingly, there has been an increase in the number of doctorates awarded by the universities and university-level institutions of higher education in India.

The large-scale award of doctorates in conventional fields of study does not, however, reflect a genuine interest in research—for most postgraduates, obtaining the doctorate marks the end of their association with research. It is better explained by the premium attached to the doctorate in appointments to teaching jobs in universities and colleges, and in career advancement from lecturer's position to that of reader. Making the doctorate mandatory for appointments to and career advancement in the teaching profession, without regard to standards, has eroded its status and quality.

Based on a review of the situation, C. P. S. Chauhan observes that "The topics undertaken for investigation are normally repetitions or linguistic transformations of some old topics of other Indian or a foreign university." Replications apart, "the topics [chosen] are not based on genuine problems of the discipline or of society, rather they involve futile mental exercise in theoretical subject matter resulting in no practical utility" (Chauhan 1999, 183). This is evident if one glances at the list of theses that have been accepted for the award of doctorates published in the *University News*, the weekly journal of the Association of Indian Universities.

All this is understandable considering that conventional doctorate holders were invariably absorbed by the university system, especially in the faculties of humanities and social sciences. While the doctorate holders in the faculty of sciences too found employment in the university system with ease, they also had employment prospects, however narrow, in research centers and laboratories outside the university system. However, with the gradual withdrawal of state patronage for higher education, the prospects of employment in the academic profession have been declining (see Jayaram 2003). Most state governments have imposed an embargo on the recruitment of teachers. The declining employment opportunities for doctorate holders in academia are sure to have two consequences: enrollment in doctoral education will decline, and the doctorate will be devalued. Doctorate holders entering non-academic and often low-paid jobs, in which their doctoral education has no relevance, is proof of this.

In India, there is a form of streaming in higher education. On completion of higher secondary schooling, the best of students take up professional education to become engineers or doctors. Only the left over take up graduate education and possibly enter other professions (like law or teaching) or semi-professions (like library or nursing). Those pursuing research as a career are rare, the best of them go abroad, and most of them do not return. These facts have to be borne in mind in reviewing the prospects of doctoral education in the country.

I have elsewhere (see Jayaram 2005) commented on the peculiar disjunction in Indian higher education: the concentration by the expanding university system on "retailing knowledge," rather than on creating and refining knowledge, which function is assigned to specialist institutes and laboratories outside the university system—like the Indian Institute of Science (Bangalore), Tata Institute of Fundamental Research (Mumbai), and the Indian Institutes of Technology (Chennai, Delhi, Kanpur, Kharagpur, and Mumbai)—and the laboratories under the umbrella of the Council of Scientific and Industrial Research (CSIR), rather than to the universities. Viewed in the light of such disjunction and the resultant absence of research-orientation in Indian university system, the UGC's recent scheme of support to "the centers of excellence" comes as a ray of hope for doctoral education.

NOTES

I thank Professor Philip G. Altbach for suggesting that I write this paper and Mr. Dinesh S. Torane for helping me with the tables.

1. In 1947, India had twenty universities and 496 colleges catering to 241,369 students. During the next fifty-six years, India built up a massive system of higher education: in 2003, there were three hundred university-status institutions (including eighteen central universities, eighty-one "deemed-to-be universities"), and 15,343 colleges. The system now employs about 436,000 teachers and caters to about 9,228,000 students (UGC 2002–03, 4, 48).

2. The University of Calcutta awarded its first doctorate degree only in 1911; that was in economics to Jajneswar Ghosh for his thesis "The History of Land Tenures in England, France, Germany and Russia and the Agrarian Question" (Datta 1989, 78).

3. Some nationalist-minded scholars like Zakir Hussain, Salim Ali, and Ram Manohar Lohia, instead went to Germany for their doctoral education.

4. It is not that scholars in India did not engage in research before 1914; but they were individual scholars at isolated colleges, or in government research institutes. The names of Sir R. G. Bhandarkar at Poona, Sir Ganganatha Jha at Allahabad, Professor Kuppuswami Sastri at Madras, Sir J. C. Bose and Sir P. C.

Ray at Calcutta, Colonel J. Stephenson and Professor S. R. Kashyap at Lahore are often recalled (see UEC 1950, 144). What is creditworthy, these scientists worked under severe handicaps, especially considering the facilities that were available to scientists in America and Britain at that time.

5. The University Grants Commission (UGC) was established by an Act of Parliament in 1956 as a centralized authority vested with the power to provide funds for and to set and co-ordinate standards of higher education. It was modeled after the British University Grants Committee (established in 1936; since abolished).

6. This was also in accordance with the Program of Action of the National Policy on Education (1986), and it was also later endorsed by the UGC's committee on pay revision under the chairmanship of Dr. R. P. Rastogi (1994–95).

7. While the UGC introduced the NET for entry-level teaching positions in 1989, it has been conducting a similar test for JRF since 1984.

8. Provisional data compiled by the UGC puts the number of doctorates awarded in 2001–02 at 11,899: arts/social sciences, 4,545 (38.20 percent); science, 4,012 (33.72 percent); commerce/management, 704 (5.92 percent); education, 427 (3.59 percent); engineering/technology, 747 (6.28 percent); medicine, 192 (1.61 percent); agriculture, 781 (6.56 percent); veterinary science, 90 (0.75 percent); law, 108 (0.91 percent); and others, 293 (2.46 percent). Subject-wise details of the doctorates in these faculties are not available yet (see http://www.ugc.ac.in/inside/statpdf/phddegree.pdf (accessed 23 March 2006)).

9. Most universities and institutes offering doctoral education have retained the nomenclature "Doctor of Philosophy" (PhD) for the degree awarded to a successful candidate. However, some universities now call this degree by the Sanskrit term *Vidyavachaspathi*.

10. Scheduled Castes and Scheduled Tribes are the traditionally indigent sections of India's population listed in the Constitution of India for protective discrimination.

11. An analysis of the data provided in the UGC's annual reports suggests that the percentage of candidates qualifying for JRF at the NET is measly. For instance, in the NET held in December 1999, only 347 out of 34,468 (or 1.01 percent) candidates were found eligible for JRF. The highest percentage of success was in the NET held in December 1993, that is, 494 out of 18,558 (or 2.66 percent). This reveals the poor quality of the candidates appearing for the NET, and it is also reflective of the poor standard of postgraduate education that they have undergone.

12. The standards of professional education are coordinated and regulated by statutory bodies such as the Indian Medical Council, the All India Council of Technical Education, the Bar Council of India, the Dental Council of India, the Pharmacy Council of India, and the Nursing Council of India. The Indian Council of Agricultural Research looks after agricultural education. The question of jurisdiction between these bodies created by acts of Parliament and the universities established by acts of Parliament or state legislative bodies has often been agitated before courts of law.

BIBLIOGRAPHY

Ashby, E., and M. Anderson. 1966. *Universities: British, Indian, and African.* London: Weidenfield and Nicholson.

Bandyopadhyay, Madhumita. 2003. "Quality Control of Doctoral Research: Role of Research Fellowships." *University News* 41(29): 1–5, 13.

Chauhan, C. P. S. 1990. *Higher Education in India: Achievements, Failures and Strategies.* New Delhi: Ashish Publishing House.

Datta, Bhabatosh. 1989. "Social Science Research: Universities and Autonomous Institutions." In *Higher Education in India: The Institutional Context*, edited by Amrik Singh and G. D. Sharma, 78–88. Delhi: Konark.

Jayaram, N. 2003. "The Fall of the Guru: The Decline of the Academic Profession in India." In *The Decline of the Guru: The Academic Profession in Developing and Middle-Income Countries*, edited by Philip G. Altbach, 199–230. New York: Palgrave Macmillan.

Jayaram, N. 2004. "Higher Education in India: Massification and Change." In *Asian Universities: Historical Perspectives and Contemporary Challenges*, edited by Philip G. Altbach and Toru Umakoshi, 85–112. Baltimore and London: The Johns Hopkins University Press.

Jayaram, N. 2005. "Beyond Retailing Knowledge: Prospects of Research-Oriented Universities in India." Paper presented at the research conference on "Flagship Universities," Center for International Higher Education, Lynch School of Education, Boston College, Massachusetts, 23–26 June.

Kaul, J. N. 1974. *Higher Education in India, 1951–91: Two Decades of Planned Drift.* Simla: Indian Institute of Advanced Study.

Ministry of Education (ME), Government of India. 1971. *Education and National Development (Report of the Education Commission, 1964–66)*, reprint edition. New Delhi: National Council of Educational Research and Training.

University Education Commission (UEC). 1950. *The Report of the University Education Commission (December 1948–August 1949)*, Vol. I. Delhi: The Manager of Publications, Government of India.

University Grants Commission (UGC). 1965. *Report on Standards of University Education.* New Delhi: University Grants Commission.

University Grants Commission (UGC). 2002a. *University Development in India: 1995–96 to 2000–01.* New Delhi: University Grants Commission.

University Grants Commission (UGC). 2002b. *University Development in India: Basic Facts and FiguresDoctorate Degrees Awarded, 1999–2000.* New Delhi: University Grants Commission.

University Grants Commission (UGC). 2002–03. *Annual report, 2002–03.* New Delhi: University Grants Commission.

· IV ·

DOCTORAL EDUCATION IN NORTH AMERICA

12 • CANADA

GARTH WILLIAMS

WITH THE COLLABORATION OF MARTHA CRAGO, JONATHAN C. DRIVER, LOUIS MAHEU, AND MARC RENAUD

> Armed with cutting edge technology from around the world, the latest tools, the latest techniques and processes learned from their work under the very best researchers, they graduate with much fanfare and go on to build the industry, institutions and society of our country.[1]—MIKE LAZARIDIS, FOUNDER, PRESIDENT AND CEO RESEARCH-IN-MOTION

Newly minted doctoral graduates, standing before the world with cap and gown at the center of a convocation hall, have come to symbolize a university's quintessential contribution to the global knowledge-based society and economy in Canada today. They represent our best hope for new discoveries and deeper understanding, for a proud place in the international intellectual community, for teaching future generations and, most especially, for national prosperity and well-being. As such, they marry the pursuit of knowledge, learning and world citizenship, on one hand, with national ambitions on the other. It is the interaction of these two forces, and the sense of importance accorded to each, that have shaped—and continue to shape—the scale and scope of doctoral education in Canada. Indeed, they must flourish or flounder together as Canadian universities with doctoral programs are all public institutions, publicly funded to serve public needs.

Yet there is no national system for supporting, governing and delivering doctoral education in Canada. Rather, the interaction of international intellectual currents and national ambitions has always been negotiated through three significantly autonomous institutions: universities, provincial governments and the federal government. Each brings different interests, resources and degrees of institutional variety to bear on doctoral education; each affects the others and none is ever without influence. When and where universities play a predominant role, intellectual currents and local cultural, social and economic variations have shaped the overall structure of doctoral education in Canada. At those times and in those areas where provincial governments have exerted more influence, regional factors have been important, while federal influence has tended to emphasize national social, economic and strategic interests. Thus, as doctoral education has evolved, growing in size and complexity in step with the country, the process has been uneven, shifting with the balance of influence between universities, provinces and the federal government, producing important variations among institutions and provinces over time.

This paper examines three periods in this evolution of doctoral education in Canada. It touches first on early developments, when limited government resources contributed to the formation of largely autonomous universities and important cultural, regional and local variations in the overall structure of doctoral education. It was at this time that universities established lasting responsibilities for developing public knowledge and providing higher education to serve Canada and the international community. At the same time, provincial governments established their jurisdiction over all postsecondary education and the federal government became involved in supporting advanced research. This arrangement of responsibilities proved to provide a durable foundation for the ever-evolving relationship between universities, provinces and the federal government.

Following the Second World War, the relationship between universities, provinces and the federal government was significantly transformed, though not entirely revolutionized, by massive public investment in higher education and advanced research. Government investment at both levels dramatically expanded the scale and scope of doctoral programs, helping mitigate institutional variations in doctoral education nation-wide. Although no single, planned or explicit negotiation took place between universities, provinces and the federal government at this time, both the new importance of public funding and modest rearrangement of governance and training responsibilities can be seen as parts of a tacit post-war social contract that is the subject of the paper's second section.[2] In a third section, the paper will examine the ways that universities, provinces and the federal government have altered that arrangement of their responsibilities since 1980, in response to globalization, before presenting, in a final section, a statistical portrait of doctoral education in Canada today.

THE EARLY YEARS: 1900–1950

In the eighteenth and nineteenth centuries, the interaction of international intellectual currents and colonial ambitions combined to inspire the creation of Canada's first universities: government chartered and assisted colleges affiliated with state sanctioned churches (the Roman Catholic Church in French Canada and the Church of England in English Canada).[3] In English Canada, however, the resentment of other churches, who quickly established their own affiliated colleges, spurred heated political debate that led colonial and, later, provincial governments to restrict support to autonomous non-denominational institutions. In the Maritimes this meant only two universities received public funding (one each in New Brunswick and Nova Scotia). In Ontario, it encouraged two colleges to secularize (Queen's University and the University of Western Ontario) and a few to federate in a large non-denominational provincial university (University of Toronto). The western provinces applied this principle too, each providing support, using public lands, to a single non-denominational university. Political interference in these institutions continued to produce controversy, however, until 1906 when a scandal at the University of Toronto prompted the Ontario government to establish a separate Board of Governors (responsible for university finances) and Senate (responsible for academic affairs) for the institution. This governance structure provided a good measure of autonomy for the institution and a minimum of controversy for the politicians. As a result, it was quickly copied in all provinces.[4]

In all institutions—even the non-denominational ones—religious influence in the intellectual community encouraged the introduction of different academic traditions in the eighteenth and nineteenth centuries. Presbyterian colleges (notably Dalhousie, Queen's, and McGill Universities) placed an emphasis on practical skills and science borrowed from the Scottish tradition of higher education.[5] In most other institutions, English and French traditions of reflective study and undergraduate teaching or the emphasis of American land grant universities on teaching and professional training dominated. Consequently, research, graduate training and doctoral education did not play a significant role in Canadian universities until the country and the intellectual community began to change at the turn of the last century.

Between 1880 and 1914, immigration, western expansion, industrial development, and the concentration of capital and people in Montréal and Toronto signaled the beginnings of a more modern, socially complex, and economically integrated Canada. These changes coincided with the introduction of social and physical sciences, disciplinary specialization and research in the international academic community. Combined, these international and national developments made the University of Toronto and McGill University in Montréal particularly fertile grounds for the introduction, via the influence of Johns Hopkins University, of the German ideal for the university as a centre of scientific research and graduate training, stimulating and supporting industrial development and economic growth. The University of Toronto awarded the first Canadian doctorate in 1900, in physics, while McGill University conferred its first doctorate, in the natural sciences, in 1909. These two institutions awarded the majority of Canadian doctorates before the Second World War.[6]

Although the number of doctoral graduates doubled in both the 1920s and 1930s, these remained very few.[7] Most Canadian PhDs trained in the United States or Britain and nearly half of all Canadian graduates found work outside the country.[8] Most public support for research and research training came indirectly from small provincial grants to the few non-denominational universities. A precedent was set, however, during the First World War for federal involvement in higher education, advanced research and doctoral training. In 1916, as part of the war effort, the federal government established the National Research Council (NRC) to fund industrial research. The NRC provided the first publicly funded research grants and doctoral fellowships in Canada and established federal jurisdiction over advanced research as part of its responsibility for economic development.[9]

Thus, by 1950, universities had established their responsibilities for conducting and managing higher education, advanced research and doctoral training. As largely autonomous, predominantly independent, institutions with limited public funding, their particular cultural traditions and local communities shaped them and their reaction to intellectual currents. Provinces had clearly defined responsibilities for chartering universities and, within specific limits, funding higher education while a small federal role in advanced research had been accepted. As a result, there was considerable variation in the funding, governance and conduct of higher education and research from one institution to another and very little doctoral study.

THE POST-WAR ERA: 1951–1980

The Second World War, and the economic and demographic booms that followed, significantly altered the scale and scope of doctoral training by encouraging much greater federal and provincial investments in postsecondary education and advanced research. Close collaboration between university researchers and the federal government during the war years proved the strategic and economic importance of scientific research. After the war, the contribution of advanced research to industrial development provided yet another argument for increased public investment. The wartime experience also reinforced a sense of obligation to create opportunities for veterans, the baby-boom generation and all who wanted to pursue higher education. This new sense of the public interest inspired new funding, new funding mechanisms and, ultimately, new governance and management structures that can be seen as parts of a tacit social contract worked out between universities and the two orders of government.

During this time, the success of universities in meeting public expectations, and the governance model applied to publicly funded institutions, helped them retain their autonomous status and influence over postsecondary education and research. In fact, it was at the urging of the National Conference of Canadian Universities (now the Association of Universities and Colleges of Canada) that the federal government, acting on its responsibility for economic development, first increased public support. It introduced direct grants to universities in 1951, increased funding for the NRC, established the Canada Council for the Arts (1957) and created the Medical Research Council (separating it from the NRC in 1960).[10] All of these initiatives encouraged the development of doctoral programs either directly, through the creation of doctoral fellowships, or indirectly, through support for institutions and provisions that encouraged professors to employ graduate students as research assistants. The federal interest in industrial and strategic research was apparent in the allocation of greater support for science, engineering and medical research rather than for the humanities or social sciences.[11] Within these parameters, however, universities ensured that federal funding agencies functioned at "arm's length" from Parliament. For the most part, these agencies awarded fundamental and strategic research grants and doctoral fellowships (approximately a third of their budgets) on the basis of peer review. In this way, they preserved a significant measure of institutional autonomy and a balance between academic interest and national ambitions.

When the first baby boomers reached university age in the 1960s, public interest in postsecondary education and business demand for an educated workforce made access to higher education and university expansion a provincial as well as a national and institutional priority. Within fifteen years, from 1960 to 1975, public funding increased universities' operating expenditures nationwide by 1,000 percent.[12] By limiting public support to non-denominational institutions, provincial governments produced rapid change in the governance structure of most colleges. Almost overnight, impoverished religious institutions secularized to serve changing public needs and access public funding. Small colleges amalgamated to form large non-denominational universities and, where no colleges existed, entirely new institutions sprang up in large and small communities. Provincial funding also brought provincial policies governing tuition fees and other measures affecting public access to postsecondary education. As a result, the contribution of student fees to university operating expenditures declined from 25 percent to 14 percent nationwide despite a huge enrollment increase.[13] At the national level, the federal government was forced to reconcile its initiatives with provincial responsibility for postsecondary education. It replaced direct grants to universities with conditional transfers to provincial governments in 1967 (1959 in Québec) and, in 1977, introduced an Established Program Financing (EPF) arrangement that gave all provinces funds to use at their discretion for medicare, hospital insurance, and postsecondary education. The same year though, it solidified its role in advanced research by creating the Natural Sciences and Engineering Research Council (out of the National Research Council) and the Social Sciences and Humanities Research Council (out of the Canada Council for the Arts). Thus, by the 1970s, a dramatic transformation had taken place in funding for higher education and advanced research in Canadian universities and both levels of government played more prominent roles in the governance and administration of funds. Yet universities retained considerable autonomy and much of their control over the content and conduct of higher education and research.

As in the past, Canadian universities turned to British, American, and French university graduates to fill their new teaching positions.[14] These scholars, all professionally trained researchers, formed graduate faculties to distinguish themselves from less qualified professors. Within these faculties, they adopted training practices that combined both the American tradition (emphasizing substantial course work) and the British and French traditions (emphasizing a long period for original research and a lengthy thesis). Generally, graduate faculties accepted students upon the recommendation of a particular department. In most universities, young Canadian doctoral students paid low tuition fees that were reduced after completion of a residency requirement, course work and a comprehensive exam in the first year or two of the program. Most had seven years to complete their degrees, demonstrate proficiency in a second language and defend their theses before committees of departmental professors with one outside examiner.

Students flooded into these new or newly enlarged doctoral programs in the 1960s. The number of graduate students rose from 6,518 in 1960 to 40,108 in 1975. In 1960, 0.9 percent of Canadians aged twenty-two–twenty-four had enrolled in graduate programs; fifteen years later, 3.3 percent pursued graduate studies.[15] Canadian universities conferred 306 doctoral degrees in 1960. Ten years later, they conferred 1,680 and enrolled 13,268 doctoral candidates in programs across the country.[16] Fourteen universities, in twelve different cities, each enrolled as many doctoral students in 1971 as the entire country had produced a decade earlier. Clearly, increased public funding made it possible for more institutions to offer doctoral programs or expand existing ones. By mitigating some of the differences between institutions in smaller centers and those in larger cities in this way, federal and provincial governments had increased educational opportunities and research nation-wide.

Despite this remarkable growth, however, no single postsecondary education or doctoral training system emerged. Institutions continued to vary as a result of their autonomous status, different scholarly traditions, different sizes and access to private resources as well as the particular needs of their local communities.[17] In 1971, the University of Toronto and McGill University still boasted the largest doctoral programs in Canada. The five largest universities (including the University of British Columbia, the University of Montréal, and the University of Alberta) trained 53.5 percent of all doctoral candidates.[18] Ten years later, the same universities taught 55.1 percent of all PhD students.[19] Within their borders, provincial governments mitigated some of these differences by providing equal funding for each student, setting common tuition levels, and providing student assistance. Yet these measures also reinforced existing provincial differences. For example, the number of graduate students choosing to study at universities in eastern and western Canada remained well below those provinces' share of the national population while the number of graduate students choosing Ontario universities remained well above and actually grew faster than its share.[20] So, while public spending transformed the scale and scope of doctoral education in Canada by reducing differences between universities, some persistent institutional and provincial variations remained.

Nonetheless, the arrangement of responsibilities for funding, governing and conducting higher education and advanced research in Canada, worked out in this period by universities, provinces, and the federal government, can be seen as parts of a tacit social contract. The federal government targeted funds to broad areas of national interest but limited its direct support to advanced research and research training. With the assistance of federal transfers, the provinces increased spending on postsecondary education and took greater control over university tuition but still provided the bulk of public funding for higher education and directed it exclusively to nondenominational institutions. Despite these changes, universities' influence in society and governance structures helped them retain much of their autonomous status as unique institutions with their own traditions and private resources, serving particular communities, managing the delivery of education, and the conduct of research.

THE GLOBAL ERA: 1981–2005

This arrangement of responsibilities between universities, provinces and the federal government changed in the 1980s as intellectual currents evolved and the global economy altered national ambitions. The new economy, spurred by the growth of multinational corporations, greater movement internationally and a revolution in communications technology, resulted in increased production and intense economic competition worldwide. It produced a global recession in 1981–82 that dramatically altered Canadian perceptions of their economic, social and political circumstances. After years of persistent inflation and unemployment in the 1970s, the recession appeared to provide conclusive evidence that post-war government policies were no longer able to assure prosperity and social stability. Canadians began to encourage their governments to reduce public spending and decrease taxes. These same developments, combined with exponential growth in advanced research and increased specialization within academe, raised new research problems that crossed provincial and national boundaries as well as disciplinary distinctions. Thus globalization altered both the context and substance of university education, advanced research and doctoral training in Canada.

Both contextual and substantial changes were negotiated through federal, provincial and institutional policies and programs. The federal government, whose role in postsecondary education and research was most closely tied to national economic policy, played a leading part by altering the means through which universities and doctoral programs might contribute to national prosperity. Provincial governments, concerned with the cost and quality of university education, sought to increase flexibility and planning within their postsecondary education systems.[21] They began to appreciate the role that research played in their own economies too and started or expanded their own programs for university research and research training. Finally though, it was the direct influence of globalization on universities themselves that had the most dramatic effect on doctoral education. Growing numbers of people sought advanced degrees and communities sought greater access to advanced research while faculty and graduate students struggled with new issues, new methodologies, costly new technologies and increasingly interdisciplinary and international research projects. Universities increasingly turned to students and the private sector for support. Thus, in response to globalization, universities, provinces and the federal government once again rearranged their collective responsibilities for funding, governing and conducting higher education, advanced research and doctoral studies in Canada.

FEDERAL FUNDING AND THE NEW NATIONAL INTEREST

Federal adjustment to the new global economy took place in two distinct phases. From 1980 to 1997 the government unilaterally reduced support for postsecondary education and university research in order to eliminate a burgeoning budget deficit.[22] It began in 1980 by capping EPF funding for postsecondary education and by revising this system of cash and tax-point transfers to the provinces in a way that would eventually have eliminated any real transfer (while still providing some justification for claims that it contributed to postsecondary education). Then in 1995 it replaced EPF with the Canada Health and Social Transfer, imposing further reductions while freeing the provinces to spend these funds as they saw fit (dropping any pretense that part of the transfer was targeted for postsecondary education). The federal government also reduced its direct support for advanced research and doctoral training in these years. In 1992 it closed the Science and Economic Councils of Canada and in 1995 cut funding to all research councils. The number of doctoral fellowships available to Canadians fell and so did registration in doctoral programs.[23] Neither funding nor registration was restored until the government reduced its deficit to zero.

In 1998 the second phase in federal adjustment to the global knowledge-based economy began as the government sought to build an economic advantage for Canada through major investments in university-based research and research training. According to then Finance Minister Paul Martin:

> There can be few things more critical to determining our economic success in the next century than a vigorous, broad-based research and development effort. The fact is the more R&D that is done in Canada, the more jobs will be created for Canadians.[24]

Recognizing, like other major industrialized countries, that technological change, larger markets and increased competition made knowledge a more important factor in the economy, the government made a series of major investments to increase the production of new knowledge and the training of highly qualified personnel in Canadian universities. However, after imposing severe restraints on all sectors of society in order to reduce its deficit, the government was no longer willing to simply assume that investment in postsecondary education, research and research training would produce long-term benefits.[25] As a result, it increasingly targeted funds to areas of national economic interest, demanding a demonstrable return on investment, greater transfer of knowledge outside academe, matching funding from other sources and higher levels of accountability.

In fact, the federal government first introduced this approach in 1989 when it created the Networks of Centers of Excellence (NCE) program (based on a similar program in Ontario). The program required close collaboration between researchers and industry but it also sought to advance new research methods, emphasizing interdisciplinary and inter-provincial team research, much like major collaborative research initiatives established at that time by the granting councils. Such programs enriched doctoral studies by exposing students, as members of large research teams, to a wider range of expertise, improved facilities and better financial support.[26] Then in 1997 the federal government set up the Canada Foundation for Innovation (CFI) to fund research infrastructure in partnership with universities, provinces and the private sector. The 1998 federal budget restored funding to the granting councils and established the Canadian Millennium Scholarship Foundation as well as other measures to assist students with the cost of higher education. In 2000 the government created Genome Canada, greatly expanded and transformed the Medical Research Council into the Canadian Institutes of Health Research (CIHR) and launched the Canada Research Chair (CRC) program to attract foreign scholars, repatriate Canadian researchers and retain academic "stars" in Canada. The CRC program significantly strengthened doctoral education by providing infrastructure and research support to funded scholars. In 2001 the government made a direct contribution to universities in order to offset the indirect costs of federally funded research (a contribution established as a permanent program in 2003).

Each of these initiatives altered the federal role in postsecondary education and research. They improved doctoral education by providing more students with better facilities and greater opportunities for funding, learning and career development. But, by insisting on greater knowledge transfer outside of academe, they also raised concerns over the control and ownership of research that universities and granting councils have just begun to address. At the same time, they further differentiated between students in the sciences, engineering and medical fields and those in the social sciences and humanities by increasingly targeting federal funds to the former. It was not until 2003 that the government provided direct support for graduate education in a way that addressed some of these concerns. That year the federal government created the Canada Graduate Scholarship (CGS) program to fund 2,000 masters and 2,000 doctoral fellowships annually. The program increased the number of federal fellowships by 70 percent (to almost 10,000) and, for the first time, supported a greater number of students in the social sciences and humanities than other disciplines (60 percent). Yet the national economic interest was still foremost in the government's mind. In the words of Minister Martin:

> The most precious commodity in today's economy is knowledge. We have invested heavily in postsecondary education and in excellence in university research. We believe that our future lies in providing young Canadians with the best education possible, with the best universities that produce the best knowledge and the best graduates, and with an education system that can compete with the best in the world.[27]

As a result, the government limited CGS scholarships to Canadians studying in Canada (a departure from other federal fellowships that allow Canadian students to attend foreign institutions). Moreover, it still has no plans to attract foreign students by allowing them to hold CGS scholarships or to work while studying in Canada.[28]

PROVINCIAL GOVERNANCE AND THE MARKET FOR IDEAS

Provincial governments faced many of the same economic, social, and political pressures as the federal government in the 1980s and 1990s. So, when the federal government withdrew support from postsecondary education, research, and research training, the provinces generally responded by reducing their level of funding to universities and by seeking new ways to improve the efficiency and accountability of their postsecondary institutions. Overall government spending on universities declined 4.5 percent despite an 18 percent increase in university enrollment.[29] Public contributions to university operating budgets declined from 81 percent, in 1986–87, to 61 percent in 2000–01.[30] These reductions shifted part of the financial burden for postsecondary education and research back onto individuals and the private sector. Moreover, they increased competition between provinces and between universities in ways that quietly accepted, for the first time in thirty years, differences based on their own resources and policy choices.

Provinces with resources and a political will to compete in the intellectual market started to differentiate themselves from those who did not. Québec, which had established its own system of research granting councils in the 1960s, had already a noticeable advantage on which to build. In the 1980s, Ontario launched a Centers of Excellence program and other targeted initiatives while Alberta directed support from its Heritage Fund to university research.[31] All three provinces sought to complement federal research funding, encourage the application of research results and support an intellectual shift towards interdisciplinary team research. As a result, doctoral students increasingly chose to study in Québec, Ontario, and Alberta. Because all doctoral programs in those provinces benefited, this trend actually reduced the concentration of doctoral studies within the largest universities, but it did not spread doctoral students across the country.[32] In Manitoba, where the provincial government chose to invest more heavily in its community colleges, the University of Manitoba saw the size of its doctoral program, eleventh largest in 1981, decline to seventeenth in 2001.[33] By then the University of Saskatchewan and Dalhousie University had also dropped out of the top fifteen, leaving only one institution among that select group, the University of British Columbia, outside of Québec, Ontario, and Alberta.

At the same time that globalization, and the federal reaction to it, increased the market influence on provinces and universities, it also increased the movement of people and ideas across international borders in a way that transformed the intellectual community as well as the market for students and researchers. These national and international trends combined in the 1980s and 1990s to encourage greater institutional and provincial interest in quality assurance. Since the 1960s Ontario universities had worked with the provincial government in the Ontario Council on Graduate Studies to assure educational quality at the graduate level. But, as they entered increasingly competitive national and international markets, all universities went farther to strengthen their internal, regional and national evaluation processes. With respect to doctoral programs, international comparisons, concern for student success and increasing costs prompted, in particular, a renewed focus on time-to-completion.[34] In 1990 universities formed a national body, the Canadian Institutional Research and Planning Association, to advance research on postsecondary education and improve methods for assessing the effectiveness and efficiency of postsecondary institutions. When John Evans, President of CFI, called for an explicit "public research contract" between universities and governments in 2001, universities took the lead in drafting a proposal.[35]

Like universities, provincial governments also increased their interest in quality assurance in response to international and national pressures. In 1990, when Canada ratified the 1979 UNESCO Convention on the Recognition of Studies, Diplomas, and Degrees concerning Higher Education in States belonging to the European Region, they joined the federal government in establishing the Canadian Information Center for International Credentials and now maintain the Center themselves. More recently, provincial decisions to allow private and out-of-province higher education providers prompted the formation of provincial quality assessment boards in Alberta, Atlantic Canada, British Columbia, and Ontario.[36] These boards are all members of the International Network of Quality Assurance Agencies in Higher Education and came together in 2005, under the auspices of the Council of Ministers of Education of Canada, to establish a Pan-Canadian Committee on Quality Assurance. There is some debate now over who, universities or governments, should take the lead on quality assurance in Canada and over what, institutions or academic programs, should be assessed—although Ontario universities recently embraced a version of degree level standards proposed by the Pan-Canadian Committee on Quality Assurance.[37]

CANADIAN UNIVERSITIES IN THE INTERNATIONAL COMMUNITY

In the 1980s and 1990s universities often found themselves caught between declining government funding and rapidly rising enrollment. Despite a decline in the traditional university-aged population in Canada, overall university enrollment increased by 30 percent as Canadians and foreign students sought advantage in the new economy.[38] Enrollment in graduate programs increased 68.6 percent while the number of doctoral candidates rose 106.9 percent nationwide.[39] The number of foreign students enrolled in graduate programs increased 84 percent. They accounted for 12.3 percent of total enrollment in 1981 and 13.4 percent in 2001.[40] In doctoral programs, the proportion of foreign students stood slightly higher at 17.9 percent in 2001.[41] During this time, the participation of women in doctoral studies also increased from 39 percent in 1994 to 46.1 percent in 2001.[42]

Universities met this demand despite government cutbacks by reducing program, faculty, and staff costs, deferring maintenance on their classrooms, laboratories, and physical plant, and by increasing their private sources of revenue.[43] Most important among these were tuition fees, that provinces allowed to increase 135 percent, on average, between 1986–87 and 2000–2001.[44] During that time all provinces introduced differential fees for international students significantly higher than those for Canadians. Some provinces (notably Ontario) also eliminated a long-standing post-residency reduction in tuition fees for doctoral candidates, adding greatly to student costs. Overall, the proportion of university operating revenues derived from tuition fees increased from 16 percent to 34 percent.[45] But universities also raised their revenues from bequests, donations, and private sector grants as well as contracts, spin-off companies, and licensing agreements to double the proportion of their revenue from all private sources to 39 percent.

These changes to university finances increased differences between institutions in two ways. They increased variations between universities in different provinces as each province adopted different tuition fee policies (in addition to providing different levels of direct support). British Columbia, Manitoba, Newfoundland, and Québec limited tuition fee increases to facilitate student access to higher education while others allowed fees to rise to help offset university expenditures.[46] But it also became clear that individual institutions had varying capacities to raise other private revenues. Smaller institutions in smaller centers absorbed more of the enrollment increases in the 1980s and, as a result, saw their operating revenues increase more than larger institutions.[47] But their expenditures also increased, they received slightly less provincial government support per student than larger institutions and had more difficulty securing private sector and federal government research funding. Conversely, universities in larger, growing and prosperous cities benefited. Most notably, the size of the doctoral program at the University of Calgary moved from fifteenth in the country in 1991 to tenth as that city grew from the nation's sixth to fourth largest by 2001.[48]

Globalization has also produced substantive changes in doctoral education as students, supervisors, and universities become increasingly integrated into international intellectual communities. By pursuing new issues and interdisciplinary research, students and supervisors have developed new methodologies, created new knowledge and understanding, redefined disciplinary boundaries, and challenged traditional departmental procedures. Universities have accommodated and encouraged interdisciplinary research by allowing students to take courses and include supervisory committee members from outside of their departments.[49] Some allow doctoral students to enroll jointly in two departments while at least one has experimented with a multidisciplinary college within the graduate studies faculty. Such interdisciplinary training is now often reflected in the degree conferred.

As interdisciplinary research takes students across provincial and national boundaries, universities have sought ways to facilitate graduate student mobility. The Canadian Association of Graduate Studies (CAGS) recently negotiated an agreement, endorsed by all institutions, to provide access to graduate programs, supervisors, libraries, and laboratory facilities for students from other Canadian universities. To bring the agreement into effect, CAGS is seeking support from the federal government for student travel and any differences in registration and housing costs from those at their home institution. CAGS hopes to extend this agreement internationally and secure permission both for Canadians to carry Canada Graduate Scholarships abroad and for international students to hold similar awards in Canada.

At present international mobility still depends on individual institutional arrangements and, as a result, is often influenced by linguistic and other cultural variables that continue to shape the intellectual community. These differences are particularly obvious in Canada because of the development, exclusively within French-speaking universities, of "co-tutelle" agreements with institutions in France. These agreements are negotiated separately for each student and make it possible for them to receive training at two institutions. Students must meet the requirements of both institutions to receive a degree that reflects the contribution of each. Recently, the Bologna process has helped Francophone universities negotiate "co-tutelle" agreements with institutions outside France by increasing the structural similarity of European universities (one of the few direct influences of the Bologna process on Canadian institutions). There is still no equivalent for students in English-speaking universities.

Today, the challenge for universities, provinces, and the federal government is to work out amendments to the tacit post-war social contract in ways that take into account the changes each introduced in response to globalization while recognizing their shared responsibilities for higher education, advanced research, and research training. That process, of arranging and rearranging responsibilities, is already more than a hundred years old in Canada. Its foundations are strong. Building on them in the global era, doctoral education has thrived. More students, and a greater diversity of students than ever before, are pursuing doctoral studies. There are more programs, offering greater financial and intellectual support, opening doors to wider networks of colleagues and partners in a larger intellectual community. Collectively, however, federal, provincial, and institutional decisions no longer aim to spread doctoral studies across the country but, rather, have accepted their concentration in provinces and cities with the necessary material, political, and intellectual resources. These changes and the persistence of support targeted by discipline are evident in the portrait of doctoral education in Canada today.

DOCTORAL EDUCATION IN CANADA TODAY

An Urban Phenomenon

In 2001 Canadian universities conferred a record number of doctoral degrees (approximately 3,660, an increase of almost 40 percent since 1991) and were engaged in training a record number of doctoral candidates.[50] There were 27,340 doctoral students that year (0.9 per thousand population), more than double the enrolment in 1981. But most of the growth came in the 1980s as from 1995 to 1998 the decline in government funding for postsecondary education, research and research training contributed to fewer students pursuing doctoral studies from 1996 to 1999.

The regional distribution of doctoral students reflects the lack of a coordinated national approach to doctoral education in Canada and the commensurate importance of urban industrial centers, institutional strength and provincial investment. Fully 71 percent of doctoral candidates studied in Ontario (39.9 percent) and Québec (31.1 percent) in 2001—both more than their shares of the Canadian population (Ontario represents 38 percent of the total Canadian population while Québec represents 24.1 percent).[51] Alberta, as a result of significant provincial investment, is the only other province to capture more than its share of doctoral students (with 10.5 percent of doctoral candidates and 9.9 percent of the population). British Columbia attracts close to its share of students (11.2 percent, relative to 13.0 percent of the population) while the other provinces fall far short (see table 12.1).

The urban, industrial and institutional influence on the concentration of doctoral studies is even more evident in the distribution of doctoral students by city. Fully 50.6 percent of all doctoral candidates study in one of Canada's three major urban centers (Montréal 21.2 percent; Toronto 19.7; Vancouver 9.7) while another 33.2 percent study in other large cities (Edmonton 7.2 percent; Québec City 6.1; Ottawa 5.2; Calgary 3.2; London 3.2; Waterloo 2.8; Hamilton 2.7).[52] Only the historic Queen's University, in Kingston, Ontario, stands out as an institution located outside of an important urban center that educates a significant percentage

TABLE 12.1. Doctoral candidates and provincial population, 2001[a]

	PhD Students		
Province	*(no)*	*(%)*	*Population (%)*
Ontario	10,900	39.9	38.0
Québec	8,510	31.1	24.1
British Columbia	3,050	11.2	13.0
Alberta	2,860	10.5	9.9
Manitoba	545	2.0	3.6
Saskatchewan	480	1.8	3.2
Nova Scotia	445	1.6	3.0
New Brunswick	270	1.0	2.4
Newfoundland	255	0.9	1.6
Prince Edward Island	10	0.4	0.4

[a] Lebel, *Statistical Report 1990–2001*, 6–7.
SOURCE: Statistics Canada, "A Profile of the Canadian Population."

of Canadian doctoral students (2.8 percent). Although ninety-one institutions are chartered to confer university degrees in Canada, only forty-six enrolled doctoral students in 2001.[53] Of these, one third (fifteen universities) trained 79.9 percent of all doctoral candidates; six universities trained more than half (51.9 percent of all candidates); while the University of Toronto alone trained 15.9 percent (almost double the next largest university).

Targeted Training

The majority of doctoral students (50 percent in 2001) pursued degrees in the social sciences and humanities (including education, arts and communication, business, management and public administration).[54] Students in the sciences and engineering accounted for 43.1 percent of doctoral enrollment while students in the health sciences made up 6.2 percent of all doctoral candidates. During the 1990s, enrollment increased significantly in business, management, and public administration (69.5 percent); arts and communications (65.5 percent); health sciences (38.2 percent); social sciences (17.9 percent); as well as the physical and life sciences (8.7 percent); in absolute terms, however, the greatest increase was in the social sciences. Enrollment in the humanities declined (by 8.9 percent), largely in the later half of the decade, while enrollment in engineering, architecture, mathematics, and computer sciences declined during the years federal funding was reduced (1995–98) before rebounding.

To support their education, doctoral candidates rely on four different sources of funding: the university, their own resources, the federal government, and their provincial governments. For all, the most common source of funding is the university. Fully 64 percent of recent graduates reported income from university teaching assistantships, 58 percent from university scholarships, and 30 percent from university research assistantships.[55] Personal savings were reported as a source of funding by 39 percent of all students, personal earnings by 33 percent, family earnings by 31.5 percent, and loans by 27.3 percent. Federal fellowships were reported by 35.2 percent of all students and federal research assistantships by 18 percent. Provincial fellowships were reported by 36 percent. Most importantly though it is clear that institutions and governments provided the largest part of most students' budgets. Fully 71.4 percent of doctoral graduates indicated that fellowships (51.6 percent) and assistantships (19.8 percent) from all sources represented their primary source of financing while 23.1 percent relied principally on personal resources of all kinds (3.8 percent loans).[56]

Government support is not distributed equally among doctoral candidates. A greater percentage of life sciences students (agricultural, biological, and health sciences) (66 percent) and science students (57 percent) draw on fellowships as their primary source of funding than students in engineering and the social sciences (50 percent), the humanities (43 percent) or any other field (26 percent).[57] Overall, women relied slightly more on personal resources of all kinds and men slightly more on teaching or research assistantships as primary sources of revenue. Men and women relied equally on fellowships.[58] As a result, 68 percent of students in the sciences and engineering graduated without any debt directly related to their graduate education.[59] This was true of 56 percent of students in the life sciences and approximately 45 percent in the social sciences and humanities. Of all those students carrying debt related directly to their doctoral studies, one third owed over $20,000 while 41 percent owed less than $10,000.[60] Students in the humanities, followed closely by those in the social sciences, carried the heaviest debt loads. Whether related to funding, or other issues, social sciences and humanities students also have the lowest completion rates (averaging 45–50 percent compared to approximately 75 percent in other disciplines) and the highest average age at time of completion.[61]

Finally, given the importance of government and institutional financing for doctoral students, it is not surprising to find that policies encouraging scientific and engineering research have had considerable impact on the distribution of doctoral students across disciplines in Canada. Fully 43 percent of doctoral students are enrolled in the sciences and engineering as compared to only 21 percent of bachelors and masters level students.[62]

Most students (75 percent) make firm plans to work or pursue further study during their doctoral program. Of these, a majority arranges employment (56 percent) while a significant number plans for postdoctoral (34 percent) or other formative training (10 percent).[63] In general, a majority of students in the humanities, social sciences, and engineering seek employment while a majority in the health and other sciences pursue further education. Of those students pursuing employment, 57 percent plan to work in the educational services industry; with 13.4 percent working in professional, scientific, and technical services; 10.6 percent in health care and social services; and 9.0 percent in public administration.[64] However, there is much greater variation in the plans of life sciences, engineering, and physical sciences graduates than those in education, the humanities, or social sciences (who account for the large number of graduates planning to work in the educational services industry) (see table 12.2). This discrepancy accounts for an important variation in salary following graduation. Although 60.4 percent of all graduates make over $55,000 per year, this figure is attained by fully 77.9 percent of graduates in education and other professional fields, 77.2 percent in engineering, and 72.7 percent in the physical sciences.[65] Over half (54.7 percent) of life sciences and social sciences (55.8 percent) graduates earn this amount while only 34.8 percent reach this level in the humanities.

The importance of government and university investment in advanced research training is even more evident among doctoral graduates who pursue further study. They predominantly take up postdoctoral fellowships offered by granting agencies (50 percent) or universities (25 percent) and almost all (87 percent) continue to work in a university setting.[66] This reflects the universities' dominant role in the national research and development undertaking.[67] The health of the Canadian research and development sector as a whole is reflected in the intention of 80 percent of Canadian doctoral students to remain in Canada.[68] Included in this number are 60 percent of all foreign students. Nonetheless, their prominence among graduates in the life and physical sciences helps account for the intention to leave Canada of one third of all students in those disciplines.

TABLE 12.2. Employment plans of doctoral graduates, by industry, 2005.[a]

Discipline/ Industry	*Educational Services*	*Science, Technology*	*Health, Social*	*Public Service*	*Goods Producing*	*Other*
Humanities	78.7	-	-	7.3	-	9.6
Social Sciences	51.1	6.1	29.3	9.6	-	-
Physical Sciences	43.6	26.6	-	12.5	10.1	-
Engineering	37.3	32.6	-	8.4	14.9	-
Life Sciences	38.9	19.9	15.8	10.1	8.5	6.8
Other	83.9	5.3	-	6.9	-	-
Total	57.0	13.4	10.6	9.0	4.6	5.4

[a] Note that "life sciences" denotes agricultural, biological, and health sciences. "Other" disciplines include, principally, education and professional fields.

SOURCE: Statistics Canada, Survey of Earned Doctorates, p. 34.

Not surprisingly then, life sciences graduates make up 40 percent of all those intending to leave and physical sciences, 21 percent. The country of choice for all was the United States.

Program Quality and Interdisciplinary Study

The interaction of intellectual and national ambitions has had a direct impact on doctoral programs themselves in recent years and affected student experience within them. By emphasizing funding for the health and physical sciences, government and institutional support reduces the need for those students to work outside of their programs, provides greater access to intellectual and material resources, and contributes to shorter time-to-completion. On average, it took doctoral students in Canada five years and ten months to complete their studies.[69] However, while all required more than five years to graduate, only social sciences and humanities students required six years or more. Doctoral supervisors and department heads identified careful student selection, student motivation, financial support, supervision, project planning, and a period of full time study as significant factors in reducing the time-to-completion for doctoral students.[70] Conversely, they noted that most students who did not complete their studies left because of a lack of financial support, poor supervision, or inadequate project preparation.

In recent years, universities have also restructured doctoral programs in order to provide intellectual experience and research training across a range of fields. For example, the Université de Montréal and the University of Toronto now offer more than thirty collaboratory or interdisciplinary programs while the University of British Columbia provides access to eleven interdisciplinary programs and one multidisciplinary unit (Green College). Universities with smaller doctoral programs also provide interdisciplinary training opportunities such as the individual and personalized programs at the University of Manitoba and Simon Fraser University. These programs provide interdisciplinary experience by encouraging students to pursue courses outside of their discipline or by including professors from more than one discipline on a supervisory committee or examination board.

A Diverse Student Community

Over the course of the 1990s, full time enrollment in doctoral programs has increased from 82.2 percent of students in 1990 to 89.6 percent in 2001 with a significant increase (3.4 percent) in 1998.[71] That year, the first members of the baby-boom "echo" generation might have qualified for doctoral studies and the federal government restored funding to the granting councils. Part-time enrollment has decreased in all fields except for engineering and architecture, where the percentage of part-time students remained small and largely unchanged. Part-time students are almost always older and include more women (60 percent).[72] Including master's level students, one quarter are in the twenty to twenty-nine-year-old age group, 40 percent in the thirty to thirty-nine-year-old age group, and 30 percent are forty or older.[73] Overall, the average age of all full and part-time doctoral graduates upon completion of their degrees was thirty-six-years-old with 20 percent in the twenty to twenty-nine-year-old cohort, 24 percent over forty years old and the remainder in their thirties.[74] Students tended to be oldest in education (forty-six-years-old on average) and younger in the sciences (thirty-one-years-old in chemistry).

The majority (53.9 percent) of all doctoral students are men.[75] Over the last decade however the number of women pursuing doctoral studies has increased steadily. In 2001 women represented 46.1 percent of all doctoral candidates whereas they represented only 35.5 percent in 1991.[76] Moreover, seven of the ten universities with the largest doctoral programs, including the four largest, enroll more women than the national average.[77] Women represent 31.3 percent of doctoral candidates in science and engineering, 57.2 percent in the social sciences and humanities, and 57.9 percent in the health sciences (the field in which women's participation has increased the most significantly in the last ten years).[78]

Foreign student participation in Canadian doctoral programs rose dramatically in the 1980s and early 1990s before peaking, in 1994, at 6,270 or

23.1 percent of total student enrollment.[79] It fell, during the years of reduced financial support for research, to 4,578 or 17.2 percent in 1999. Those numbers increased slightly, with funding, to 17.9 percent, in 2001. However, foreign student enrollment has increased markedly since then with continued funding and, possibly, reaction to American immigration policy following the events of September 11, 2001. In 2003 foreign student enrollment surpassed its previous peak for the first time since funding was restored, reaching 6,738 or 21.1 percent of all doctoral students. This sensitivity to national and international forces reflects the influence of globalization on doctoral training and presents a challenge, for institutions and policy makers, who must react quickly with imperfect information.

The distribution of foreign students and their significance in doctoral programs is not even across the country. In 2003 fully 66.6 percent of all foreign students registered in one of the ten universities with the largest doctoral programs in Canada, a level of concentration very similar to that of Canadian students.[80] However, only four of those ten universities enrolled more foreign students than the national average. For the most part, smaller institutions in the Atlantic and western provinces attract a greater percentage of their doctoral students abroad. Foreign students are predominantly male (approximately 75 percent) and are more common in the sciences and engineering (fields that attract approximately 75 percent of all foreign students.)[81] They represent 45.6 percent of all students in the sciences and engineering, 25.4 percent in the social sciences and humanities, and 24.1 percent in the health sciences.[82]

CONCLUSION

Doctoral education in Canada today reflects much of its evolution over the past hundred years. Its growth has been uneven, driven by changing intellectual currents and national interests negotiated through universities, provinces and the federal government. Yet, as the national interest in postsecondary education, advanced research and research training has increased, so has the scale and scope of doctoral education. Today, in the global era, the national interest has made doctoral education a much larger undertaking, involving more resources, more people and more complex, interdisciplinary and international research than ever before. Such strength should encourage Canadians in the years ahead to consider anew their place in the intellectual community. Doctoral education in Canada need no longer be principally about tapping international scholarship. It can also be about Canadian leadership in the world.

This shift in emphasis opens new possibilities and creates new opportunities to address fundamental questions about the shape and contribution of Canadian scholarship. Is it still in the national interest to focus resources largely on the natural, life and applied sciences or would Canadians and Canadian scholarship benefit from a robust investment in the social sciences and humanities as well? Is it only possible, and only beneficial to the country and the intellectual community, to support and conduct higher education, advanced research, and research training in large urban centres? Is it still possible, even responsible, to build intellectual strength at home without contributing to the intellectual community worldwide? And finally, do Canadians and Canadian scholars need a more coordinated approach, at home and abroad, to postsecondary education, advanced research and doctoral studies? As universities, provincial governments and the federal government continue to arrange and rearrange their responsibilities they will be called on to answer such questions with the highest of ambitions. Their answers will help determine Canada's place in the world, help shape the international intellectual community and help sketch the limits of scholarship for tomorrow's doctoral candidates.

NOTES

This paper was commissioned by the Canadian Association for Graduate Studies.

1. Mike Lazaridis, "The Importance of Basic Research," *Re$earch Money*, Vol. 18, No. 18, (November 22, 2004), 8.

2. In 2001, John Evans suggested that an explicit social contract for scientific research (a "public research contract") be established between universities and governments given the increased role governments had come to play in funding advanced research and the increased expectations of performance and accountability this placed on universities. John Evans, *The 2001 Killam Annual Lecture: Higher Education in the Higher Education Economy: Towards a Public Research Contract* (Halifax: Trustees of the Killam Trusts, 2001). However, the concept of a tacit social contract governing the arrangement of responsibilities between universities and governments in the years following the Second World War is borrowed from Ben Martin, "The Changing Social Contract for Science and the Evolution of Knowledge Production," in Aldo Beuna, Ammon Salter and Edward Steinmuller, eds. *Science and Innovation: Rethinking the Rationales for Funding and Governance* (Cheltenham: Edward Elgar, 2003).

3. McGill University was a notable exception to this rule. It was established as a private non-denominational institution in 1821. Much of the information in this paragraph is drawn from Glen Jones, ed. *Higher Education in Canada: Different Systems, Different Perspectives* (New York: Garland Publishing, Inc., 1997) and Tom Pocklington and Allan Tupper, *No Place to Learn: Why Universities Aren't Working* (Vancouver: UBC Press, 2002).

4. Glen Jones, "Higher Education in Ontario," in Jones, ed. *Higher Education*, 139.

5. Discussion of various postsecondary traditions is borrowed from Pocklington and Tupper, *No Place*, 19–36.

6. A. B. McKillop, *Matters of Mind: The Ontario University, 1791–1951* (Toronto: University of Toronto Press, 1994), 346.

7. In 1920 there were twenty-four doctoral degrees conferred in Canada; in 1930 there were forty-six; and in 1940 there were seventy-five. Statistics Canada, "Degrees Awarded by Canadian Universities and Colleges, by Sex, Canada, Selected Years, 1831–1973," *Historical Statistics of Canada*, Catalogue 11–516-X1E, Section W: Education, Series W504–512 (Ottawa: Statistics Canada, 1983).

8. McKillop, *Matters*, 344.

9. David Cameron, "Post-secondary Education and Research: Whither Canadian Federalism?" in *Taking Public Universities Seriously*, ed. Frank Iacobucci and Carolyn Tuohy (Toronto: University of Toronto Press, 2005), 277.

10. University activism at this stage was important as it gave institutions and academics a measure of control over federal government initiatives. Much of the information in this and the succeeding paragraph is drawn from Cameron, "Post-secondary Education," 277–282.

11. The practice arose of allocating approximately 50–55 percent of federal research funding directed through the granting councils to the sciences and engineering, 35–40 percent to medical research and 10–15 percent to the humanities and social sciences. It is not clear how this division was first established.

12. Statistics Canada, "Degrees Awarded by Canadian Universities."

13. *Ibid.*

14. Pocklington and Tupper, *No Place.* See also Howard Clark, *Growth and Governance of Canadian Universities: An Insider's View* (Vancouver: University of British Columbia Press, 2003).

15. Statistics Canada, "Summary of total full-time enrolment, by level of study, related to relevant population, Canada, selected years, 1951 to 1975," *Historical Statistics of Canada*, Catalogue 11–516-X1E, Section W: Education, Series W10–20 (Ottawa: Statistics Canada, 1983).

16. Statistics Canada, "Degrees Awarded by Canadian Universities." Jean Lebel, *Trends in Graduate Enrolment and Graduation at Canadian Universities* (Ottawa: Canadian Association for Graduate Studies, 2001), 1.

17. For a different interpretation see Pocklington and Tupper, *No Place.*

18. H. H Jacobs, *1972 Statistical Report* (Ottawa: Canadian Association of Graduate Schools, 1972), 30.

19. L. C. Payton, *1982 Statistical Report* (Ottawa: Canadian Association of Graduate Schools, 1982), 26.

20. Between 1960 and 1975 the provincial distribution of the total population varied little. Approximately 10 percent of Canadians lived in the Maritime provinces, 28 percent in Québec, 35 percent in Ontario, and 27 percent in western Canada. In 1960, 4.1 percent of graduate students studied in the Maritimes, 30.4 percent in Québec, 39.9 percent in Ontario and 25.6 percent in the West. Fifteen years later, 6.1 percent studied in the Maritimes, 27.7 percent in Québec, 44.5 percent in Ontario

and 21.7 percent in the West. Statistics Canada, "Full-time University Enrolment, by Sex, Canada and Provinces, Selected Years, 1920 to 1975," *Historical Statistics of Canada,* Catalogue 11–516-X1E, Section W: Education, Series W340–438 (Ottawa: Statistics Canada, 1983). Statistics Canada, "Population of Canada, by Province, Census Dates, 1851 to 1975," *Historical Statistics of Canada,* Catalogue 11–516-X1E, Section A: Population and Migration, Series A2–14 (Ottawa: Statistics Canada, 1983).

21. See articles on each province in Glen Jones, *Higher Education.*

22. Cameron, "Post-secondary Education," 279–82.

23. Enrolment dropped in four successive years, from 1996–1999. Jean Lebel, "Table 1: Graduate Enrolment in Canada, 1990–2001," *Statistical Report 1990–2001* (Ottawa: Canadian Association for Graduate Studies, 2004), 1.

24. Paul Martin, *Budget Speech,* (Ottawa: Department of Finance Canada, 1998).

25. David Wolfe, "Innovation and Research Funding: The Role of Government Support," in *Taking Public Universities Seriously,* ed. Frank Iacobucci and Carolyn Tuohy (Toronto: University of Toronto Press, 2005), 318.

26. Overcoming isolation during doctoral studies in this way has proven to reduce attrition. Barbara Lovitts, *Leaving the Ivory Tower: The Causes and Consequences of Departures from Doctoral Study* (Lanham: Rowman and Littlefield Publishers, 2001) noted in Martha Crago, *Pre-Budget Submission to the House of Commons Standing Committee on Finance (*Ottawa: Canadian Association for Graduate Studies, 2003), 3.

27. Paul Martin, *Budget Speech* (Ottawa: Department of Finance Canada, 2003).

28. Crago, "Pre-Budget," 3.

29. Statistics Canada."Changing Patterns of University Financing," *Education Quarterly Review,* Vol. 9, No. 2, (2003): 11. Catalogue 81–003.

30. *Ibid.*

31. See articles on Québec, Ontario, and Alberta in Jones, *Higher Education.*

32. Universities with the five largest doctoral programs enrolled 55.1 percent of all doctoral candidates in 1981 but only 47.7 percent in 1991 and 45.7 percent in 2001. Jacobs, *1972 Statistical Report,* 34–35; Payton, *1982 Statistical Report,* 29–32; Lebel, *Statistical Report 1990–2001,* 8.

33. Manitoba, *Priorities for Advanced Education* (Winnipeg: Manitoba Education, Training and Youth, 2001). Payton, *1982 Statistical Report,* 29–33. Lebel, *Statistical Report 1990–2001,* 6–8.

34. These initiatives also led to program changes that seek to provide greater support for students. Edward Holdaway, "Organization and Administration of Graduate Studies in Canadian Universities," *The Canadian Journal of Higher Education,* Vol. 24, No. 1, (1994): 1–29.

35. John Evans, *The 2001 Killam Annual Lecture.*

36. In Alberta, the Private Colleges Accreditation Board (established in 1984) was replaced by the Campus Alberta Quality Council in 2004. In Atlantic Canada, the provinces refocused the Maritime Provinces Higher Education Council mandate on quality assurance in 1997. Ontario established the Postsecondary Education Quality Assessment Board in 2000 and British Columbia formed the Degree Quality Assessment Board in 2003.

37. Donald Baker, *On the Need for High Quality Colleges and Programs,*

(Moncton, New Brunswick: Association of Canadian Community Colleges Annual Conference, 2005).

38. Association of Universities and Colleges of Canada, *Trends in Higher Education* (Ottawa: Association of Universities and Colleges of Canada, 2002), 8.

39. Payton, *1982 Statistical Report*, 28. Lebel, *Statistical Report 1990–2001*, 1. Jean Lebel, *35th Statistical Report 1994–2003* (Ottawa: Canadian Association of Graduate Studies, 2005), 3.

40. Payton, *1982 Statistical Report*, 70. Lebel, *Statistical Report 1990–2001*, 36. Lebel, *35th Statistical Report 1994–2003*, 39.

41. The presence of non-Canadian students in doctoral programs is higher than the national average in Atlantic Canada (38.8 percent), Western Canada (36.9 percent) and Québec (34.7 percent). It is lower, at 31.1 percent, in Ontario). Lebel, *Statistical Report 1990–2001*, 36, 50. Lebel, *35th Statistical Report 1994–2003*, 39.

42. Lebel, *35th Statistical Report 1994–2003*, 15.

43. Association of Universities and Colleges of Canada, *Trends*, 14.

44. Statistics Canada. "Changing patterns," 11.

45. *Ibid.*

46. At present, tuition fees for doctoral programs vary from a low of $2,502.45 per year (three semesters), reduced to $936 per year post residency, at the Université de Montréal; to a high of $6,176 per year with no post residency reduction at the University of Toronto. International students pay $13,617.45 per year, reduced to $936 per year post residency, at the Université de Montréal while, at the University of Toronto, they pay $10,970 per year with no post residency reduction.

47. Statistics Canada. "Changing patterns," 13.

48. Lebel, *Statistical Report 1990–2001*, 6–8. Statistics Canada, "A Profile of the Canadian Population: Where We Live," *Census, 2001* (Ottawa: Statistics Canada, 2002). Catalogue 96F0030XIE2001001.

49. Holdaway, "Organization and Administration of Graduate Studies," 1–29.

50. Lebel, *Statistical Report 1990–2001*, 65.

51. *Ibid.*, 6–7. Statistics Canada, "A Profile of the Canadian Population."

52. Lebel, *Statistical Report 1990–2001*, 8.

53. *Ibid.* Association of Universities and Colleges of Canada, *Trends*, 80.

54. Lebel, *Statistical Report 1990–2001*, 9.

55. Statistics Canada, *Survey of Earned Doctorates: A Profile of Doctoral Degree Recipients, Culture, Tourism and the Centre for Education Statistics Research Papers* (Ottawa: Statistics Canada, 2005). Catalogue 81–595–MIE2005032, 10, 27.

56. *Ibid.*, 28.

57. *Ibid.*, 11–12.

58. *Ibid.*, 28.

59. *Ibid.*, 31.

60. *Ibid.*, 13.

61. Roberta-Anne Kerlin, *Towards a Theory of Women's Doctoral Persistance* (PhD Thesis: University of Victoria, 1997). Statistics Canada, *Survey of Earned Doctorates*, 9.

62. Conversely, there is a much greater enrolment of bachelors and masters

level students in the social sciences and humanities (72 percent) than doctoral students in those disciplines (50 percent). The health sciences enroll 7 percent of bachelors and masters level students and 6.2 percent of doctoral students. Association of Universities and Colleges of Canada, *Trends,* 80. Lebel, *Statistical Report 1990–2001*, 9.

63. Statistics Canada, *Survey of Earned Doctorates,* 14.

64. *Ibid.*, 34.

65. *Ibid.*, 35.

66. *Ibid.*, 17, 36.

67. Universities now account for approximately 17 percent of all R&D activity in Canada. Association of Universities and Colleges of Canada, *Trends,* 41.

68. Statistics Canada. *Survey of Earned Doctorates,* 18.

69. *Ibid.*, 25.

70. Holdaway, "Organization and Administration of Graduate Studies," 1–29.

71. Lebel, *Statistical Report 1990–2001*, 61.

72. Association of Universities and Colleges of Canada, *Trends,* 5.

73. *Ibid*, 4.

74. Statistics Canada, *Survey of Earned Doctorates,* 9.

75. If foreign students (most of whom are male) are removed from these calculations the number of Canadian men and women enrolled in doctoral programs converges slightly more than described here. Lebel, *Statistical Report 1990–2001*, 14. Statistics Canada, *Survey of Earned Doctorates*, 8.

76. Lebel, *Statistical Report, 1990–2001*, 14.

77. *Ibid.*, 28.

78. *Ibid.*, 29.

79. Lebel, *Statistical Report, 1994–2003*, 3, 39.

80. *Ibid.*, 10, 48, 25.

81. Statistics Canada, *Survey of Earned Doctorates,* 9.

82. Lebel, *Statistical Report 1990–2001*, 51.

BIBLIOGRAPHY

Association of Universities and Colleges of Canada. 2002. *Trends in Higher Education*. Ottawa: Association of Universities and Colleges of Canada.

Axelrod, Paul. 2002. *Values in Conflict: The University, the Marketplace, and the Trials of Liberal Education*. Montréal: McGill-Queen's University Press.

Barnetson, Robert, and Alice Boberg. 2000. "Resource Allocation and Public Policy in Alberta's Postsecondary Education System." *The Canadian Journal of Higher Education* 3, No. 2: 57–86.

Beach, Charles, Robin Boadway, and Marvin McInnis, eds. 2005. *Higher Education in Canada.* Montréal: McGill-Queen's University Press.

Bourdages, Louise. 2001. *La persistence aux études supérieures: Le cas du doctorat.* Sainte-Foy: Les Presses de l'Université du Québec.

Cameron, David. 1991. *More Than an Academic Question: Universities, Government and Public Policy in Canada*. Halifax: Institute for Research on Public Policy.

Canadian Association of University Teachers. 2005. *CAUT Almanac of Post-Secondary Education in Canada, 2005*. Ottawa: Canadian Association of University Teachers.

Clark, Howard. 2003. *Growth and Governance of Canadian Universities: An Insider's View*. Vancouver: University of British Columbia Press.

Crago, Martha. 2003. *Pre-Budget Submission to the House of Commons Standing Committee on Finance*. Ottawa: Canadian Association for Graduate Studies.

Goodale, Ralph. 2004. *Budget Speech*. Ottawa: Department of Finance Canada.

Harrison, Trevor, and Jerrold Kachur. 1999. *Contested Classrooms: Education, Globalization and Democracy in Alberta*. Edmonton: University of Alberta Press.

Holdaway, Edward. 1994. "Organization and Administration of Graduate Studies in Canadian Universities." *The Canadian Journal of Higher Education* 24, No. 1: 1–29.

Iacobucci, Frank, and Carolyn Tuohy, eds. 2005. *Taking Public Universities Seriously*. Toronto: University of Toronto Press.

International Association of Universities. 2004. *Sharing Quality Higher Education Across Borders: A Statement on Behalf of Higher Education Institutions Worldwide*. May.

Jacobs, H. H., R. A. Lebrun, and B. G. Hogg. 1972. *1972 Statistical Report*. Ottawa: Canadian Association of Graduate Schools.

Jones, Glen. ed. 1997. *Higher Education in Canada: Different Systems, Different Perspectives*. New York: Garland Publishing Inc.

Jones, Glen, Patricia McCarney, and Michael Skolnik. 2005. *Creating Knowledge, Strengthening Nations: The Changing Role of Higher Education*. Toronto: University of Toronto Press.

Kerlin, Roberta-Anne. 1997. *Towards a Theory of Women's Doctoral Persistance*. PhD Thesis: University of Victoria.

Lebel, Jean. 2001. *Trends in Graduate Enrolment and Graduation at Canadian Universities*. Ottawa: Canadian Association for Graduate Studies.

Lebel, Jean. 2004. *Statistical Report 1990–2001*. Ottawa: Canadian Association for Graduate Studies.

Lebel, Jean. 2006. *35th Statistical Report 1994–2003*. Ottawa: Canadian Association for Graduate Studies.

Martin, Paul. (1998–2003, annual pub.). *Budget Speech*. Ottawa: Department of Finance Canada.

McKillop, A. B. 1994. *Matters of Mind: The University in Ontario, 1791–1951*. Toronto: University of Toronto Press.

Payton, L. C. 1982. *1982 Statistical Report*. Ottawa: Canadian Association of Graduate Schools.

Pocklington, Tom and Allan Tupper. 2002. *No Place to Learn: Why Universities Aren't Working*. Vancouver: University of British Columbia Press.

Statistics Canada. "Degrees Awarded by Canadian Universities and Colleges, by Sex, Canada, Selected Years, 1831–1973." *Historical Statistics of Canada* 11–516-X1E, Section W: Education, Series W504–512.

Statistics Canada. 2001. "Bachelor's Graduates Who Pursue Further Postsecondary

Education." *Education Quarterly Review*, Vol. 7, No. 2.: 22–36. Catalogue 81–003.

Statistics Canada. 2003. "Changing Patterns of University Financing." *Education Quarterly Review*, Vol. 9, No. 2: 9–17. Catalogue 81–003.

Statistics Canada. 2005. *Survey of Earned Doctorates: A Profile of Doctoral Degree Recipients.* Ottawa: Culture, Tourism and the Centre for Education Statistics Research Papers. Catalogue 81–595-MIE2005032.

Tremblay, André and Sylvie Paquette. 2000. "Changements institutionnels en éducation supérieure: Un nouveau paradigme?" *The Canadian Journal of Higher Education*, Vol. 30, No. 2: 1–56.

Waite, P. B. 1994, 1998) *The Lives of Dalhousie University*, Vols. I and II. Montréal: McGill-Queen's University Press.

Woodside, Willson. 1958. *The University Question: Who Should Go? Who Should Pay?* Toronto: The Ryerson Press.

13 • UNITED STATES OF AMERICA

MARESI NERAD

INTRODUCTION

During the last fifteen years doctoral education in the US has received sporadic, yet considerable, public attention. Since the early 1990s organizations and stakeholders—those with a direct interest in the quality of doctoral education and concern about the production and employment of the next generation of highly educated scholars and professionals in the US labor market—have voiced criticism.

The major criticisms include the under- and over-production of PhD recipients; a doctoral education that is mainly oriented to provide for the next generation of professors; the lack of training in professional skills needed for collaborations and working in organizations; the inadequate preparation for teaching in the different types of US higher education institutions; the long time-to-doctoral-degree in some fields, an overall low completion rate; and the lack of information about employment outside of the academy. These tumultuous years for doctoral education mirror previous eras in the evolution of doctoral education in the US, when graduate education had to respond to demands from national forces as well as to the internal demands and dynamics of their own universities.

Thus the purpose and structure of US doctoral education today faces numerous challenges. These challenges include: managing the intricate link between doctoral education and the institutional research missions of the university; undergraduate education; the labor market; funding; accountability and governance; and most recently, pressures from the global economic market. In this paper I will provide an overview of the history of graduate education in the United States, the current structure of graduation at most US universities, recent challenges and changes within doctoral education and national responses to those challenges and changes.

FORMS—DEVELOPMENT AND SCOPE OF US DOCTORAL EDUCATION

History: A little over a hundred years ago, in the late nineteenth century, leading US college educators turned to the German university as a model for inspiration to reform the inherited British undergraduate college into a place for advanced learning and training in original research. They borrowed selectively and reworked the German ideas to fit the needs and ideas of the time. The results became new creations with only little resemblance to the original inspiration. The advanced degree served, and still serves, almost exclusively as the gateway into the professoriate. Therefore, in US universities the PhD[1] from its inception entailed, in most cases, substantial research training. Most strikingly the US version concocted a novelty never imagined in Germany until recently: the distinction between undergraduate and graduate study.[2] At the individual discipline level, undergraduate and graduate education is housed under one roof, the "department." As a way to coordinate the various graduate programs, US universities established the "graduate school," a central administrative unit that oversees all masters and doctoral education, and more recently houses post-doctoral training in a campus setting.

Purpose and Goals: While different debates about doctoral education have accompanied its development in the US, the primary purpose and goal of doctoral education has been preparation of the next generation of university professors who will become productive researchers and innovators, and in turn become teachers of the following generation.

Infrastructure: In the United States over four hundred institutions award doctoral degrees and the number is steadily increasing. Between 1995 and 2003 the number of US universities conferring doctoral degrees climbed from 376 to 423.[3] However, fifty of these institutions award about 50 percent of all doctoral degrees. As a result, doctoral education is primarily concentrated in a few institutions—the major research universities—of which the majority are members of the American Association of Universities.[4]

Funding: The US has public and private universities. Public institutions are part of the public higher education system and are under the sovereignty of the fifty US states. Initially, the states provided property, building, equipment, and instructional salaries for all of their public universities. Private institutions are funded by endowments, philanthropy, investments, and property holdings, and student fees. Once a student is accepted into a doctoral program in a private institution his or her studies are funded similarly to a student in a public institution. In both the public and private institutions doctoral education is funded by various sources. Teaching and advising is funded by the state through salaries to academic instructional staff, the graduate professors. Research is largely funded by the US federal government[5] through research grants and contracts including laboratory instrumentations to individual professors and campuses. Research is also funded by private foundations and internal university allocations. Doctoral students are funded through a few national government, private foundation, and individual campus graduate student fellowship programs. Many doctoral students are funded through teaching assistant (TA) positions within their departments that last for at least one year or up to four years, as in the humanities. These TAs are provided by the state. Practically all science, engineering and many social science students are funded as research assistants (RA) on professors' individual research grants or through traineeships from governmental grants. In addition, universities have additional financial support mechanisms such as fee and tuition fellowships or waivers. Students can also apply for federal support through the student loan program. According to the 2003 *Summary Report of the Survey of Earned Doctorates* (SED) graduating doctoral students reported that their primary financial support came from these areas: 20 percent from fellowships; 30 percent from research assistantships; 20 percent from teaching assistantships; and 30 percent from financing their studies on their own, by working various jobs on or off campus, including financial support from their employers, or from foreign governments.[6]

Demographics: Approximately 4 percent of all undergraduates in the US go on to obtain a doctorate. Presently about 40,000 PhDs are awarded annually in the U.S. The growth in PhD production began during the 1960s (when about 10,000 PhDs were awarded) with the onset of the Vietnam War. Many men deferred the draft by going to graduate school—and thus the early 1970s show a dramatic increase in doctorate awards (nearly 30,000 PhDs). This PhD increased production rate leveled off over the 1980s (the number remained about the same) and began to increase again in between 1990 and 1998 to nearly 43,000 PhDs. Fueling the increase in PhDs, particularly in humanities and arts, has been the widely publicized, but false prediction of a shortage of PhD recipients in the late 1980s to fill the positions of retiring faculty. This increase in the PhD production rate during the 1990s was further fueled by higher enrollments in the life sciences, physical sciences, and engineering largely due an increase in the influx of international students in these fields. Since 1970 the life sciences experienced

TABLE 13.1. Percent of Women PhD Recipients by Major Field

Field/Year	*1973* *N=33,755**	*1983* *N=31,281**	*1993* *N=39,505**	*2003* *N=40,590**
Physical Science	7%	14%	21%	27%
Engineering	1%	5%	9%	17%
Life Science	18%	31%	42%	48%
Social Science	21%	40%	50%	55%
Humanities	29%	44%	48%	51%
Education	25%	50%	59%	66%
Prof./Other	13%	29%	36%	50%
Total	18%	34%	38%	45%

* N equals all PhDs awarded.
SOURCE: CIRGE, UW Seattle, 25 August 2005;. From "Doctorate Recipients from United States Universities: Summary Report 2003," p. 49.

the largest consistent increase, to over 8,000 PhDs awarded in 2003. Education experienced the most consistent decrease of doctorates awarded since the 1970s, by a drop of slightly over 8 percent, from about 7,200 to 6,600 doctorates, a field with relatively few international students. The rapid increase in the physical sciences and engineering fields experienced during those years was followed by a slow but steady decrease since the late 1990s.

Doctoral education in the US has seen a significant change in the demographics of doctoral students. Regardless of age and other employment status, all individuals enrolled in a graduate education program in the US have a student status within the university, regardless also of employment as a teaching or research assistant. Women's degree achievement in doctoral programs since WWII has steadily increased, and reached close to parity in 2003 (45 percent).[7] The largest increase occurred during the last thirty-three years. In 1970 the proportion of women earning PhDs was 13 percent, and in 1983 and 1993, it increased to 38 percent. (See table 13.1.)

Women's PhD acquisition since the year 2000 surpassed men's in the fields of education, social sciences, and the professional fields, and is equal to that of men in the humanities and nearly equal to that of men in the life sciences.[8]

While the vast majority of doctorate recipients are racially identified as white, the year 2003 saw the largest percentage of doctorates being earned by individuals identified as racial/ethnic minorities who were historically underrepresented groups in higher education. Nineteen percent or 4,753

TABLE 13.2. Doctorates Awarded to Racial/Ethnic Minority U.S. Citizens for the Last Three Decades: 1973–2003

Race/Year	*1973* *N=22,956**	*1983* *N=25,020**	*1993* *N=28,408**	*2003* *N=26,931**
Black	3%	4%	4%	7%
American Indian	0%	0%	0%	1%
Asian	4%	4%	7%	8%
Hispanic	1%	2%	3%	5%

* N equals all PhDs who identified their race/ethnicity.

SOURCE: CIRGE, UW Seattle, 30 August 2005, NSF Web CASPAR; From "Survey of Earned Doctorates/Doctoral Record File," via Web CASPAR, http://caspar.nsf.gov.

of all recipients were minorities and included Blacks, Asians, Hispanics, Native American Indians, Hawaiians, and Pacific Islanders. (See table 13.2.)

International students are those students who come to the study in US institutions on a full-time basis. Officially they are called "non-US citizens on temporary visa." The proportion of international students rose from 10 percent in 1973 to 27 percent (10,585) in 2003. (See tables 13.3 and 13.4.)

Although the number of international applicants has dropped since 2002, there has been no reduction in doctorates awarded to international students because it takes on the average five to seven years from entrance to graduate school to doctoral degree completion (including master's degree). Until 2002 roughly 50 percent of the international PhD students remained in the US after degree completion.[9] The five largest countries of origin are: the People's Republic of China, Korea, India, the Republic of China (Taiwan), and Canada.

Despite the increase in PhD production, the ratio of PhDs to bachelors degrees has stayed fairly stable between 3.5–4.3 percent during the last twenty years, at 3 percent when we count only degrees awarded to US citizens and permanent residents. About 25 percent of the US population holds a bachelor's degree and 1.5 percent holds a doctoral degree, including MDs and JDs.

Although the number of faculty at US colleges and universities has steadily increased during the last thirty years, the number of tenure-track faculty has not increased in relation to the increase in the undergraduate and graduate student population.[10] The number of "other faculty," referring to the non-tenure track group of annually appointed lecturers, instructors, and affiliates (who are often part-time) is steadily increasing.[11]

TABLE 13.3. Percent of International PhDs by the Last Three Decades

1973	10% (N=3,209*)
1983	15% (N=4,540*)
1993	25% (N=9,973*)
2003	26% (N=10,585*)

* N equals total international PhDs awarded.

SOURCE: "Doctorate Recipients from United States Universities: Summary Report 2003," p. 54.

TABLE 13.4. International PhDs by Major Field for the Last Three Decades

Field/Year	*1973 N=3,209**	*1983 N=4,540**	*1993 N=9,973**	*2003 N=10,585**
Physical Science	21%	20%	24%	21%
Engineering	20%	26%	28%	27%
Life Science	20%	17%	20%	21%
Social Science	16%	13%	11%	11%
Humanities	8%	8%	6%	7%
Education	9%	12%	6%	6%
Prof./Other	5%	5%	6%	6%

* N equals total international PhDs awarded.

SOURCE: "Doctorate Recipients from United States Universities: Summary Report 2003," p. 54.

Overall, the median age of doctoral recipients in the US is in the early 30s. In 2003 the median age was 33.3 years. Individuals receiving their doctorates in science and engineering fields are generally the youngest, with a mean age of 31.8 years, while for those in the humanities the median age is closer to the mid 30s (34.5). Education doctorates are generally the oldest with a mean age of early 40s.[12]

Program Structure[13]: After completing an undergraduate degree, which is generally a four-year course of study, an individual is qualified to apply for further education at the graduate level. Masters and doctoral education (also called graduate education) takes place in highly decentralized and semi-autonomous units, mainly in departments of doctoral-granting universities and colleges. If a person chooses to go on for a doctorate degree, he or she has various program options. For some programs the procedure is to obtain a master's degree and then apply to continue on for the doctorate. Other programs allow the applicant to apply directly to a doctoral degree program. While great variety exists among doctoral programs, two basic structures are common. One pertains primarily to social science and humanities fields, the other to science and engineering. Both general types of programs have a highly selective admissions process. In general, a quarter of all applicants are admitted.

Admission criteria are based on the undergraduate grade point average; the scores on a national graduate entrance exam—which includes a verbal, analytical, and quantitative component; letters of recommendation from undergraduate professors; and a "Statement of Purpose" essay. For the social science and humanities the typical program involves up to three years of course work—mainly seminars. Many doctoral programs require a certain number of fixed core courses along with a fairly large number of electives. The end of this period is marked by taking general exams and writing a major publishable article, which together serve to demonstrate the knowledge of the field acquired during the coursework years. Usually after passing the exam and completing the article, students embark upon developing their dissertation proposals. These proposals are formally reviewed. Thereafter students are engaged in their original research. This period of time does not necessarily need to take place at the home university, and often it is spent in the field—for example in archives, museums, or libraries—anywhere in the world. The completion of the dissertation is in most instances a formal presentation by the student to the dissertation committee, which consists of between three to five faculty members, with one person who must be from outside the program. The dissertation manuscript must be signed by the dissertation committee signaling its approval. At present the average time-to-degree in the social sciences and humanities ranges between five to eight years for social sciences and five to nine years in the humanities.

Science and engineering doctorates follow a similar sequence of course studies, dissertation development, and research. However, an essential preliminary step is an examination at the end of the first year of doctoral study in which the students have to demonstrate basic advanced knowledge of the field. In many programs this exam functions as a way to ensure that only qualified students continue. At the end of year two, or in some cases year three, students take a general exam that includes the presentation of dissertation research and at least a publishable research paper. During the entire period of doctoral study, the students work in their main dissertation advisor's laboratory, usually paid as research assistants. Given that in these laboratories major research is taking place, doctoral students work side by side with their advisors, the advisor's post-docs, and undergraduate students, on research that is likely to shape their dissertation. Completion of the dissertation culminates in a defense, usually at the end of year five and up to year seven. One significant distinction between the fields of study is the nature of their financial support. Social science and humanities students rarely have the opportunity to be paid to work on their dissertation. Instead they are often employed as teaching assistants. However, this employment is, in most cases, not directly related to their dissertation. In many science fields a post-doc position (usually between two and four years) has become a requirement or a preferred option to enter a professorial career path.

The Department—Home of the Graduate Program: The graduate faculty members are those professors who are likely to teach both undergraduate and graduate classes. For graduate education (both masters and doctoral) a faculty member serves as advisor to a doctoral student most often from entrance to exit. In the humanities, social sciences, and education, students often choose their main advisor and dissertation committee at the time they begin working on their dissertations. Graduate professors oversee the many issues facing graduate students, such as admission decisions, allocation of fellowships and assistantships, awards for exceptional graduate students' teaching, initiation of program revisions, and the overall monitoring of student progress. Every department has one administrative assistant dedicated to graduate student matters. Often this person holds a permanent staff position so that he or she is able to offer continuity to the graduate students and to the program as a whole.

Program Quality Assessment: Departments are subject to periodic review, generally every seven to ten years. This review covers both undergraduate and graduate programs and its procedure varies among universities. The graduate component of these department reviews, which are undertaken by neighboring departments within the same university and faculty from the same discipline from other universities, consists of a qualitative and a quantitative assessment of the masters and doctoral programs. Usually the departmental review is part of the responsibility of the graduate school, undertaken by the "graduate council"—an academic senate sub-committee. In addition, the department chair annually reviews faculty members for the purpose of promotion. This promotion review includes an assessment of publications, teaching evaluations, and in many cases the level of doctoral students' satisfaction with advising provided by the faculty member. It also includes doctoral students' academic achievement and honors, assistance to graduate students in their professional development (such as publishing, teaching, and grant writing), and the students' presentation skills at national and international conferences.

National Assessment of Doctoral Education Programs: The national assessment of doctoral programs in the US began over seventy-five years ago (in 1925). A number of national associations began conducting reputational studies by asking raters, who were usually professors in various fields, about the esteem in which they held doctoral programs. The results were then ranked. Since 1982 the National Research Council, a "think tank" of the National Academies, has undertaken such assessments. While the last assessment, in 1995, expanded the quantitative research methods, nevertheless it spurred widespread criticism of creating a "horse race" mentality through the ranking of programs.[14] NRC therefore appointed an advisory committee to examine past methodology used. In 2003 the committee published its recommendations. It pointed out five major weaknesses of previous assessments: (1) a flawed measure of educational quality, derived from unclear questions posed to faculty respondents that resulted in "research reputation" and "program quality" being interchanged; (2) the obsolescence of data because of the ten-year cycle; (3) a poor dissemination of results; (4) the use of outdated or inappropriate taxonomy of fields; (5) the inadequate validation of data accuracy. NRC is currently undertaking a new and widely improved research doctorate assessment to be completed in 2007–08.

Although the NRC assessment was widely criticized, institutions and individual doctoral programs have taken the results very seriously because the assessment stood as a proxy of program quality. High quality programs attract high quality students, more research money, and are less likely to lose faculty or funding, and/or to be abolished altogether. In response, institutions are refining their quality measures. Institutional data collection has become a primary concern. Many graduate schools have introduced exit questionnaires that are completed by doctoral recipients. These questionnaires ask recipients to assess their satisfaction with their degree programs. In addition, various professional accreditation organizations produce their own department and doctoral program assessments in order to maintain a high quality of doctoral education. In all, these various means of quality assessment are a guarantor of ongoing systemic renewal and improvement.

Graduate School and Graduate Dean: The graduate school is closely linked to the research agenda of the university. Universities vary in how they ensure that policies and procedures that govern the research activities of the university are directly responsive to the needs of the graduate programs. In some instances the positions of vice-president for research and graduate dean are shared by the same person. In other cases, particularly where large medical schools exist, these two positions are filled by two different people. Regardless, the graduate dean and the vice-president for research are in the inner circle of the president of the university.[15]

The graduate school monitors student progress, grants degrees, collects dissertations, and approves new degree programs. The graduate school plays additional important roles on campus, from establishing policy and procedures to determining financial support, to developing mechanisms for quality assurance. It supports intellectual development and advocates for the academic staff in their roles as advisors, as well as for the graduate students, with a focus on student retention, time-to-degree, career development, and doctoral job placement.

WEAKNESSES AND CRITICISMS OF US DOCTORAL PROGRAMS

In the late 1980s, articles in major publications such as the *New York Times* and the *Wall Street Journal* heralded a forthcoming shortage of PhD recipients by the 1990s due to massive faculty retirements and an anticipated increase in the college-bound population. These articles were based on a 1989 book by the president of the Andrew Mellon Foundation and the 1990 publication of a presidential address of the American Association for the Advancement of Science.[16] In response many universities planned expansions to their graduate education programs in rapid succession. However by 1995, the end of the Cold War, a worldwide recession, and a federal government forced to reduce a budget deficit called a halt to plans of expansion. Universities soon began curtailing PhD production in those fields with a limited academic job market. For many universities, working to realign their PhD production in terms of national and international forces represented the beginning of a major re-thinking of PhD education in general.

This major re-thinking gained additional momentum with the 1995 publication of an influential and widely quoted report by a committee of the National Academies, *Reshaping Graduate Education of Scientists and Engineers.*[17] This publication was highly critical of the current state of doctoral education. From 1995 on, a number of forces for change began to come together: The National Academies Report, increasing criticism from doctoral students (through the establishment of graduate student unions), and the demand for greater accountability by state governments concerning doctoral education outcomes generated national attention and resulted in a national convening of major doctoral education stakeholders in Washington, DC in the summer of 1995. For the next five years invigorating and necessary attention was paid to doctoral education, culminating in a major national conference in 2000. This conference, organized by *Re-Envisioning the PhD* under the leadership of Jody Nyquist and funded by the Pew Charitable Trusts, articulated a call to reevaluate doctoral education, to determine whether this education is indeed appropriate to prepare scholars and researchers to meet the demands of society and the global world, to better understand the criticisms of doctoral education in the United States, and to develop strategies to address the criticisms. The major criticisms of US doctoral education that have arisen over the past fifteen years can be summarized in the following list regarding doctoral student training. Briefly, doctoral students are believed to be:[18]

- educated and trained too narrowly;
- lacking key professional skills, such as collaborating effectively and working in teams, and lacking organizational and managerial skills;
- ill-prepared to teach;
- taking too long to complete their doctoral studies and in some fields many are not completing their degrees at all;
- ill-informed about employment outside academia; and
- having too-long a transition period from PhD completion to stable employment.

FORCES AND STIMULI OF CHANGE

Changes in higher education's wider social, political, and economic contexts shape the content and operation of doctoral education. Powerful forces converge at the intersection of doctoral education and university research in particular.[19] The labor market, state higher education governing boards, federal and state research funding and student aid policies, and the public have demanded that the university be increasingly accountable for the use of public tax dollars. Graduate students, within their national organization (NAGPS) and within their disciplines' national professional associations such as the MLA, have played a more dominant external role in shaping institutional policy and program structure. The internal forces that have shaped graduate education include advancement in knowledge; individual departments, which differ widely from each other in size, wealth, program structure, and outlook regarding the purpose of doctoral education; a student body that in recent years has become increasingly diverse in gender, ethnicity, citizenship, and age and has formed graduate student unions; and the increasing intra-institutional competitive pressure to improve or maintain programs that are regarded highly in academic quality by their peers.

Since 2001, due to a change in the leadership of the US government, followed by changed national priorities after the terrorist attack on September 11 of 2001, graduate education again had to cope with external forces and a further reduction in funding by state and federal governments. Exceptions are areas of national priorities, such as biotechnology, and areas of military and national security. Most recently, the reduction of international students coming to study in the US is of concern to universities and national organizations that focus on the production of the country's highly trained labor force. As US science and engineering has become increasingly more dependent on international students and scholars, the United States needs to compete more strenuously for international talents to come to US programs. Also, US students need to be prepared to work in a global arena and be able to address global scientific challenges in a time of increasing global tension.

Recently, Ronald Ehrenberg, Director of the Cornell Higher Education Research Institute, succinctly stated what the nature of the connection of federal funding is in regards to graduate education, the economy and international students:

1. Research and development lead to innovation and economic growth.
2. Graduate students in general and foreign graduate students in particular, play a major role in the production of research and innovation
3. Attempts to make statements about shortages of PhD-level scientists and engineers are almost certainly doomed to fail and miss the point that what is optimal from the perspective of different actors in the market (individuals contemplating graduate study, individual professors, academic departments, and employers), is not necessarily optimal for the nation as a whole.
4. Financial stresses faced by American higher education institutions have serious implications for the future flow of US graduates into PhD programs.
5. The mobility of college graduates in general, and PhDs in particular, will cause states to under-invest in their public higher education sys-

tems and provides a strong argument for an increased federal role in graduate education.[20]

INITIATIVES AND INNOVATIONS

These criticisms gave impetus to a flurry of national and local initiatives in doctoral education by the National Science Foundation, the Alfred Sloan Foundation, the Ford Foundation, the Council of Graduate Schools, the Pew Foundation, the Woodrow Wilson Foundation, the Carnegie Foundation for the Advancement of Teaching, and a number of individual university programs. Private foundations, reflecting the particular US higher education system, fund all but one of the national initiatives, and a number of single-institution ones as well. These initiatives include:

1. National Science Foundation: The Integrative Graduate Education Research and Traineeship program (IGERT), and Alliances for Graduate Education and the Professoriate (AGEP)
2. Council of Graduate Schools: Professional Master's Program, Professional Science Master's Program; Responsible Conduct of Research Project; the Doctoral Completion Project; Preparing Future Faculty/ Preparing Future Professionals
3. The Carnegie Foundation for the Advancement of Teaching: Carnegie Initiative on the Doctorate
4. Pew Foundation Charitable Trust: Re-envisioning the PhD
5. The Woodrow Wilson National Fellowship Foundation: The Responsive PhD, including the Humanities at work program
6. CIRGE/Ford Foundation national PhD career path and educational outcome surveys

The National Science Foundation's "Integrated Graduate Education and Research Traineeship" (IGERT) initiative proposes the creation of doctoral programs that are centered on theme-based research. The goals are:

a. To provide funding for doctoral students that is more independent of the faculty advisor by tying the funding to the doctoral program and not the faculty advisor;
b. To build doctoral programs that are interdisciplinary;
c. To educate and train doctoral students in problem-oriented and theme-based research programs;
d. To provide access for doctoral students to professionals in their field who work outside of academia;

e. To organize the structure of the program so students learn the maximum range of professional skills, from learning how to teach, to working in teams, publishing, developing presentation skills, and learning organizational skills; and

f. To bring diversity to doctoral programs.

This initiative provides funding primarily for students rather than faculty. With the shifting of funding away from faculty to students the emphasis is placed on the learning environment. With this shift NSF hopes to reduce time to doctoral degree and to create a future generation of scholars who are better prepared to address the large-scale problems of industrialized societies that cannot be solved by a single disciplinary focus or by a single researcher. This program is intended to catalyze a cultural change in graduate education, for students, faculty, and institutions, by establishing innovative new models for graduate education and training in a fertile environment for collaborative research that transcends traditional disciplinary boundaries. It is also intended to facilitate diversity in student participation and preparation, and to contribute to the development of a diverse, globally-engaged science and engineering workforce. Since 2003 it has included an international perspective. At present 125 programs at sixty-five universities are or were funded for five years, with a possibility to apply for renewal. Each program was granted $2.9 million, largely for student stipends, evaluations, and curriculum development.

The National Science Foundation's "Alliances for Graduate Education and the Professoriate" (AGEP) initiative is designed to increase the number of US citizens and permanent residents entering the science, engineering, technology, and math fields. AGEP has the specific goal to increase the number of under-represented minority graduate students in these fields and consequently the number of underrepresented minorities in faculty positions.

The Council of Graduate Schools (CGS) has a number of initiatives and programs that are designed to respond to changes in graduate education. The "Professional Master's Program" initiative helps institutions develop and provide a master's degree for people who are interested in pursuing careers in the business, government, and non-profit (BGN) employment sectors and who will start work at the entry level. This initiative responds to employer needs for an entry-level work force that has stronger skill sets than workers with bachelors degrees, as well as student needs for a degree that helps them compete successfully for jobs in the BGN sector. The professional master's is particularly well-suited for the liberal arts undergraduate major who is not pursuing either a PhD or professional degree (law, social work, engineering, etc.).

A similar initiative, but geared more explicitly for the sciences, is the "Professional Science Master's Program," funded by the Sloan Foundation, Council of Graduate Schools, and the Ford Foundation. It is an initiative that proposes a better match between the career options and the career opportunities of graduate students in the sciences and social sciences. This program responds to the criticisms of doctoral education time-to-degree, high attrition rates, the limited academic job market, and students' desire for nonfaculty positions, by providing an alternative route to a terminal science master's degree. This initiative funds institutions to develop a new type of science master's degree that equips people to work outside of academia. It targets major research universities as well as masters-focused institutions to develop two-year masters programs that are heavily oriented toward interdisciplinary course work and strong interaction with employers.

CGS also sponsors a project aimed at educating scientists and their students about the professional norms and ethical standards for responsible conduct of research. This project helps to ensure that all scientists are informed about the ethical requirements of research. It is underwritten by the US Department of Health and Human Services' Office of Research Integrity and by a grant from the National Science Foundation.

Another important project spearheaded by CGS and funded by Pfizer Inc. and the Ford Foundation is the "PhD Completion Project." This project is designed to help institutions develop strategies to address doctoral completion rates and attrition. It further supports evaluation of the strategies so that institutions can determine what strategies work and why. Participating institutions will have their graduate deans present results of the project and share information nationally.

"Preparing the Future Faculty" (PFF) initiative was originally initiated and funded in 1993 by the Pew Charitable Trusts Foundation and coordinated by the Association of American Colleges and Universities and Council of Graduate Schools. Currently the Council of Graduate Schools coordinates this program as a core part of its mission. The initiative's goals are to prepare current doctoral students for their role as future faculty and to prepare students, in a few cases, for their roles as professionals in their fields outside of academia. Today about 295 institutions participate. The majority are masters and bachelors institutions, with forty-three doctoral granting universities also participating. The initiative sponsors seminars and workshops to introduce doctoral students to the different types of institutions of higher education, to their responsibilities as teachers, researchers, and to providing a service to the academic community. It places students into internships at these various institutions, where they teach under the mentorship of an established professor. Thus doctoral students have multiple mentors. It also offers pedagogical workshops. Since 1998, the PFF works together with disciplinary associations. These associations select the participating doctoral programs.

Another initiative is the "Carnegie Initiative on the Doctorate," sponsored by the Carnegie Foundation for the Advancement of Teaching. It is designed to support departmental efforts in structuring their doctoral programs. This initiative addresses the disciplinary communities of six fields: chemistry, education, English, history, mathematics, and neurosciences. It fosters discipline-based conceptual work. Departments that apply for and are selected to participate in this initiative receive advice and funding for two of their members to attend meetings with their counterparts in other participating programs, where they share experiences and information about restructuring their programs. They do this work in collaboration with their professional associations. In short, this initiative tries to stimulate a debate about the structure of doctoral programs by engaging the national association of a discipline in such a conversation.[21]

The "Responsive PhD," coordinated and funded by the Woodrow Wilson National Fellowship Foundation, is an initiative that focuses not directly on students or departments. Rather, it intends to support the initiators of change at a university, that is, department deans, divisional deans, and department chairs. It provides information on best practices in graduate education by bringing participating members together to share their experiences with their own best practices, particularly on the implementation process. The foundation funds the information-sharing meetings and provides some financial support to institutions that wish to implement one of the best practices. The Responsive PhD has identified four issues for a national agenda. The first one is to improve the diversity in graduate education and the professoriate. The second is to ensure that academic knowledge is used for social challenges and to promote "public scholarship." The third is to understand the impact of globalization on doctoral education. And the fourth is to prepare doctoral students for a range of careers.

The Woodrow Wilson Foundation also created the "Humanities at Work" project that consists of a two-year postdoctoral fellowship program, practicum grants of $1,500 for graduate students, and a public scholarship grant for faculty. The primary goal of this project is to increase society's awareness of the value of humanities education.[22]

The Ford Foundation has funded the University of Washington's Center for Innovation and Research in Graduate Education to undertake national surveys on graduate education outcomes, including the career paths of PhD recipients (Social Science PhDs—Five + Years Out) and the evaluation of graduate education of these PhD holders. The intersection of family and career in the life of PhDs is a major topic in the analyses of the career path both for men and women. Increasingly the PhD leads to multiple career possibilities inside and outside of academia that are very satisfying to PhDs.

These initiatives and research activities address various forces that impact doctoral education. They represent different approaches and strategies in the effort to bring about desired changes and by so doing, they target different constituent groups: students, departments, deans, and universities. These initiatives furthermore vary significantly in scope and impact. They all acknowledge the major criticisms of the doctoral program and provide a platform for dialogue on innovation and change. Except for the NSF-funded initiatives they offer minimal financial incentives for implementing these best practices. Mostly they appeal to a moral imperative that there is a need for change and to the goodwill of campus administrators. They all provide advice and the promise of national visibility, thus raising the status of participating departments.

CONCLUSION: WHAT INFORMATION IS NEEDED?

Over the last decade, a robust body of research on doctoral education has grown to inform practices in doctoral education. It has begun to move forward a rationale for an incentive structure to bring about change in a system where there are competing pressures and structures that tend to perpetuate the status quo. But more work in this domain is essential to ensure continued improvement. The innovations in doctoral education that address the changing population of students, new methods of learning, and emerging new disciplines do produce best practices, but additional studies are needed to discern the outcomes and the mechanisms for institutionalizing change. We continue to need improved understanding of what works and what does not. Many innovations are still largely local, and changes in practices are not broadly understood. The development of interdisciplinary curricula is largely done by trial and error. Different models for learning that preserve disciplinary depth and go beyond the traditional disciplinary boundaries while allowing students to prepare for a variety of careers in a changing global context warrant systematic investigation. The definition of what is a successful outcome for a PhD's education needs to be rethought. As new types of programs emerge that try to meet the demands of the labor market, it is important to define what the unique contribution of the PhD education is, and how success should be measured both for society and the individual. Changing doctoral education is difficult in a decentralized system with the absence of an incentive structure. Innovation and institutional reform most likely will be achieved in the US when linked to the competitive races for scientific priorities, resources, and reputation.[23]

NOTES

I would like to thank Bianca Bernstein, Suzanne Ortega, Debra Stewart, Mimi Heggelund, Rebecca Aanerud, and Karalynn Ott for their comments and editorial suggestions, and Sheila Huang for producing the tables and graphs.

1. In the following PhD (Doctor of Philosophy) and doctoral degree are used. There are a number of professional doctorates that are not PhDs, but are included in the numbers cited, for example the doctor of education (EdD), the doctor of social work (DSW), the doctor of public health (DPH), but *not* the doctor of jurisprudence (JD), nor the medical doctor (MD).

2. James Turner and Paul Bernard, "The German Model and the Graduate School: The University of Michigan and the Origin Myth of the American University," in *The American College in the 19th* Century, ed. Roger Geiger (Nashville: Vanderbilt University Press, 2000).

3. NORC, *Doctorate Recipients from United States Universities: Summary Report 1995*, 3, and 2003, highlights, and NORC, Summary Report 2003.

4. Currently sixty US universities and two Canadian universities are members.

5. The National Science Foundation (NSF), the National Institutes of Health (NIH), the Department of Energy (DOE), United State Department of Agriculture (USDA), and National Aeronautic and Space Administration (NASA).

6. NORC, *Summary Report of the Survey of Earned Doctorates, 2003.*

7. The 45 percent figure includes all women; when we look at just US citizens and permanent residents, we see that 51 percent of doctoral degrees went to women.

8. NORC, *Summary Report of the Survey of Earned Doctorates Degrees*, 2003.

9. D. Gupta, M. Nerad, and J. Cerny, "The Road Home: Exploring the Choice to Stay or Return of International PhDs," *International Higher Education*, Spring 2003.

10. The tenure system in the US is a promotion system in which professors progress to a permanent position. In order to achieve the permanent position a faculty member must be in a tenure-track position.

11. *Chronicle of Higher Education* Almanac, Issue 2005–6, 25; see also Baldwin and Chronister 2001; Gappa and Leslie 1996; Sommer 1994.

12. NORC. *Summary Report, Survey of Doctorates, 2003.*

13. See addendum.

14. *Assessing Research-Doctorate Programs: A Methodology Study*, 5.

15. See Organizational Charts.

16. Both predicted a serious shortfall of PhDs in the arts and traditional science, as well as the natural sciences and engineering for several decades to come. William G. Bowen and Julie Ann Sosa, *Prospects for Faculty in the Arts and Sciences* (Princeton, NJ: Princeton University Press, 1989); 8 Richard Atkinson, "Supply and Demand for Scientists and Engineers: A National Crisis in the Making," *Science*, 27 April 1990: 425–32.

17. COSEPUP 1995.

18. M. Nerad, "The PhD in the U.S.: Criticisms, Facts and Remedies," *Higher Education Policy*, Vol.17, No. 2.; Jody Nyquist and Bettina Woodford, "Re-envisioning the Ph.D.: What Concerns Do We Have?" Seattle, Washington, CIDR web site, http://depts.washington.edu/cidrweb/.

19. Patricia Gumport, "Graduate Education and Research: Interdependence and Strain," in *American Higher Education in the Twenty-First Century*, ed. Philip Altbach et. al. (Baltimore: Johns Hopkins University Press, 2005).

20. Ron G. Ehrenberg, "Graduate Education, Innovation and Federal Responsibility," *Communicator*, CGS Vol. XXXVIII, No 6, July 2005, 1ff.

21. Chris Golde and George Walker, 2006.

22. The Woodrow Wilson National Fellowship Foundation, *Diversity and the Ph.D. A Review of Efforts to Broaden Race and Ethnicity in U.S. Doctoral Education.* Princeton, NJ: Woodrow Wilson National Fellowship Foundation, May 2005.

23. Irwin Feller, "Interdisciplinarity As a Component of the Reform of American Graduate Education," presentation to the NSF workshop on the future of graduate education, 19–20 March 2003.

BIBLIOGRAPHY

Altbach, Philip G. 2004. "The United States: Present Realities and Future Trends." In *Doctoral Studies and Qualifications in Europe and the United States: Status and Prospects*, edited by Jan Sadlak. Bucharest: UNESCO-CEPES.

Atkinson, Richard. 1990. "Supply and Demand for Scientists and Engineers: A National Crisis in the Making," *Science*, 27 April: 425–32.

Bowen, William G. and Julie Ann Sosa. 1989. *Prospects for Faculty in the Arts and Sciences.* Princeton, NJ: Princeton University Press.

Chronicle of Higher Education Almanac, Issue 2005–6, p. 25.

Ehrenberg, Ron G. 2005. "Graduate Education, Innovation and Federal Responsibility." *Communicator*, CGS Vol. XXXVIII, No 6 (July): 1ff.

Feller, Irwin. 2003. "Interdisciplinarity As a Component of the Reform of American Graduate Education." Presentation to the NSF workshop on the future of graduate education, 19–20 March.

Golde, Chris and George E. Walker, eds. 2006. *Envisioning the Future of Doctoral Education. Preparing Stewards of the Discipline. Carnegie Essays on the Doctorate.* San Francisco, CA: Jossey-Bass.

Gumport, Patricia. 2005. "Graduate Education and Research: Interdependence and Strain." In *American Higher Education in the Twenty-First Century*, edited by Philip Altbach et. al. Baltimore: Johns Hopkins University Press.

Gupta, D., M. Nerad, and J. Cerny. 2003. "The Road Home: Exploring the Choice to Stay or Return of International PhDs." *International Higher Education*, Spring issue.

Kanpol, Barry. 1997. *Issues and Trends in Critical Pedagogy*. Cresskill, NJ: Hampton Press.

National Research Council. *Assessing Research-Doctorate Programs: A Methodology Study*, 5.

Nerad, M. 2004. "The PhD in the U.S.: Criticisms, Facts and Remedies." *Higher Education Policy*, Vol.17, No. 2.

NORC. 1995. *Doctorate Recipients from United States Universities: Summary Report 1995*, 3.

NORC. 2003. *Summary Report of the Survey of Earned Doctorates.*

Nyquist, Jody, and Bettina Woodford. 2000. "Re-envisioning the Ph.D.: What Concerns Do We Have?" Seattle, WA: CIDR web site, http://depts.washington.edu/cidrweb/.

Turner, James, and Paul Bernard. 2000. "The German Model and the Graduate School: The University of Michigan and the Origin Myth of the American University," in *The American College in the 19th Century*, edited by Roger Geiger. Nashville: Vanderbilt University Press.

The Woodrow Wilson National Fellowship Foundation. 2005. "Diversity and the Ph.D. A Review of Efforts to Broaden Race and Ethnicity in U.S. Doctoral Education." Princeton, NJ: Woodrow Wilson National Fellowship Foundation.

INTERNAL ORGANIZATION OF US UNIVERSITIES

Example 1

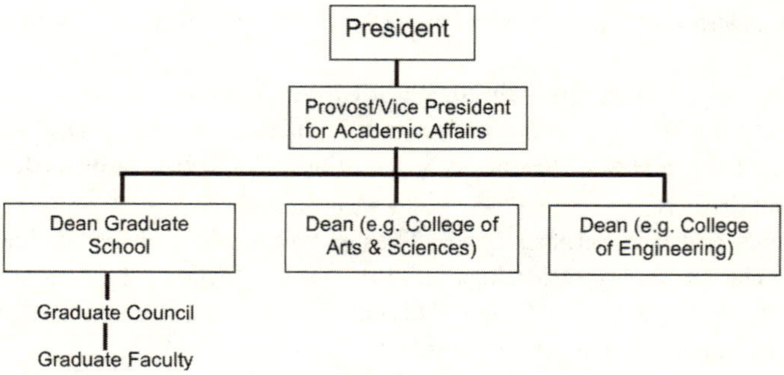

Example 2

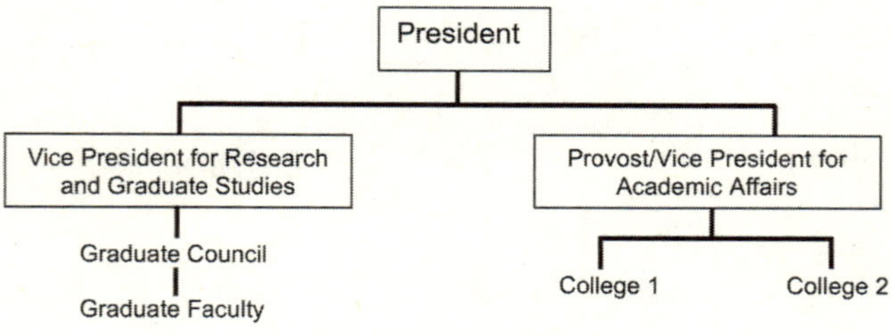

SOURCE: CIRGE, University of Washington

BASIC STRUCTURE OF US PhD PROGRAMS

Social Sciencies and Humanities

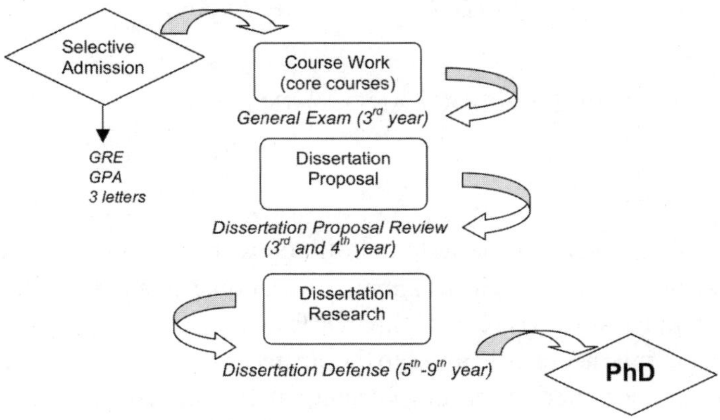

Physical, Life Sciences and Engineering

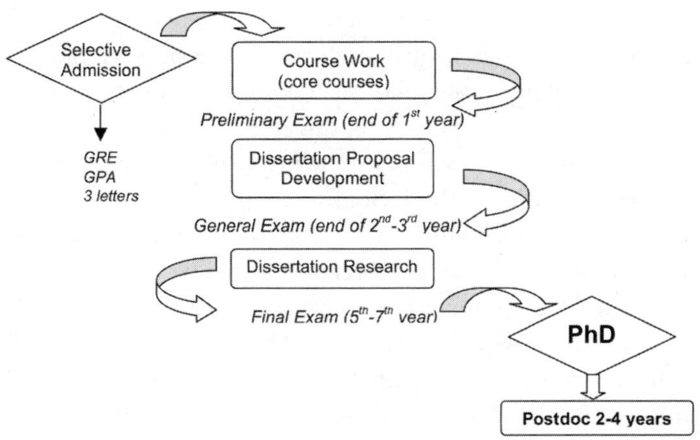

SOURCE: CIRGE, University of Washington

CONCLUSION

GLOBALIZATION AND DOCTORAL EDUCATION—TOWARD A RESEARCH AGENDA

MARESI NERAD AND THOMAS TRZYNA

Universities have always been global institutions; they functioned in a common language (Latin) and served an international clientele of students. In fact, universities have come full-circle from the Medieval Ages as being centers of international learning, to the nineteenth and twentieth centuries rising as nation-state universities pursuing national interests, and now again as international centers of scholarship and learning in a time of globalization. Globalization, defined as "the intensified movement of goods, money, technology, information, people, ideas, and cultural practices across political and cultural boundaries" (Holton 2005, 14) is a multi-faceted process that affects each country differently. In spite of these differences, can we say that the forms of doctoral education are converging? Globalization certainly is changing doctoral education, but are programs of doctoral education simultaneously influencing the process and nature of globalization by producing new generations of researchers and leaders? Within this context, the purpose of this chapter is not to propose definite conclusions but rather to draw on the preceding empirical chapters and the collaborative work of the doctoral education experts who met in Seattle at the University of Washington in 2005 to outline an agenda of research needed for future-oriented doctoral education worldwide.

We begin by developing a conceptual framework for understanding doctoral education within globalization. This provides the context for considering key dimensions of globalization in doctoral education that are illuminated by the work presented in this book: commoditization, the market economy, the Mode 2 educational model, brain drain, the use of English, standardization, quality assurance, and the Bologna Accords. We focus on national and institutional responses to globalization, and on the ways that these responses are affecting the education of individual doctoral students. When, in the following, we refer to specific countries, we are referring to the country chapters in this volume. We then synthesize the innovations described in this volume into an outline of the likely characteristics of future-oriented doctoral education. We conclude with the research agenda that emerged from the 2005 conference and was articulated in the "Seattle Declaration." This research agenda identifies topics critical to understanding the current dynamics of doctoral education and for shaping the future of doctoral education in a global context that preserves diversity.

CONCEPTUAL FRAMEWORK

The Unequal Context of Doctoral Education

It is important to note that this discussion takes place in a world where doctoral education and research agendas are unevenly distributed. In the late twentieth century, a few research universities mainly in resource-wealthy countries have become powerful academic institutions. One index of that power is the controversial Shanghai Jiao Tong University annual rating of the research productivity of world universities as measured by international awards, publications in major journals, and citations listed in major citation indexes. By that rating system, seventeen of the top twenty world research universities were in the United States, two in Britain, and one in Japan. None are in Latin America, Africa, or Australasia, other than Japan. Past colonial systems still cast shadows across higher education in countries as the chapters in this volume on South Africa and India show. A number of nations are reeling from "brain drain." Some authors have questioned, indeed, whether recent developments in globalization and especially in the commercialization of higher education constitute neocolonialism (Altbach and Knight 2007) by which major research universities dominate the minds and the universities of people in poorer nations through such means as IT systems, journals, and advanced technology. Moreover, research questions that may be important in the developed world may not be equally important in other nations. In a global higher education system where a few nations dominate the international research and publishing agenda, it is difficult for other nations and scholars to identify or lead distinctly different research agendas. No single chapter in this book speaks about inequality per se, but reading through the entire volume, inequality of resources and positioning in the global context strikes one as a reality.

Globalization and Rule Sets

Some scholars and observers argue that globalization will free higher education from a narrow national outlook and foster needed changes. These same scholars claim that market forces, technological innovations, the expansion of the private sector in higher education, and a shift from elite to mass higher education will permit everyone to compete on a basis of equality. Others, as noted above, claim that on the contrary, globalization strengthens worldwide inequality, fosters the franchising of higher education institutions, and tends to keep academic power in the hands of the wealthy universities of the developed countries.

Governments, business organizations, and other entities, including universities, regularly make decisions about the extent to which they will expedite or resist globalizing flows of resources, information, and individuals. The geopolitical analyst Thomas P. M. Barnett refers to the complex mix of policies, practices, and other characteristics that define an entity's relationship to globalization as that entity's "rule sets." (Barnett 2006).

In a general sense, entities that choose to accept and even embrace globalization adopt rule sets that make their boundaries more porous to globalizing flows. At a national level related to economic trade, for example, those rule sets would include free-trade agreements, standardization of currency, laws protecting importers and exporters of goods, economic and legal transparency, rapid processes for business licensure, and unimpeded "offshoring" of work to persons and businesses in other countries. Such rule sets aim to ease transnational interactions by turning processes and products into "commodities" with no distinct local features. In a fully globalized economy, all goods would be treated the same, all financial instruments would be equivalent, laws would be the same from nation to nation, and national boundaries would create no obstacles to the pursuit of profit or competitive advantage.

Conversely (continuing to use the economic sphere as an example), those who resist globalization establish barriers to the free flow of goods, services, information, and individuals. For example, they create tariffs or other trade barriers; they do not conform their financial instruments to the standards of others; their laws have localized characteristics that can complicate or interfere with transnational interactions; and they limit offshoring of economic activity.

To the extent that nations or entities adopt rule sets that make one nation or entity's practices very much like another, with no localized characteristics to add friction to the globalizing flows, the world can be described as "flat," to use Thomas Friedman's widely quoted description. (Friedman 2005)

Doctoral education, as many of the authors of papers in this volume have said, is not immune to the forces of globalization and the issues those forces raise. Institutions offering graduate education and their state and private sponsors are constantly in the process of defining rule sets that either facilitate or impede globalization, whether or not their deliberations regarding those rule sets actually use the word "globalization." As the chapters in this book show, some university systems and nations are adopting rule sets that "flatten" the world of doctoral education, making it look more alike, while others are holding on to local policies and practices. Still others are acceding to globalization and at the same time formulating new local policies to ease what they consider to be undesirable localized impacts of globalization.

Internationalization

Some scholars use the world "internationalization" in reference to educational programming and institutional practices, suggesting that it is different than "globalization." Internationalization may include proactive implementation of programs and services of international education exchange, international research collaborations, joint degrees, and other institutional behaviors (Knight 2006).

For the purposes of this chapter, we will suggest that to the extent that universities intensively "internationalize" their practices, they are applying rule sets that facilitate globalization, and to the extent that they do not internationalize they may be adopting positions that resist globalization. There may be differences in intentions or in how practices are understood between "internationalizing" and "globalizing," but the overall impact can be seen as either supporting or impeding globalization, or as accepting globalization while also acting to ameliorate some of its perceived negative consequences.

DIMENSIONS OF GLOBALIZATION IN DOCTORAL EDUCATION

Commoditization

The "commoditization" of education in general is a much remarked-upon phenomenon. With regard to doctoral degrees within a context of globalization, commoditization may mean the elimination of any purely local characteristics or qualities of a degree program so that the degree's value, significance, and utility can be assessed by anyone, anywhere, and so that an economic value can be placed on that degree by anyone with adequate expertise in educational credentials. Degree holders then become "sellers," in a broad or even international "marketplace," of what their degrees represent in terms of knowledge, skills, and other attributes. The more each degree is commoditized, the less difficult it becomes for the seller to market the product, because there is less need to explain relative worth by translating credentials from one culture and educational system to another. At the same time, "buyers" of degree holders are happier because the transaction is easier and the value of the commodity is better understood, so the whole transaction becomes easier, more efficient, and less risky. The world marketplace, for degreed individuals that is, then becomes "flatter."

Universities and their sponsors may like or dislike, reject or embrace this phenomenon, but commoditization will affect them regardless of their preferences. Universities may choose to work to modify the larger phenomenon of commoditization in some way that is based on their values, judgment, and experience, but they will also be faced with localized decisions about what rule sets to adopt in relation to the increasing degree to which doctoral education will be viewed as a commodity.

In this context, pursuing doctoral education for the sake of curiosity, exploration, or the love for a specific field seems to be disappearing, relative to doctoral education aimed at solving specific intellectual and social challenges and for the development of specific industries that can compete effectively with other nations. In other words, doctoral education is becoming a commodity that has value only if it can be bought and sold in the public marketplaces of research, development, policy formation, and social and institutional change. In a society where knowledge is an economic driving force for innovation, through doctoral education research universities become regional economic forces. Will doctoral education only be valued if it is connected to the global economy and the priorities of that economy? While commoditization is not specifically named in any of the chapters of this volume, it is part of the globalization phenomenon.

The Market Economy

Market forces are also mandating that newly trained holders of doctorates have, in addition to their content knowledge and research skills, specific additional skills that will make them effective participants in economic development. Nations throughout the world are increasingly investing in higher education to produce knowledge and to stay abreast of new technologies that are driving economic growth in the most developed nations. Nations that fall behind in this process run the risk of being left out of the emerging world economy. New PhDs are increasingly expected to be competent writers, speakers, managers, and team members, so that they can communicate research goals and results and participate effectively in corporate as well as university research and development.

Where there is strong national resistance to changing the model of doctoral education, private universities can adjust more rapidly to the new global expectations. The growth of private universities, as the chapters on Mexico and Japan have shown, has been stimulated by some of these forces. At the same time concerns about the quality of some private, international universities have led some nations, particularly in South America (see chapter on Brazil), to examine carefully the credentials and programs of new private sector universities that apply to offer educational programs within their borders.

In many nations (see chapters on Japan and Mexico) the appearance of private universities constitutes a major shift in thinking about higher education, because universities have in the past been funded only by state and federal governments and have been controlled by those governments. Where tuition has been free or almost free, as it has been in Europe, the emergence of private institutions and for-profit universities changes education from a social entitlement to a privilege that not only must be earned through merit, but also must be purchased.

The same market forces can also direct national resources toward specific national agendas, as doctoral education in Iceland and Scandinavia (see chapter on Nordic countries) has been focused on the development of strong high-technology sectors in those nations.

"Mode 2"

Perhaps no emergent trend in doctoral education reflects adaptation to global market economies as strongly as the impetus toward what has been called the "Mode 2" educational model (Gibbons et. al. 1994). In the old, or "Mode 1" model of doctoral education, an individual student performed research on a topic of mostly his or her own choice, or, as is often the case in science and engineering, on a topic given by the advisor—but the research was always directed by one "master" professor. In 1995, US major policy bodies complained about the number of new doctorates who were supposedly in perpetual postdoctoral positions or underemployed. Even if these concerns were overblown, as CIRGE research on career outcomes of PhDs has shown, they triggered changes in graduate education, such as the introduction of the National Science Foundation funded Integrated Graduate Education and Research Traineeship (IGERT) program (see chapter on USA). From the standpoint of wise use of national investments, these PhDs without appropriate positions constitute a waste of national resources. As we learned from other chapters in this book, this same problem has been endemic in other nations, as has the related problem of students who drop out of doctoral programs and of students who take extraordinary amounts of time to complete doctorates.

Mode 2 doctoral education is characterized by a team of students and senior researchers working together on a project that has marketable value as defined either by government or private interests. Dissertations in the sciences are starting to be replaced by a series of journal articles. Research teams are often interdisciplinary, and in many cases the research work itself involves teams from many nations and cultures, and from many different universities. Mode 2 doctoral research can also involve collaborations among universities, corporations, and other entities.

Mode 2 doctoral education is emerging more rapidly, where the traditional departmental structure of universities can be an impediment to the new approaches to university governance, organization of research, interdisciplinary networks, and other innovations. In general, the mode of research and doctoral education that has been common in the natural sciences and engineering is now becoming the norm or standard for doctoral education, even in the social sciences and humanities. These changes present challenges to many traditional assumptions about doctoral education in nations such as Germany, where the dissertation director has played such a dominant role (see chapter on Germany), and England (see chapter on UK), where doctoral research has been highly individualistic. Where there has been concern about the number of department members necessary to maintain a successful doctoral program, Mode 2 doctoral education offers the possibility of organizing world-class doctoral study through networks of cooperation with scholars and universities across the globe as well as with scholars in many different academic disciplines, as the chapter on Brazil informs us.

Brain Drain

Perhaps the most discussed impact of global market forces on doctoral education is the phenomenon of "brain drain," in which countries lose their doctoral students to opportunities in other countries. A particularly notable case of this kind of brain drain is found in the chapter on Mexico, where development of national universities and research institutions has to an important degree been limited by the proximity of the United States of America and its large number of doctoral programs and research universities. The same is true for South Africa (see chapter on South Africa), as young minds are leaving once-excellent research universities.

Some nations are considering new educational policies that will both assure a return on national investments in doctoral education and may limit the free flow of students across national borders; requiring a return to one's home country after degree completion. Some nations try to resist the substitution of their national language with English and request that the dissertation be written in the country's language. There are complex relationships between market demands and national economic priorities that affect the financing of doctoral education, including national priorities for creating and sustaining universities and programs.

The Use of English

Increasingly, the global language of doctoral education is becoming English. In many nations, including European nations, doctoral courses are taught in English and research papers are prepared and presented in English. Scientific journals are published primarily in English. Internet communication is mainly in English. The language of scholarship and research has become English. Against this tide, some nations have built dikes of one kind or another. Brazil invests in the continuance of a Portuguese-language culture by offering free or reduced tuition to scholars from other Portuguese-speaking nations (see chapter on Brazil).

The new communication technologies are intensifying the development and growth of intellectual and scholarly networks worldwide, and communication between networks is mostly done in English. This movement furthers the divide between the local communities communicating in local languages and the scholarly community communicating in English. The Internet has no borders, and the Worldwide Web has made access to libraries, scholars, journals, and other information sources, increasingly in English, both universal and instantaneous, so long as an individual lives in a place where there is access to the Internet. Of course this trend privileges English as the primary language of international research and communication and increases the "digital divide" between North and South and the divide between the scholars and local communities.

Increasing Standardization

Worldwide, trends can be seen toward the establishment of a common model of doctoral education. Chapters in this volume by Australia, the UK, Germany, the European University Institute, and the Nordic countries discuss, for example, convergence toward common definitions of degrees in terms of names, increased agreement regarding the purpose and standard of the research dissertation as contributing to new knowledge, the introduction of common curricular elements such as formal coursework in research methods, professional development workshops, and ethics research training, and a movement toward more interdisciplinary research preparation.

The gradual adoption of a single European standard for the length of the baccalaureate, masters, and doctoral degrees, as well as more clarity about the relationship between baccalaureate and doctoral education is also evidence of broad, if not international, standardization (see chapter on the Bologna Process).

Rule sets still under negotiation in many nations focus on such matters as competitive admissions standards, the need for outside examiners, for oral examinations, and the number of years necessary for a doctoral degree. Although there are advances to a converging model of doctoral education, we don't know what we are losing: different modes of learning? Better adapting to local needs?

Quality Assurance

Nations and other entities are developing and establishing internationalized mechanisms to vouchsafe the quality of doctoral degrees. Japan, for example, is adopting a quality control system similar to the one in place in the United States. Both Japan and Germany divert national funding to a smaller group of universities judged to be good candidates to compete at the highest levels of international excellence in research productivity and doctoral training. These are examples of accepting a new international standard, as is the gradual redefinition or disappearance of the licentiate degree in parts of Europe.

Overall, many universities are operating increasingly in a managerial mode similar to businesses and are applying quality standards through outcomes assessment systems that include matrices of measurable objectives. Benchmarking is also becoming more common.

While the application of benchmarks and outcomes assessment can promote quality, such management strategies can also produce risk-averse behaviors.

As universities in some nations focus their efforts on quality initiatives for competing more effectively in the global research marketplace, US and European institutions are responding with new initiatives to maintain their present strengths. In this way the entire process of globalization within higher education is cyclical and self-reinforcing.

However assessment is carried out, it is clear that assessment schemes are attempting to assure some form of reliable quality that has validity across national borders. Among the input measures, competitive admission is becoming more common. Throughput measures include more emphasis on mandated coursework in all programs, assessment of doctoral supervisors, and assessment of departmental capacity to offer doctoral work. Output measures include such traditional factors as time-to-degree, completion rates, and employment of doctorates, but increasingly output is measured in terms of contributions to identified research agendas.

Among recent innovations are the British Code of Practice, the move in Australia to multiple dissertation advisors, and the adoption of Mode 2 research. All of these changes have implications for the financing of doctoral education, the benchmarks that students must reach to maintain their grants, and the productivity standards that research teams and thesis directors must maintain to continue their own research funding and university support. The managerial mode of university management is feeding on quality assurance. To what degree these new management models will dampen creativity, initiative, and innovation remain to be seen and will need to studied.

The Bologna Accords

The Bologna Declaration of 1999 can be seen as a prototype of embracing globalization. While the Bologna Declaration may be the culmination of nearly fifty years of discussions within the European Union, the Prague Communiqué of 2001 and the Berlin Communiqué of 2003 added objectives to the Bologna Declaration that standardize doctoral education in Europe, or as the Europeans call it, "harmonize" the proposed length of time to the doctorate and add program components addressing market forces. The proposed changes will allow the mobile PhD degree holder to "sell" his or her degree in all of the European Union countries. Most significantly, the European Union member countries vouched to allocate 3.2 percent of the GNP by 2010 to research and development in their countries. This money will flow, and already is flowing to a significant degree, into the doctoral degree-granting universities and result in noticeable change.

The authors of the chapters on European countries describe the often rapid and drastic current and future influence of the Bologna agreement on their doctoral education, particularly Germany. Certainly the process has led to significant innovations and to the establishment of a common platform of understanding in such areas as doctoral supervision, the definition of degrees, guidelines for the length of study, provisions for mobility across national boundaries, provisions for collaboration among scholars and universities, new funding formulae, and new expectations for the outputs of doctoral education and research, as measured in terms of national economic and development objectives. Other nations entering the discussion of doctoral education are well advised to study this European model.

CHARACTERISTICS OF THE NEW DOCTORATE

In summary, taking together the changes and innovations described in this volume into a synthesis, future-oriented doctoral education will be characterized by many of the following characteristics:

1. Graduate students will be prepared for a variety of career possibilities in academe, government, industry, or non-profit organizations.
2. Ideally, they will be offered three years of funding including research and teaching assistantships—with clear benchmarks and performance standards to be met at various stages of the degree process.
3. Students will be encouraged to work with multiple mentors.
4. Graduate education will begin with a general graduate education course on epistemology—on different ways of knowing.
5. General graduate education will include a course on "environmental literacy" and ethics.
6. Even within a single discipline, graduate education will include some interdisciplinary or multidisciplinary components.
7. Future-oriented graduate programs will have collaborative projects with other universities, research centers, or industrial research organizations.
8. Ideally, students will be expected to carry out some portion of their training or research in another country.
9. International graduate students will need to be fully integrated into the university's graduate curriculum so that learning becomes a two-way street, where students also learn from their international peers.
10. Graduate students and postdoctoral fellows will receive professional development training such as experience in teamwork, grant writing, and time and project management. They will receive training in presentation, communication and leadership skills.
11. Ethics education will become integral in all fields, not only in science and engineering graduate programs.
12. Graduate students will need to master more than one language.
13. World citizenship education will become a goal.

THE "SEATTLE DECLARATION"

During the course of the 2005 Seattle conference, the doctoral education experts from six continents and fourteen countries set a milestone for sharing information widely, shaping new research on global trends, and promoting innovations in doctoral education worldwide. They created a guiding document, dubbed "the Seattle Declaration." This declaration set a research agenda in doctoral education and was to steer the continuing conversation about where doctoral education has been and where it is going in the future.

Recognizing the complexities of the global higher education context and its effect on graduate education and working towards a more equal higher education system both within nations and worldwide, particularly in the context of the North-South divide, the Seattle Declaration provides a framework and support for universities to lead societies in shaping doctoral education to meet the needs of the twenty-first century in a global world and to create conditions to educate global citizens. We want to educate doctoral students who are *world citizens*, who cross national boundaries without seeking to assimilate and homogenize but instead accept differences and embrace diversity. If we do not care about understanding the current dynamics of doctoral education and contributing to shaping the future of doctoral education as both global and diverse, we might lose the world capacity to harness and engage the human capacity for innovation and imaginative problem solving at a time when the problems facing humanity are increasingly complex, global, and fundamentally social. We need diverse perspectives to understand global dynamics. We need diverse perspectives to form the basis for cross-cultural communication. If doctoral education doesn't educate people well, then we waste brainpower.

The Seattle conference participants announced seven commitments to guide their efforts and the research agenda until the next such meeting which was held in 2007. (The full "Seattle Declaration" is provided in the appendix.) These commitments include:

1. Be active players in international collaborations that foster the development and continuous improvement of doctoral education—for students and for institutions globally.
2. Forge effective global networks of doctoral education experts, examining patterns of change and outlining an agenda for international research and innovations to improve doctoral education and share best practices.
3. Understand the two-way influence of doctoral education on the global economy and of globalization on doctoral education.

4. Develop strategies resolving the tension between nation building and the need for international cooperation, by preserving native culture and language and reducing "brain drain."

5. Strive for international consensus on what comprises doctoral education and what competencies the degree should confer.

6. Create, share, and apply internationally meaningful comparative data on doctoral education and evaluate doctoral education across national boundaries.

7. Identify policies that promote excellence in doctoral education and simultaneously prepare for world citizenship that fosters diversity.

BIBLIOGRAPHY

Altbach, Philip. *Tradition and Transition: The International Imperative in Higher Education.* Chestnut Hill, MA: Boston College, Center for international Higher Education, Lynch School of Education, 2007.

Barnett, Thomas P. M. *A Blueprint for Action: A Future Worth Creating.* New York: G. P. Putnam and Sons, 2006.

Friedman, Thomas L. *The World is Flat: A Brief History of the Twenty-First Century.* New York: Farrar, Straus and Giroux, 2005.

Gibbons, M., C. Limoges, H. Nowotney, S. Schwarzman, P. Scott, and M. Trow. *The New Production of Knowledge: The Dynamics of Science and Research in Contemporary Societies.* London: Sage, 1994.

Holton, Robert J. 2005. *Making Globalization.* New York: Palgrave MacMillan.

Knight, Jane. "Internationalization: Concepts, Complexities and Challenges." In International Handbook of Higher Education, edited by James Forest and Philip Altbach. Springer, 2006.

APPENDIX A

PAST DIFFERENCES, CURRENT COMMONALITIES, AND FUTURE TRENDS IN DOCTORAL EDUCATION IN SELECTED COUNTRIES*

PAST DIFFERENCES

1. In many countries doctoral education did not have a formalized admission process nor explicit admission standards.
2. In some countries, access to the doctorate was possible only after completing a master's degree.
3. In most cases dissertation research was undertaken without a structured doctoral program.
4. Only one dissertation supervisor worked with the person who wanted to undertake a doctoral dissertation.
5. Particularly in Europe, a person with a doctorate had the possibility to enter into a variety of careers—in government, industry, business, nonprofits, and academia. If academic employment was the immediate next step after the doctorate, it was not an appointment to professor.
6. The only available data on the doctorates were the numbers of degrees awarded by discipline. There was no collection of data on time-to-degree nor on attrition.
7. Quality assurance was assessed at the student level in the form of the quality assessment of the dissertation.
8. Countries around the world that granted a doctoral degree varied widely in terms of resources and positioning in the global context.

CURRENT COMMONALITIES

1. All countries agree that the defining feature of the PhD is an original piece of research embodied in an original dissertation.

*The Forces & Forms of Change Network (2005): Australia, Brazil, Canada, Denmark, Germany, Iceland, India, Japan, Mexico, New Zealand, Norway, South Africa, United States

2. All doctorates are expected to have substantial knowledge in their area of study.
3. A minimum of 3 years time for the doctorate is required in most countries.
4. Doctoral education increasingly takes place within a structured program with required courses.
5. Most countries have external dissertation/thesis examiner(s); the examiner(s) can be from outside the institution and/or outside the country.
6. The average time to a doctoral degree varies between 4–7 years.
7. During the last decade, all countries have increased their PhD production. Women's participation in doctoral education has steadily increased. The enrollment of international students in science and engineering programs has increased steadily in most countries, but the increase is particularly notable in countries outside the US.
8. All countries show some form of response to the Bologna process, the European Union's rapidly moving program of higher education reform.

FUTURE TRENDS

1. In all countries, there is a shifting emphasis in the purpose of the doctoral degree from being solely for knowledge creation to being also preparation for employment.
2. In a number of countries, access to the doctoral program may occur after three years of study at the university or after the bachelor's degree.
3. Many countries have moved to explicitly stated admission standards.
4. In a number of countries doctoral students are fully funded during the entire duration of studies, including studying abroad.
5. All countries agree that transferable/professional skills and competencies (teaching, leadership, communication, project management, working in teams), should be included in doctoral studies; however, implementation of training in such skills is uneven.
6. Graduate schools/graduate research schools have been introduced into universities where none existed before.
7. Many countries have introduced a supervision panel, which consists of more than one dissertation supervisor.
8. Concern with diversity among students and faculty exists in a few countries.
9. Formal doctoral program evaluation procedures and mechanisms are being introduced.

10. The introduction of professional doctorates (nursing, business administration, etc.) is proliferating.
11. Various forms of international involvement/collaborations regarding doctoral education are emerging. They range from joint doctoral degrees to the requirement of spending research time in another country.
12. All countries have become aware of the need to collect data on doctoral education beyond the mere number of degrees awarded. A particular emphasis seems to be on collecting information on the employment of recent PhDs.
13. The need to introduce interdisciplinary studies and research preparation is a topic of discussion in all countries.
14. In a number of countries, governments have introduced specific innovations in doctoral education through their national research councils in the form of major research grants.
15. Policy debates in a number of countries are concerned with how to make dissertation research more socially relevant.

APPENDIX B

THE SEATTLE DECLARATION

SEPTEMBER 2005*

We, the *Forces and Forms* network, in order to increase the world's capacity for solving global problems and meeting human needs, declare our commitment to understanding the role of doctoral education in globalization. This declaration is a call to reflect upon the forces shaping doctoral education worldwide and a call to act upon the forms of doctoral education worldwide. It defines a framework for shaping doctoral education to meet the needs of the 21st century and for creating the conditions to educate doctoral-level researchers as world citizens.

We acknowledge that doctoral education is a resource for economic competition between nations and that the current distribution of intellectual capital tends to magnify global inequality.

We believe that doctoral education should be a resource for social cooperation and the mitigation of inequality.

We are committed to understanding what forms of doctoral education are needed to produce socially relevant knowledge, promote international cooperation, and bring to fruition diverse ways of knowing.

Many factors motivate the need for a global understanding of doctoral education. These include growing interest in doctoral education as a source of innovation and competitive advantage in the global economy; expansion of doctoral education in small countries and developing nations; increasing diversification of international students' destinations for doctoral study; internationalization of the labor market and global competition for PhD scientists and researchers; and increasing awareness of

*This workshop was organized by the Center for Innovation and Research in Graduate Education (CIRGE) with funding from the National Science Foundation, the Ford Foundation, and the University of Washington's Graduate School and College of Education.

life-threatening problems, such as global warming and nuclear proliferation, that can only be confronted with international cooperation.

In light of these trends, as doctoral education researchers, policy makers, funders, and administrators, we believe we can promote the improvement of doctoral education worldwide through the following activities:

- Participating actively in international collaborations;
- Forging global networks to examine patterns of change in doctoral education;
- Defining an agenda for international research on innovations in doctoral education;
- Sharing research findings and best practices;
- Studying the role of doctoral education in globalization;
- Developing strategies for preserving native cultures and reducing "brain drain" while also strengthening local connections to international science and scholarship;
- Striving for international consensus on what doctoral education is and the competencies a PhD degree should confer;
- Creating, sharing, and applying internationally meaningful comparative data on doctoral education;
- Evaluating doctoral education across national boundaries; and
- Identifying policies that promote excellence in doctoral education and simultaneously foster diversity.

This Seattle Declaration is one result of a comprehensive effort to assess doctoral education as a critical force in responding to and shaping trends in globalization. Initiated by the Center for Innovation and Research in Graduate Education at the University of Washington, Seattle, three *Forces and Forms of Change in Doctoral Education Worldwide* workshops will take place. For doctoral education experts these meetings will provide the basis for understanding how, and how well, graduate education is responding to global trends. For the first conference, in 2005, more than 30 doctoral education experts from 6 continents and 14 countries convened at the University of Washington in Seattle, Washington, USA. This first conference was a milestone for sharing information widely, shaping new research on global trends, and promoting innovations in doctoral education worldwide.

SIGNATORIES

Barbara Evans - Australia
Dean, Graduate Studies,
University of Melbourne

Terry Evans - Australia
Professor and Associate Dean
of Research, Deakin University

Helene Marsh - Australia
Dean of Post Graduate Studies,
James Cook University

Simon Schwartzman - Brazil
Instituto de Estudos do Trabalho
e Sociedade, Rio de Janeiro

Russolina Zingali - Brazil
Associate Professor, Instituto de
Bioquimica Medica, Universidade
Federal do Rio de Janeiro

Renato Ribeiro - Brazil
Evaluation Director, Professor,
CAPES-Brazilian Ministry of
Education, University of São Paulo

Marc Renaud - Canada
President Social Sciences &
Humanities Research Council
of Canada

Louis Maheu - Canada
Dean of Higher Education,
University of Montreal

Jonathan Driver - Canada
Dean of Graduate Studies,
Simon Fraser University

Hans Siggaard Jensen - Denmark
Professor & Executive Research
Director, The Danish University of
Education

Hans Jürgen Prömel - Germany
Vice President for Research,
Humboldt-Universität zu Berlin

Barbara Kehm - Germany
Professor, Managing Director, Center
for Research on Higher Education

Hans Kristjan Gudmundsson - Iceland
Director, Rannis - The Icelandic
Center for Research

Andreas Frijdal - Italy
Head of Academic Service, European
University Institute

Tetsuo Shoji - Japan
Professor and Associate Dean for
Research, Tohoku University

Kumiko Hirabayashi-Tansho - Japan
Head of Research Cooperation
Division II, International Program
Department, Japan Society for the
Promotion of Science (JSPS)

Shinichi Yamamoto - Japan
Professor and the Director of Research
Center for University Studies, Tsukuba
University

Mauricio Fortes - Mexico
Director General Adjunto de
Investigación y Normas, CENEVAL

Armando Alcantara - Mexico
Professor of Center for University
Studies, National Autonomous
University of Mexico

Salvador Malo - Mexico
Director General, CENEVAL

Graham Smith - New Zealand
Distinguished Professor in Indigenous
Education, University of British
Columbia

Linda Tuhiwai Smith - New Zealand
Director National Research Center of
Excellence for Maori Development

and Advancement, University of Auckland

Morten Levin - Norway
Department of Industrial Economics and Technology Management, Norwegian University of Science and Technology

Toko Mayekiso - South Africa
Professor Head of School, School of Human and Community Development, University of the Witwatersrand, Johannesburg

Ahmed Bawa - South Africa
Deputy Vice Chancellor of Research, Knowledge Production & Partnerships; Professor of Physics & Education, University of KwaZulu-Natal

Jeroen Bartelse - The Netherlands
Deputy Director, Netherlands Association of Universities

Howard Green - United Kingdom
Chair, UK Council for Graduate Education, Senior Adviser to the Vice Chancellor, Staffordshire University

Maresi Nerad - USA
Associate Graduate Dean, Associate Professor and Director, Center for Innovation and Research in Graduate Education (CIRGE), University of Washington, Seattle

Walter Schaffer - USA
NIH Research Training Officer, Office of Extramural Research, The National Institutes of Health

Myan Baker - USA
Consultant & Facilitator, Center for Innovation and Research in Graduate Education (CIRGE), University of Washington, Seattle

Bianca Bernstein - USA
Division Director, Division of Graduate Education, Education and Human Resources (EHR), National Science Foundation

Suzanne Ortega - USA
Vice Provost and Graduate Dean, University of Missouri/University of Washington, Seattle

Debra Stewart - USA
President, Council of Graduate Schools

Mimi Heggelund - USA
International Coordinator, Center for Innovation and Research in Graduate Education (CIRGE), University of Washington, Seattle

CONTRIBUTORS

ARMANDO ALCANTARA, Professor, Instituto de Investigaciones sobre la Universidad y la Educación (IISUE), Universidad Nacional Autónoma de México, graduated from the School of Psychology at UNAM, obtained a master's degree from Stanford University, and his PhD from the University of California, Los Angeles. He is currently a full-time professor at IISUE and has been visiting scholar and visiting professor at Boston College and the Universidade Federal de Goiás, Brazil. Alcantara is a member of Mexico's National System of Researchers. His most recent book is *Entre Prometeo y Sísifo: Ciencia, Tecnología y Universidad en México y Argentina* (2005), and he has also published several chapters in books and articles on topics related to higher education, comparative education and science, and technology policies. Alcantara served as Secretary General of Mexico's Council of Educational Research, and is currently president of the Mexican Society for Comparative Education (affiliated to the World Council of Comparative Education Societies). He is also a member of the editorial boards of various educational journals.

JEROEN BARTELSE, Vice Director, The Association of Universities in the Netherlands (VSNU), completed his dissertation research (in 1999) on institutional reform in European higher education. He has worked with the Netherlands Organisation of Scientific Research, in consultancy projects at CHEPS, and later as a policy advisor to the Executive Board of the University of Twente. He co-authored a 2001 report, "Academic Careers: a Comparative Perspective," prepared for the Dutch Advisory Council for Science and Technology Policy on academic careers. He also co-authored the chapter "A Portrait of the Researcher as a Young (Wo)Man" in The Institutional Basis of Higher Education Research (2007).

AHMED BAWA, Professor of Physics and Deputy Vice Chancellor of Research, Knowledge Production and Partnerships, University of KwaZulu-Natal, South Africa, recently served as a Professor and Distinguished Lecturer in the Department of Physics and Astronomy of Hunter College, City University of New York. Professor Bawa has also spent many years in academic administration in South Africa, including four years as deputy vice chancellor of academic affairs at the University of Natal. In 2002 the Ford Foundation appointed him as program officer of higher education and scholarship in the Southern Africa (Johannesburg) Office. Trained in theoretical physics, Professor Bawa teaches and conducts research in particle physics and on social and intellectual issues concerning the production of knowledge in society.

BARBARA EVANS, Pro-Vice Chancellor (Research Training) and Dean of Graduate Studies, University of Melbourne, Parkville, Australia, has been Dean of the School of Graduate Studies (SGS) at the University of Melbourne, a research-intensive university with approximately 43,000 students and over 3,000 PhD students, since 1997. She has been the convener of the Australian Council of Deans & Directors of Graduate Studies (DDOGS) and of the Universitas 21 DDOGS networks, and an invited speaker at recent meetings of the US Council of Graduate Schools (CGS), the UK Council of Graduate Education (UKCGE), the Canadian Council of Graduate Schools (CAGS) and the European Universities Association (EUA). Also a specialist in animal physiology, Professor Evans has published widely in the field of comparative cardiovascular and respiratory physiology and is the author/editor of three award-winning biology textbooks for tertiary and senior secondary school students.

TERRY EVANS, Associate Dean of Education (Research), Faculty of Education, Deakin University, Geelong Victoria, Australia, is Associate Dean (Research) and Professor in the Faculty of Education at Deakin University, Geelong, Australia. His current research and publication focuses on doctoral education, although he also has a longstanding record in open and distance education. He is a co-editor, with Carey Denholm, of *Doctorates Downunder: Keys to Successful Doctoral Study in Australia and New Zealand* (Melbourne, ACER, 2006) and *Supervising Doctorates Downunder:*

Keys to Effective Supervision in Australia and New Zealand (Melbourne, ACER, 2007).

MAURICIO FORTES, Deputy Director of the National Evaluation Center in Higher Education (CENEVAL), professor, Instituto de Física, Universidad Nacional Autónoma de México, graduated from the School of Science at the National University of Mexico in 1967 and obtained his PhD in Physics from the State University of New York at Stony Brook in 1973. In 1974 he joined the Institute of Physics at the National University of Mexico where he is currently full-time professor. At the National University of Mexico, he served as Dean of the Graduate School. He was also President of the Mexican Academy of Sciences where he advanced several novel programs to improve science education and initiated the national program on Science Olympiads. He also established several collaborative programs with the U.S. National Academy of Sciences and the National Research Council. Most of these focused on education issues, student and faculty mobility, as well as a peer-review program to examine PhD programs at the National University of Mexico. He served as part of the steering committee that created the InterAcademy Council (a consortium of the world's academies of sciences). He has also served as President of the US/Mexico Foundation for Science and President of the National Council for Social Participation in Education. Since July 2002, he served as Deputy Director of the National Evaluation Center in Higher Education (CENEVAL) in charge of research projects, the standard setting program and the quality assurance procedures. In this capacity, he contributed in several studies and publications based on the psychometric results obtained at this Center and in the creation of new tests and instruments based on competences.

ANDREAS FRIJDAL, Head of Academic Service, European University Institute, Florence, studied chemistry (RUCA) and economics at the Free University Brussels and also obtained his PhD in Economics there. He has worked in the Economics Department of the Free University Brussels in the Centre for Financial Economics. He later set up the university's R&D sector and focused on specializing in research management. In 1985 he moved to the European University Institute, Florence (Italy), where he was responsible for research management before becoming head of the Academic Service. While there, he published various reports on research management, doctoral education and the development of European Studies programs for the European Union and other governmental bodies. Over the last ten years he has focused on the training of researchers in his function as head of Academic Service, responsible for the implementation of the doctoral and postdoctoral program.

HOWARD GREEN, Senior Partner in higher education consultancy Postgraduate Directions, United Kingdom, was until recently senior adviser to the Vice-Chancellor at Staffordshire University, Professor of Urban Planning, and chair of the UK Council for Graduate Education. He is now senior partner in the Higher Education consultancy Postgraduate Directions, which specializes in postgraduate development. He is also principal of D. Howard Green Consulting, a consultancy which provides an interface between Higher Education and the development industry in regeneration matters. An urban planner, Green graduated from Cambridge in 1969 and researched with Peter Hall in Reading, gaining a PhD in 1974 and subsequently professional qualifications in planning. His current research is concerned with urban policy and partnership building in Europe, about which he has written and lectured widely. He was one of the founder members of the Franco-Britannique Planning Group. Green has also researched and written extensively on issues concerning postgraduate education. *Doctoral Study in Contemporary Higher Education,* co-authored with Professor Stuart Powell, was published by the Open University Press in July 2005. His next book, *The Doctorate Worldwide,* co-edited with Stuart Powell, was published by SRHE and Open University Press in 2007.

HANS KRISTJAN GUDMUNDSSON, General Director, RANNIS—The Icelandic Center for Research, Reykjavik; Former Rector and Chairman of the NorFA board. Since April 2003 Hans Kristjan Gudmundsson has been the general director of the Icelandic Centre for Research, a governmental organization that runs the Icelandic competitive public funding system for research, development, and innovation, and supports the science policy system by gathering, analyzing and providing information. Gudmundsson is a physicist with a doctoral degree in solid state physics (TechnD) from KTH, Stockholm. After a research career at the University of Iceland and the Iceland Technology Institute, IceTec, in Reykjavik, Gudmundsson served seven years as a scientific counselor at EFTA and the Icelandic Mission to the EU in Brussels. During the period 1999–2003, he was the Rector of NorFA, the Nordic Academy of Advanced Study.

MIMI HEGGELUND, International Coordinator, Center for Innovation and Research in Graduate Education (CIRGE), University of Washington, Seattle, Washington, USA. As a member of the Center for Innovation and

Research in Graduate Education at the College of Education and the University of Washington (UW) Graduate School, Heggelund organizes the series of international conferences on the Forces and Forms of Change in Doctoral Education Worldwide. She also facilitates the work of the Forces and Forms Global Network, which focuses its attention on the global, regional, and international forces that play a major role in the development of doctoral education. She also coordinates the UW-Jordan Education Trust Partnership (JETP). Heggelund earned her PhD from the UW College of Education and has worked on several international teacher education programs that include developing a teacher training program for one hundred teachers and faculty from Indonesia and assisting in the preparation for accreditation of the UAE Academy in Abu Dhabi.

JEROEN HUISMAN, Professor in Higher Education Management and Director of the International Centre for Higher Education Management (ICHEM), University of Bath, United Kingdom, graduated from the University of Groningen, the Netherlands (educational sciences) and holds a PhD from the University of Twente, the Netherlands. He is editor of Higher Education Policy and co-editor of Tertiary Education and Management. His research interests include Europeanization and internationalization; diversity in higher education; organizational change; and management and leadership in higher education.

NARAYANA JAYARAM, Professor and Director, Institute for Social and Economic Change, Bangalore, India, is on the Steering Committee of the International Network on the Role of Universities in Developing Areas (INRUDA), He is the Managing Editor of Sociological Bulletin (Journal of the Indian Sociological Society) and the Editor of ICSSR Journal of Reviews and Abstracts: Sociology and Social Anthropology. He has published extensively on the sociology of higher education in India, and his books include *Higher Education and Status Retention, Sociology of Education in India, Social Conflict* (co-edited with Satish Saberwal), and *The Indian Diaspora.*

BARBARA M. KEHM, Professor of Higher Education Research, International Centre for Higher Education Research (INCHER-Kassel), Kassel University, Kassel, Germany, is a professor at the International Centre for Higher Education Research at the University of Kassel. She is also the Managing Director of that Centre. She is responsible for an international masters program in higher education studies and is currently in the process of establishing a doctoral program in this field, both exclusively taught in English. Kehm had worked as a researcher (wissenschaftliche Mitarbeiterin) at the University of Kassel from 1990 until 1996. From 1996 on, she was active as a senior researcher at the Institute for Higher Education Research of the University of Halle-Wittenberg, and from 2001 she coordinated research projects at the same institution. She was a member of the EAIR (European Association of Institutional Research) executive committee and is now the Secretary of CHER (Consortium of Higher Education Researchers) and the chair of the executive committee of the German Society for Higher Education. She is also a member of the editorial boards of four international higher education journals. She has carried out several large-scale projects for international organizations such as UNESCO, OECD, and the Council of Europe.

SALVADOR MALO, Research Director, Instituto Mexicano para la Competitividad, graduated from the School of Science at the National University of Mexico and obtained his PhD in Physics from the Imperial College of Science and Technology, University of London. Early in his career, he worked at the International Atomic Energy Agency in Vienna, Austria. After that, he held several positions at Mexico's Instituto Mexicano del Petróleo (an oil industry-related technical and research centre), including Vice-President of Research. In 1983 he joined the Mexican Department of Education where he initiated several programs to promote the development of graduate studies in Mexican state universities and of research in Mexico, one of these being the well-known Sistema Nacional de Investigadores. In 1990 he moved to the Universidad Nacional Autónoma de México (Mexico's National University) where he first served as Secretary General, then as Vice-President for Management, and later as Vice-President for Budget and Planning. In addition to his duties in these positions, he became actively involved in international activities: He was a member of the Mexican Task Force Group for Collaboration in Higher Education in North America, and a board member of the Consortium for North American Higher Education Collaboration. In 2002 he was appointed Director General of the Centro Nacional de Evaluación para la Educación Superior (Mexico's Centre for the Assessment of Higher Education) where he launched a collaborative project involving sixty universities in thirteen different countries dedicated to the comparison of degree requirements, assessment procedures, number of academic credits, and research activities in six professions. Since May 2006 he has been Research Director at Mexico's Institute for Competitiveness.

HELENE MARSH, Dean of Graduate Research Studies, James Cook University, Townsville, Australia. As James Cook University's Dean of Graduate Research Studies, Marsh is committed to cross-disciplinary research. She has collaborated widely with colleagues in other disciplines, and many of her students are supervised by staff from disciplines other than biology—including anthropology, biochemistry, geography, and statistics. Marsh's research interests include the application of ecology to the management of marine, coastal and terrestrial wildlife species. Her current research also addresses management of Indigenous resources and environmental monitoring, and methodological problems. Additionally, Marsh is currently leading a program at the Marine and Tropical Science Research Facility, Queensland Australia, which studies species of conservation concern in the Great Barrier Reef region.

MARESI NERAD, Associate Graduate Dean; Director, Center for Innovation and Research in Graduate Education (CIRGE), and Associate Professor, University of Washington, Seattle, Washington, USA. Since fall 2002, Nerad has been the founding director of the Center for Innovation and Research in Graduate Education (CIRGE), the first such center for studies on graduate education in the US and worldwide. Since 2003 Nerad has been Associate Graduate Dean, Graduate School, University of Washington. Her research and teaching in the Educational Leadership and Policy Studies Program, College of Education at UW, in the higher education program of the college, focuses on graduate and postdoctoral education reforms; impact of globalization on students, faculty, structure, and organization of Graduate Education; international trends in doctoral education, women in higher education, and others. From 1988 until 2001, Nerad was in charge of research at the Graduate Division at the University of California-Berkeley. She has directed three US career-path studies of PhDs, "PhDs—10 Years Later," (biochemistry, computer science, electrical engineering, English, mathematics, and political) funded by the Mellon Foundation and NSF, "Art History PhDs—A Decade Later," funded by the Getty Grant Foundation, and "Social Science PhDs—Five + Years Out," (anthropology, communications, geography, history, political sciences, sociology) funded by the Ford Foundation.

RENATO JANINE RIBEIRO, Evaluation Director, CAPES-Brazilian Ministry of Education, and Professor of Ethics and Political Philosophy, University of São Paulo, São Paulo. As Evaluation Director at CAPES (Coordination for the Improvement of Higher Education Personnel, a part of the Brazilian Ministry of Education), Ribeiro is responsible for the evaluation of the almost 2,000 doctoral and masters degree programs that presently exist in Brazil. Ribeiro has also been a full professor of Ethics and Political Philosophy at the University of São Paulo since 1993. Additionally, he has served on the council of CNPq (National Council for Scientific and Technological Development, Brazil); the Brazilian National Research Council (1993–97); and council and board of SBPC, the Brazilian Association for the Advancement of Science (1995–2003). Ribeiro won the Jabuti Prize for Best Essay in 2001 for "A sociedade contra o social: o alto custo da vida social no Brasil" (Society versus the Social: The High Cost of Social Life in Brazil). He is currently writing about the development of democracy in the context of an authoritarian legacy. In spring 2005, Ribeiro was the first visiting professor to hold the Center for Brazilian Studies' Rio Branco Chair, a post endowed by The Brazilian Ministry of Foreign Affairs in 2003.

THOMAS TRZYNA, Professor of English and member of the Washington Educational Research Center at Seattle Pacific University, Seattle, Washington, USA, is an educational consultant and researcher who has taught at Seattle Pacific University, the University of Washington, and Ohio State University. He assists US and foreign universities with their development. He earned his BA at UC Berkeley and his PhD at the University of Washington.

GARTH WILLIAMS, Principal, Public Knowledge Canada, Ottawa, Canada, holds a doctorate in the social-cultural history of Canadian politics. He has fifteen years of experience in research policy and public affairs. He has coordinated national consultations and provided policy analysis on postsecondary education and research policy for national research organizations in Canada. In 2004 he founded Public Knowledge Canada to help researchers and research institutions build public recognition and influence for their work while helping government, voluntary sectors and business organizations access, interpret and use leading-edge research.

SHINICHI YAMAMOTO, Professor and Director, Research Center for University Studies, University of Tsukuba, Tokyo, is a professor and the director of the Research Center for University Studies, Tsukuba University, Tokyo. His main interest is the analysis of the various functions of the higher education system, including university research, administration and management. After graduation from the University of Tokyo, he served on the Ministry of Education (Monbusho) for seventeen years, where he obtained administrative experience in school education, university and research management, and international affairs. He served the National Science Foundation as a research fellow from 1988–89. He has also been involved in several Organization for Economic Co-operation and Development (OECD) activities, including research training, university funding and other areas, and was at CSTP (Committee on Science and Technology Policy) in 1992–2003. He is a member of the Board of the International Basic Science Program (IBSP) of UNESCO.

INDEX